MONROE R. LAZERE, LL.B., Columbia University, is President of the Lazere Financial Corporation, which he founded in 1951. He is Chairman of the Board of the Association of Commercial Finance Companies of New York, Inc., and a Vice President of the National Commercial Finance Conference, Inc. Mr. Lazere is the author of several articles on credit and finance and conducts a course in commercial financing at Cornell University.

CONTRIBUTORS

Philip Cohen
Harry L. Goldstein
T. Carter Hagaman
Robert L. Krause

Monroe R. Lazere
Joseph S. Lesser
Robert Martin
Eli S. Silberfeld

COMMERCIAL
FINANCING

Edited by

MONROE R. LAZERE
LAZERE FINANCIAL CORPORATION

NATIONAL COMMERCIAL FINANCE CONFERENCE, INC.
NEW YORK

Library of Congress Catalog Card Number 67–30356

PRINTED IN THE UNITED STATES OF AMERICA

Preface

In a very real sense, this volume is a summary of the accumulated experience of an industry of lenders. Primarily the emphasis has been placed on secured lenders, who collateralize their loans by security interests in personal property. As is indicated here, such lenders now include banks as well as non-bank institutions. Originally, however, and in historical terms very recently, such lenders were almost exclusively non-bank organizations. Necessarily, therefore, much of this volume has been culled from the experience of such non-bank lenders. To that extent, this book has been the offspring of that industry's trade association, the National Commercial Finance Conference, Inc. In acknowledging my heavy debt to others, therefore, I must first refer to the Conference and its continuing educational programs directed toward seeking new and refining old lending techniques. In this respect, the work has been almost a cooperative enterprise.

Since commercial financing deals with various credit techniques utilized in financing commerce or trade, the term properly may be deemed to include industrial financing. Advance factoring is clearly a financing device. Maturity factoring, although not strictly a financing device, expedites business transactions, deals with credit, and provides a module or building block for advance factoring. Accordingly, it is felt that all of these techniques appropriately may be discussed as part of an up-to-date treatment of commercial financing.

At bottom, the successful administration of these techniques is dependent upon sound intuitive judgment and broad insightful experience. The first comprehensive verbalization of them was successfully undertaken by Walter S. Seidman, specifically commissioned by the Conference. His book was developed as he conducted a college course on the subject of finance companies and factors. It existed during 1948–1956 in mimeographed editions and in 1957 was published in printed form. Thereafter, no author on the same subject can avoid being in his personal debt. Now a Vice President of The First National City Bank of New York, he also has been kind enough to read and criticize parts of this work in typescript. I am, therefore, doubly grateful to him.

Since 1957, the field of commercial financing has undergone three fundamental and far-reaching modifications. First, the commercial banks have increasingly expanded their secured lending activities. For many of them, it has become an area for new business development, rather than merely a technique for working out an originally unsecured loan that exhibits difficulty in repayment. Second, the Uniform Commercial Code—then an innovation in a few states—has been almost universally adopted by the fifty states. This has resulted in new legal terminology, new language in agreements, new forms, and some new administrative mechanics for old credit techniques. And finally, some credit devices that were then relative rarities have become very popular. The dollars outstanding in such loans have become rather considerable. No text on the subject can now be complete without discussions of the fields of industrial time sales, equipment leasing, interim real estate financing, and the development of FCIA insurance in export financing. It seemed, therefore, that a new book on commercial financing would serve a useful purpose.

Other individuals have been very helpful. Professor Homer Kripke, of the New York University Law School, was enlightening in his writings, in our personal discussions, and in his specific comments on portions of the book. In addition to contributing a chapter hereof, Eli S. Silberfeld, General Counsel to the Conference, has provided fruitful comments on several other chapters. Madison M. Myers, of James Talcott, Inc., and Lawrence Seder, of G. D. C. Leasing Corporation, presented thoughtful comments on equipment leasing. The work also benefited from my discussions with Joshua L. Rednor, of Max Rothenberg and Company, regarding specific accounting problems.

Louis Freidenberg, of Coleman and Company, was extremely helpful in connection with the chapter on factoring. John F. Rand, of A. J. Armstrong and Company, Inc., contributed important materials on import and export financing. Gerald J. Grossman, of Commercial Trading Corporation, helped with the chapter on perfecting liens under pre-Code law. Leonard Machlis, Secretary of the National Commercial Finance Conference, Inc., was valuable as a source of material and invaluable in reiterating the need for an updated book on commercial financing. His enthusiasm for such a book was infectious, and his bland assumption that I would do it was flattering. This exhortatory combination made an utterly unreasonable undertaking appear to be a routine project.

To Dean Robert A. Beck and Professor Gerald W. Lattin, of Cornell University, I must express my appreciation for affording us the opportunity of testing the material in the course on commercial financing which they bravely innovated in Ithaca. In this connection, I am also indebted to Harry K. Weiss, of Helmsley-Spear, Inc., a fellow Cornellian and my opposite number in a parallel real estate course, for suggesting the Cornell course. He also served as gadfly and goad by repeating, upon each personal encounter, the simple but literally moving question "How is the book coming?" As I conclude this preface, I eagerly await our next meeting.

The pleasure of acknowledging the assistance of all the above named bears the corresponding obligation of absolving them from any responsibility for errors of fact or law, as well as lack of clarity or style. Let such exoneration here be recorded.

As later appears, many of the chapters were written by operating practitioners in specialized areas. To fully cover his area, each contributor had to define his field, contrast it with others, and describe operational and legal developments. Since the world of business is a continuum, such developments and problems relate to several fields. Further, each chapter was designed to stand alone for specific but full reference for the field covered. Necessarily, therefore, a certain, but I trust sufficiently limited, repetition is found in the text. As conceived and executed, however, it should present a unified whole.

To the specialized practitioners who have written specific chapters I wish to express my gratitude for their tolerant attentiveness to my suggestions and their patient acceptance of my cajoling. Patently, a certain amount of verbal pushing and pulling (sometimes popularly described as nagging) was necessary to achieve accommodations of theory, style, and deadlines. It is a tribute to their patience that we have concluded the task and have remained good friends.

Since I am professionally engaged in the field of commercial financing, the time required to write or edit the materials herein was necessarily extracted from other areas of activity. My office colleagues were extremely helpful in taking up the slack resulting from my being otherwise engaged. The typing load was assumed by my secretary, E. Carole Guevara, who developed an unusual facility for following and collating sometimes unrelated scraps of material scrawled or dictated in odd moments.

Without the continuing support of my family, the work would

not have been concluded, or even undertaken. Periodically, my wife and children understandingly and patiently awaited my return from the confines of the den. To Muriel, Eric, and Cathy, therefore this book is affectionately dedicated.

MONROE R. LAZERE

New York, New York
October, 1967

Contents

COMMERCIAL FINANCING

1

Credit and
Credit Institutions

Monroe R. Lazere
President, Lazere Financial Corporation

MEANING AND FUNCTION OF CREDIT

Credit has been variously described as man's confidence in man and as the lifeblood of our economy. The importance of credit may be readily derived from the following figures. In 1966, the Gross National Product (abbreviated GNP) was 739.6 billions of dollars. That is, the total of goods sold and services rendered in the American economy was valued at that figure. During that year, the total amount of currency in circulation was approximately 44.7 billion dollars or substantially less than 10 per cent of the GNP. It must also be recognized that the GNP includes only sales of final products and does not include intermediary sales (e.g., manufacturer to wholesaler to retailer). It also excludes certain governmental "transfer payments" such as pensions, social security benefits, and interest on government debt. But all the figures—and they are substantial—represent additional financial transactions that were recorded during the year.

This tremendous volume of transactions resulting in a flow of goods and services was made possible through the use of credit. Instead of dollars changing hands at the conclusion of each transaction, credits were utilized and canceled each other, thereby reducing the amount of currency moving through the economy. The term "credit" derives from the Latin verb "credere" meaning "to believe" or "to trust." In English usage, it can convey either of two meanings. One is a potential ability to borrow money or obtain goods upon a promise to pay in the future. This is what is meant by the phrase "his credit is good." In the present discussion "credit" refers to the actual utilization of the potential. The credit has in fact been issued. This is the meaning that will hereafter be attached to the term.

A credit is the legal right to receive money. The opposite side of the same coin is the obligation to pay money. Every credit involves a debt. Every creditor has a debtor. The terms are reciprocal in the same sense as the terms "purchase" and "sale." Both describe the same transaction but from different vantage points. It is the issuance of such credits (and assumption of such debts) plus the ultimate cancellation thereof that make possible the flow of goods and services without exchanges of currency in the same dollar amount.

Prerequisites for Credit System

It has been estimated that more than 90% of the business transactions in the American economy are accomplished by credit. For a society to function thus, some basic elements must be present:

1. *An accepted code of conduct.* It must be anticipated that debtors will pay their obligations without costly collection effort.
2. *Legal machinery for enforcement of claims.* Creditors with claims against non-paying debtors must be enabled to bring to bear the force of society to effect collection. This assists the creditor and also helps preserve the credit system.
3. *A reasonably stable monetary unit.* The money received by the creditor next month or next year must have a purchasing power equal to that money's present purchasing power. Otherwise, the creditor cannot project the future value of the present promise and is therefore understandably disinclined to extend credit.

Types of Credit

There are, of course, manifold types of credit. For example, A ships B some merchandise on thirty-day terms. That is, B may pay A for the merchandise thirty days after the merchandise is received. A is extending B mercantile or trade credit as a supplier. Again, C works for D. C does not receive his salary at the end of every day. The employer, D, pays C every week or every two weeks. C is extending credit to D, although it is only for administrative convenience.

But this discussion will be limited to the types of credit provided by financial institutions of various types. As will later become apparent, the types of credit available through each financing institution are related to the source of funds of that institution.

Business' Need for Credit

Let us now change our focus from the over-all economy to the particular business entity. Almost every business enterprise starts with a capital investment. The capital or equity investment represents the funds provided by the ownership interest or interests. As the volume of business of the enterprise increases, the cash-flow requirements increase in order to support the operation.

Obtaining the operating cash with which to finance its growth presents a major problem to a small business. Surprisingly, however, this aspect of small business operation frequently receives the least attention from the small entrepreneur. He is most often production-oriented or sales-minded. But forecasting and providing for the financing of growth is the touchstone of a successful small business operation. The flow of cash may be viewed as the blood circulating in the body. Proper circulation permits proper growth; an inadequate cash flow may result in atrophy of certain limbs or areas; and a failure of circulation can obviously lead to the decline and possible death of the enterprise. Just as the blood brings oxygen to the parts of the body and carries away the wastes, so does cash flow bring fresh labor, materials, and ideas to the components of the business entity, and carry away finished goods and clear away outmoded procedures or other blockages to proper business growth.

Obviously one solution to the cash flow requirement would be to constantly increase the over-all equity investment to provide this flow, but this would frequently be beyond the means of the owners. To seek equity capital from others may permanently dilute the present owner's share of the enterprise while his need for operating cash may be temporary or perhaps seasonal. Additionally, in many situations, it would reduce the leverage for earnings on invested capital. However, increasing the equity investment is often the proper move.

Although there are methods of raising equity capital to service a growing business, equity financing is outside the scope of this book.

Equity financing involves underwriters, convertible debenture or stock issues, and the like. One of the major problems of small business in the modern economy is its limited access to the capital markets and the resultant difficulty in arranging for equity financing. The tax impact on profits makes the accumulation of capital through earnings more difficult. Hence the accumulation of capital frequently does not keep pace with the growth requirements of a small business.

This book centers around the lender-borrower relationship. Frequently the funds provided by lenders are described as increases in "working capital." This phrase, however, has a specific definition in accounting. It is the difference between current assets and current liabilities. Short term loans (secured or unsecured) increase cash and current liabilities in virtually equal amounts, thereby leaving working capital unchanged. Long term loans (secured or unsecured) increase cash without corresponding increases in current liabilities, thus increasing working capital. Further, the term "capital," as we have just seen refers to ownership investment or equity position. To avoid such ambiguity, therefore, the lender-borrower relationship shall hereafter be described as providing "operating cash."

Under the lender-borrower arrangement, the lender does not take an ownership or equity position in the enterprise. Rather, the lender's funds constitute a loan which must ultimately be repaid. For the use of such funds, the lender is compensated at an agreed rate. The funds thus employed by the borrower enable him to utilize his invested capital more effectively by increasing his cash flow, thereby increasing the earnings on his invested capital. The provider of such operating cash shall hereinafter be referred to as the lender or financer. This will distinguish the financer from the financier who provides or arranges for the acquisition of equity capital funds as defined above.

Throughout, references will be made to small business. The Small Business Administration, created by the Federal Small Business Administration Act of 1953, has given this term a very specific definition in terms of volume and/or invested capital and/or number of employees. But the definition herein encompasses a broader area. A small business is here defined as any enterprise whose growth-financing requirements are not built into its pricing structure. The noted economist Gardner C. Means has pointed out that some giant corporations provide for such growth financing in their pricing schedules. This obviously requires some extended study of market potential, tooling and production costs, and financial projections and can therefore only be done by extremely large enterprises. Other businesses—though larger than the SBA definitions—require growth financing from non-price structured sources. These are here considered to be small businesses and are the chief source of clientele for the credit devices herein discussed.

TYPES OF CREDIT INSTITUTIONS

In describing the major types of credit institutions, one is immediately faced with the problem of evolution and change. As the economy evolves and as the means of communication and transportation change, the traditional functions of various institutions are modified, and credit institutions are no exception. In addition to external forces (changes in the physical methods by which business is conducted) credit institutions are subject to what may be described as internal, organic, or structural changes which derive from improved knowledge coupled with more sophisticated analysis of economics and the functioning of the institution itself. Such changing frontiers of knowledge are as important in the evolution of credit institutions as the changes in technology of transportation and communication. Included in these forces of change, of course, are the developments in computers and data processing which enable business institutions to obtain faster and more accurate information on their own operations, as their volume of transactions expands.

Hence the following descriptions of credit institutions are to be viewed as snapshots of moving bodies. The representations are as at a given historical moment and are subject to evolutionary development and change.

Investment Bankers

The investment banker is an intermediary between the business enterprise and the capital market. This institution is not a bank in the popular sense of the term, for it deals primarily with the merchandising of securities (stocks and bonds) of the business entity. Frequently this is done in a manner very similar to the method of a mercantile wholesaling enterprise. The investment banker purchases the issued securities at a price satisfactory to the business enterprise and then proceeds to sell them to individuals or to institutional investors such as pension funds or mutual funds. This is called an underwriting. The investment banker may also serve as an adviser in the planning of a security issue and then broker the sale of the entire issue via a private placement to a single institution or a group of institutions. Since a history of sound operation is a major consideration, this type of funding usually requires a rather large and well-established business entity.

Life Insurance Companies

Because of the striking growth of the industry, the accumulation of assets in life insurance companies has been rapid and substantial. It has been estimated that these companies are accumulating assets at the rate of $6 billion per year. The outflow of their funds can be statistically predicted. Hence a part of their portfolio is available for long-term financing in the form of mortgages on industrial, commercial, and housing real estate. They also make term loans to businesses but require substantial enterprises with long earnings records and dealing in markets not subject to rapid change. The average small or medium-sized business would not qualify.

Union and Corporate Pension Trusts

Like the insurance companies, these trusts have experienced a rapid and large accumulation of assets and have a statistically predictable outflow. Their standards of investment are also similar to those of the life insurance companies.

Commercial-Paper Houses

These firms merchandise or broker sales of short-term promissory notes of the borrower to individuals or institutions or other business entities. Only large firms with long histories of sound operation are eligible for this type of financing.

Mutual Savings Banks and Savings and Loan Associations

These two kinds of institutions function similarly. The mutual savings banks were originated by public-spirited community leaders to encourage thrift and to manage "the savings of mechanics, laborers, servants and others." The inclusion in mutual savings bank titles of "Five Cents" or "Dime" indicates their orientation toward modest but steady and long-range savings. Mutual savings banks are owned by their depositors and are found mostly in New England and the

Middle Atlantic seaboard states where industrialization (and therefore industrial workers-savers) developed earliest in America. To expand their influence into other geographical areas, their trade association is urging the adoption of Federal chartering of mutual savings banks.

The savings and loan associations were originally developed as co-operative efforts to encourage individual home ownership. As a result, they created the monthly amortized home loan. They may be mutual associations or stock corporations, depending on the law of the state in which they are chartered. If Federally chartered, they must be mutual associations.

The source of funds of both institutions is the deposited savings of thrifty individuals. The withdrawal turnover is understandably slow. Technically both types of institutions are entitled to from thirty to ninety days' notice of withdrawal. In practice, however, they permit withdrawals upon demand. Their loans are primarily in long-term real estate mortgages with an emphasis on individual home owners. Indeed, savings and loan associations are limited by law to investments in home mortgages and United States Government securities.

The Federal Deposit Insurance Corporation provides insurance up to $15,000 per depositor for mutual savings banks. Similar insurance is provided for savings and loan association depositors by the Federal Savings and Loan Insurance Corporation. Both insurers are government agencies created to protect and encourage deposits in the respective institutions.

Government-created Credit Sources

The Small Business Administration, established by the Small Business Administration Act of 1953, makes loans, provided such loans are not commercially available. More recently it has encouraged banks to undertake and manage such loans, with the SBA assuming the risk, either by providing virtually all the funds or by guaranteeing the loan to the bank.

Some communities have created area redevelopment associations to attract industry to areas of under-employment, in an effort to provide jobs in those areas. Such associations—in conjunction with local banks—provide long-term and short-term financing as inducements to business firms to persuade them to locate in the depressed areas.

In 1958 Congress passed the Small Business Investment Company Act creating the SBIC's. These companies are capitalized with nongovernment funds (either privately or publicly acquired), and they obtain some interesting leverage from SBA matching debentures. Their function is to make long-term (more than five years) loans to small business and take equity positions in such enterprises.

Factors

One of our oldest financial institutions, the factor was originally a businessman, not a financer. The term "factor" stems from the Latin verb "facio" and literally means "he who does things." It originally referred to an agent for a property owner, following the Roman practice of entrusting property management to others.

It was in connection with the growth of the wool industry in England beginning in the late fourteeth century that the commercial factor was developed as an institution. The factor served as a commission merchant or selling agent for the mill. Because of the slowness of transportation and communication in those days, geographical distances were cumbersome obstacles for business transactions. The factor would therefore advise the mill of the styles and merchandise most popular in the local market. The mills would ship merchandise in bulk to the factor who would sell it in his area and assume the responsibility for the credit worthiness of his customers.

Since he was guaranteeing credit and billing in his own name, the factor could ease the financial burden of the mill by remitting to the mill a high percentage of uncollected accounts. Experience indicated that a 20–25% reserve would be sufficient to cover disputes and claims for defective merchandise. Those claims would also be settled by the factor, but subject to the mill's consent, since such claims remained the mill's responsibility. Additionally, he would frequently make advances to the mill on the merchandise shipped. The amount advanced was usually 50% of the estimated sales value of the merchandise, and the commission on sales was about 5% of volume.

The development of American mills led to the development of factors for those mills. A factor, located in New York, for example, would represent several New England mills. With a number of mills each producing one type of product which might have a limited season, the factor developed the practice of making pre-seasonal advances to the mills to assist them in creating the inventory of merchandise that could be sold during the season.

With the improvement of communication and transportation, and the onset of increased competition, the mills developed their own sales and shipping organizations. While this replaced the business functions of the factor, the mills continued to subscribe to his financial services. Modifications of procedure resulted. Invoices now bore the seller's name plus a legend indicating the assignment to the factor and requesting payment to the factor. Merchandise was no longer in the factor's possession. Hence the factor's advances were secured by liens created either by warehousing the merchandise or relying on the legal device of the "factor's lien."

The factor also provided an additional service by subletting space in his own offices to the various mills he factored. The sublet space served as offices for the mill's salesmen and permitted rapid access to the factor's credit decisions and advice on potential customers. The firms became known as "departments" which gave rise to the designation of "departmental risk" to indicate a credit risk that the factor had not approved but that the mill assumed. More recently, no doubt because of the ease of telephone communication, the mills have rented their showrooms away from the factor's office. As the factoring procedures became more recognized and accepted, factoring was extended to other industries in addition to textiles. Manufacturers (as well as wholesalers) of shoes, hats, furniture, and other merchandise now utilize the services of a factor.

Within the last few years, several commercial banks have undertaken factoring functions. Thus, an institution that originated as a non-lending, mercantile operation has evolved into a financial operation dealing with the advancing of funds and guaranteeing of credit and has been adopted as an additional function of the commercial bank. This evolution is particularly noteworthy since it differs from that of some other credit devices that were pioneered by non-bank lenders because the commercial banks were unable to adapt to the techniques required. In those instances—for example, automobile financing and accounts receivable financing (see below)—the refinement of technique and acceptable loss record compiled by non-bank lenders encouraged commercial banks to enter the field.

Commercial Banks

The most familiar and oldest type of credit-granting institution is the commercial bank. The earliest records of civilization reveal depositary and money-lending functions in the economy. Individuals owning gold would place it in the custody of special persons for safekeeping. These custodians would also serve as moneychangers and moneylenders.

Modern commercial banking is said to date from 1587, when a public bank was established in Venice. This was at the time of the Renaissance when trade and commerce again began to flourish in the Mediterranean area. The techniques and practices there developed spread to Amsterdam, then Hamburg, and influenced the growth of banking in England and ultimately in America.

In the seventeenth century, British merchants and tradesmen developed the practice of depositing their money and bullion for safekeeping in vaults of the local goldsmiths. The goldsmiths were artisans in precious metals, who also served as moneychangers. The smiths would issue receipts for the gold. Gradually the merchants and traders began to write drafts ordering the smith to transfer specified quantities of gold to specified persons or to their order. Further, goldsmiths' receipts gradually evolved from personalized receipts to promissory notes payable to bearer. This was an early form of bank note and was used in the settlement of debts.

Thus the smith found that he could issue notes in excess of the actual store of precious metal, since the actual demand for the metal was less than the amount physically in custody. He could lend money by issuing his own note (receipt) and require repayment with interest within a short term. He was, in short, creating money.

In the United States, the commercial bank is the only financial institution permitted to accept demand deposits. In a perhaps overly simplified analogy, the custody of the demand deposit by the modern commercial bank produces a situation similar to that of the goldsmiths of England's seventeenth century. The commercial bank does not have to retain *all* funds for immediate demand. It can make loans by making a bookkeeping entry increasing the amount on deposit with it by the borrower. It thereby creates money. Significantly the ability of an institution to accept and create demand deposits enables that institution to create money. The other lending institutions here discussed make loans by transferring to the borrower funds already on deposit and representing accumulated savings of some type. For the health and control of the economy, this distinction is vital. The extent to which money can be thus created and the regulation thereof through the Federal Reserve System are beyond the scope of this study. Suffice it here to say that the source of funds of the commercial banks has been capital, surplus, and undistributed profits (designated as capital accounts) plus demand deposits.

Significantly, the demand deposits are frequently more than ten times the capital accounts of the bank. Historically, therefore, the demand deposit greatly influenced the type of loan that the commercial banker made, for in order to insure that sufficient funds would be available to meet any demand, he (like the goldsmith) made short-term liquid loans. Traditionally this meant that commercial bank loans were required to be short term and self-liquidating. That is, the borrower in the course of a one-year cycle had to convert the proceeds of the loan into merchandise or services, then into sales, then into collections from sales (i.e., cash again) with which to retire the original loan. Thus the commercial loan theory of bank credit provided for increasing the money supply as the production needs of the economy increased and decreasing the money supply, through retirement of these loans, as the production cycle concluded.

Commercial Finance Companies

Early in the twentieth century, the commercial finance company was created to fill a gap between the traditional lending practices of the commercial banks and the financing requirements of businessmen. The idea originated in Chicago in 1904 when an enterprising seller of encyclopedias found himself short of cash. Since he was selling his books on the installment plan, he found his receivables mounting rapidly as his sales increased. Having exhausted available sources of credit, he sought a lender who would advance cash against his receivables. He found such a person and they became partners.

They recognized the value to businessmen of financing of receivables and formed a company to offer such services. They intended to operate in the same manner as the factors by having the account debtor (the borrower's customer) pay the finance company directly. This mode of operation met with considerable resistance from their potential clients who feared that such notification would be interpreted as an indication of financial weakness. Notification factoring, they said, had historically developed in the textile field and was accepted in that field. But in other industries, it would be construed as a confession of insolvency. So the new finance company hit upon a plan of having the borrower assign the receivables to the lender but collect its own receivables normally. By agreement, however, the borrower was designated the agent for the finance company and was obliged to turn over all collections to the finance company in the form in which they were received. This mode of receivables financing became known as "non-notification accounts receivable financing" to distinguish it from factoring. The demand for this type of financing grew, and the number of finance companies supplying this service increased rapidly. The source of funds of finance companies was and is the invested capital of private individuals, supported by bank lines from the commercial banks. In the case of large finance companies, long-term subordinated debt from insurance companies is available, as are funds from the commercial paper market.

The prevailing view of banking was known as the commercial loan theory of bank credit. This theory held that fixed plant and equipment should be financed only out of accumulated savings and not through bank credit. Only loans for productive commercial (as opposed to investment, consumption, and speculative) purposes should be financed by bank credit. Proper financing by bank credit would expand the money supply with increases in production and contract it with decreases in production. In 1913, when the Federal Reserve Board was created, it naturally made paper for short-term productive purposes eligible and paper resulting from extending credit for consumption, investment, or speculative purposes ineligible for rediscount at Federal Reserve Banks.

The Federal Reserve Board at that time permitted a commercial bank to rediscount its loans only by presenting eligible third party-paper (not the particular bank's own note). Hence if the banks were to finance receivables, some negotiable paper had to be created. An effort was made, therefore, to popularize the device of the trade acceptance. A trade acceptance is a negotiable draft made by the seller on the buyer at the time the goods are shipped. The buyer accepts the draft upon receipt of the goods and thus creates a special negotiable note resulting from the sale of goods. This negotiable instrument sets forth the amount of the obligation and maturity date, just as a note does. Sellers requesting buyers to accept such drafts met severe resistance, since the buyers were insulted by the request and were not inclined to co-operate. The buyers felt that by ordering and accepting the merchandise they undertook to pay and no signed instrument was necessary to re-inforce their promises. Hence the then traditional banking requirements of "paper" resulted in the banks' inability to finance receivables.

During the twenties, the volume of receivables financing handled by the commercial finance companies increased. Immediately after World War I large corporations were engaged in programs of mergers and expansion by equity and debenture offerings. The banks were concentrating on financing these growth programs, and were not pursuing accounts receivable financing. Commercial banks were investing heavily in loans on such corporate securities and also investing in long-term corporate bonds.

With the onset of the depression in the thirties, some of the banks began to utilize accounts receivable financing. But they were utilizing it primarily as a device to secure an originally unsecured loan where the borrower was in financial difficulty and unable to retire the original loan in accordance with its terms. Receivables financing therefore became associated in the minds of bank officers with financial distress. This of course conditioned their thinking on the subject and inclined them against accounts receivable financing as a credit device for banks. Consequently the finance companies continued their growth in this area.

As the finance companies flourished they developed additional techniques for providing further financial assistance to their clients. They provided such additional accommodation by means of liens on equipment and inventory. As the industry grew, it refined its techniques for administering its collateral and moved into new areas and simpler formulae for financing undercapitalized small business enterprises. With emphasis on collateralized loans, the commercial finance companies developed reputations for imaginative and inventive financing arrangements for the small business, with increasingly streamlined procedures.

Sales Finance Companies

In the twilight of the 19th century and dawn of the 20th century, Detroit was giving birth to the automobile industry. The concepts of interchangeable parts and assembly line production were being put into operation. The volume of cars rolling out of the factories was beginning to mount. Hence the problem of financing the distribution and sales of automobiles began to receive attention.

The prevailing commercial loan theory of banking again had an effect. This doctrine considered unsound the financing of items of consumption by commercial banks. So the financing of purchases of automobiles on the installment plan was left to the non-bank financers. Naturally, those commercial financing companies already functioning developed sales finance departments, division, or subsidiaries.

In 1915 the Guaranty Securities Company was organized in Ohio by the Willys Overland Company for the express purpose of financing installment sales made by Willys Overland Automobile dealers. Success immediately followed, and in 1916 the company undertook such financing on the sales of all makes of cars.

The success of the first sales finance companies encouraged competition and many such finance companies were organized. Success in the field of automobile financing encouraged the companies to venture into new fields. They financed sales of radios, refrigerators, washing machines, furniture, dryers, vacuum cleaners, and other items more modernly known as consumer durables.

As the volume of automobile sales increased, the dealers found themselves facing the problem of financing their inventory of automobiles. The problem arose because of the seasonal peaks and valleys of consumer sales and requirement of the auto manufacturers that the dealers accept an even flow of the manufacturers' production. The sales finance companies therefore developed the "floor plan" device. This consists of a trust receipt arrangement in which the finance company maintains a lien on the inventory of cars in the dealer's showroom and/or warehouse. This readily led to the package deal under which the sales finance company providing the floor plan financing would receive the financing on all consumer installment sales generated by the dealer.

The same device was later applied to the financing of sales of other consumer durables such as washing machines, dryers, television sets, and other appliances. These procedures function in the same way today.

MOTION IN THE PICTURE

As previously indicated, the credit institutions here discussed are subject to the same process of change as other human institutions. Perhaps the most dramatic evolutionary change has been exhibited in the field of commercial banking.

The conventional commercial loan theory of banking has been abandoned. During 1933–35, as a result of the depression, the banking structure was overhauled. The Federal Deposit Insurance Company was organized to insure deposits up to $5,000; then $10,000; and later $15,000. Federal Reserve System banks were required to belong to the FDIC, others could. To encourage banks to join the System, the Federal Reserve Board at that time eased many restrictions on the National Banks. It permitted commercial banks to make real estate loans. It encouraged mutual savings banks and Morris Plan banks (specializing in consumer loans) to join the System. And finally it permitted, in certain circumstances, member banks to borrow from the Federal Reserve Banks on their own notes. No longer was eligible third-party paper required. These changes were clearly designed to encourage the banks to assist in the process of capital formation, and in the process the commercial loan theory of banking gradually expired.

Further, the commercial banks are now increasingly staffed by officers too young to have been conditioned by the 1929 depression and its aftermath. The new officers are growth minded and aggressive. In consequence, the commercial banks have, during the last ten years, increasingly entered the fields of small personal loans, automobile financing, accounts receivable financing, and, more recently, equipment leasing and factoring. Indeed, in 1957 the Credit Policy Commission of the American Bankers Association formally recognized and announced that the need for accounts receivable financing did not necessarily indicate financial distress, but could simply result from the growing pains of a successful operation.

Additional forces are at work. A lowering percentage of demand deposits has spurred commerical banks into competing for savings accounts and certificates of deposit. This decrease arises in large measure from the desire of giant corporations to obtain yields for idle funds. Hence the banks must pay interest on certificates of deposit. Also, they compete for deposits by offering interest on individual savings accounts. This in turn impels them to seek higher yield investments and to offer services such as factoring, leasing, and accounts receivable financing. Whether the operational costs of properly administering revolving loans secured by current assets substantially offset the higher gross yield remains at this time an unsettled question.

The line of demarcation between finance company loans and bankable loans is therefore currently shifting, and a new line may shortly be set. But there can be no doubt that both institutions will continue to function side by side. Nor can it be doubted that newer and administratively more difficult loans will continue to be pioneered by the finance companies. It is unnecessary here to discuss where this shifting line will, from time to time, settle. Suffice it to say that different loans require different criteria.

UNSECURED AND SECURED LOANS

The traditional unsecured loan from a commercial bank is measured by the strength of the borrower's balance sheet and his projected capacity to repay the loan on short term. The well-known and traditional three C's of credit are here involved: Capital, Character, and Capacity. Obviously, in many situations, the amount of loan which a particular enterprise can liquidate within a short cycle may not constitute sufficient accommodation for the borrower's requirements. Hence the fourth "C" may be added—collateral.

Loans may be made on pledged collateral. Collateral consists of assets belonging to the business entity that are pledged to the lender to secure the loan. As indicated above, the amount of such a loan is frequently beyond the capacity of the borrower to retire on short term. Hence, in the event of default, the lender may recoup his loan by liquidating the collateral. Naturally, however, the lender does not desire or even anticipate such a default. The collateral is pledged to protect the lender in the event of unforeseen difficulties.

Generally speaking, the types of collateral offered will shape the nature and administration of the loan. Pledged current assets—receivables and inventory—usually result in a revolving type of credit under which the amount of loan fluctuates with the ebb and flow of the current asset or assets. Pledged fixed assets—equipment and real estate—usually result in an initial advance of an agreed amount, with repayments of interest and principal scheduled periodically over the term of the loan. The significance of the differences in loan arrangement will become more apparent as the discussion proceeds.

2

Unsecured Bank Credit

T. Carter Hagaman
Assistant Vice President, Irving Trust Company

THE BANKING SYSTEM

Traditional economists divide the nation's money supply into two components—currency in circulation and demand deposits in commercial banks.[1] The amount of currency in circulation is determined by the Federal government, but the volume of demand deposits depends to a significant degree on banks' lending policies. To keep our illustration simple, we will suppose that the country has only one bank, Bank A.

Bank A's balance sheet looks like this:

Cash	$40	Deposits	$30
		Capital	10
	$40		$40

At this point, Bank A is earning no income. Then Company B walks in to borrow $20. The loan is made and the proceeds are credited to Company B's account. Now the bank statement looks like this:

Cash	$40	Deposits	$50
Loans	20	Capital	10
	$60		$60

Both assets and liabilities of Bank A have been increased by making the loan, and money in the form of a demand deposit has been created. Deposit creation is something only banks can do.

---

[1] There are other definitions of the money supply, but we will stick to the simple case and disregard time deposits throughout this discussion.

Other lenders are in the same boat as Finance Company F. Its balance sheet looks like this before making a new $20 loan:

Cash	$ 30	Borrowings	$ 85
Loans	70	Capital	15
	$100		$100

and like this afterward:

Cash	$ 10	Borrowings	$ 85
Loans	90	Capital	15
	$100		$100

Finance Company F's cash was reduced by the amount of the new loan.

Let us return a moment to Company B's loan at the bank. The company did not borrow to leave the money on deposit; it wants to buy $20 worth of goods from Company C. When it does, it writes a check for $20 payable to Company C. Company C deposits the check in its account at Bank A. As a result, Bank As' statement is unchanged.

Limits on Ability to Create Deposits

What sets a limit to a bank's ability to increase deposits by making loans? There are several forces at work here. The bank is limited by the amount of its capital from acquiring too many deposits. Bank A with $50 of deposits and $10 of capital still has room for expansion, but at some point—probably between $100 and $150 of deposits, supervisory authorities will require more capital.

Bank A also has to provide liquidity against the possibility of withdrawals. Since there are actually many banks in the country, Company C (who sold the goods to Company B) could have deposited its check in another bank. In that case, Bank A's balance sheet would look like this:

Cash	$20	Deposits	$30
Loans	20	Capital	10
	$40		$40

Making the loan still created deposits, but another bank got the benefit. Another key factor in limiting banks' ability to create deposits is the Federal Reserve System. The Federal Reserve System is our central bank and has responsibility for regulating monetary policy. There are several ways it can do this:

First, the Federal Reserve System (Fed) sets reserve requirements for all member banks. This means that for every dollar of demand deposits a bank has, it must keep a specified percentage on deposit at the Fed. These requirements are presently $16\frac{1}{2}\%$ for large banks in cities designated as reserve cities by the Fed and 12% for all other member banks. Non-member banks must follow state laws and keep reserves on deposit with other banks.

Second, the Fed influences the amount of loanable funds banks have by buying or selling government securities. These transactions are called open market operations. If the Fed sells government securities that it holds, it absorbs cash from the banks and leaves them holding securities. The money it absorbs cannot go into loans. Even if the government securities are bought by companies, they must draw down their deposits in order to pay for the securities, and the same result is achieved. To stimulate lending, the Fed can buy securities, providing the banking system with loanable funds.

Third, banks are permitted to borrow from the Fed subject to various rules. Borrowing takes place at the "discount window" of Federal Reserve Banks. The Fed can change the rate at which banks may borrow and may also tighten or relax the rules. When rediscounting (as this borrowing is called) is cheap and easy, banks can increase their level of loans because the Fed is providing additional liquidity.

Bank Credit in the Business Economy

As of December 31, 1965, commercial banks across the country had about $200 billion in loans outstanding. Of course, only a portion of these loans were to businesses. For example, about $49 billion of this amount was in the form of real estate loans and another $45 billion was in loans to individuals. Only $71 billion was in business and commercial loans, and this figure rose significantly in 1966. These figures can be compared with current notes and accounts payable by United States corporations of $157.4 billion at the end of 1965.[2]

These figures are only intended to offer a more concrete illustration of something we already know—that commercial banks are a major source of business credit. Another illustration of the role of the banking system is shown in the quotation from the *Monthly Review* of the Federal Reserve Bank of New York:

Despite the continued strong showing of overall bank lending, commercial banks have recently experienced a reduction in their share of the private credit markets. Thus, while net funds raised by domestic non-financial

[2] *Federal Reserve Bulletin* (June, 1966).

borrowers other than the Federal Government have continued to grow sharply, bank credit to these borrowers has moderated. In the first half of 1965, bank credit reached a record 50 per cent of total household, business and state and local government borrowing, but this ratio dropped in the second half of 1965 and then declined to only slightly more than 30 per cent in the first quarter of this year. . . . This banking development was paralleled by an even sharper decline in the credit market share of other groupings of financial intermediaries, as direct credit extended by the nonfinancial sectors . . . advanced to a record 40 per cent of the market.[3]

Volume of Unsecured Lending. The most recent data available on secured vs. unsecured bank lending is a study by the Fed in 1955 and 1957. A survey in October, 1957, showed that two-thirds of the number and one-half of the amount of all business loans outstanding at member banks were secured or endorsed, and that nine-tenths of the number and half the amount of secured loans were to borrowers with assets of less than $1 million. This data suggests that unsecured borrowing is related to the size of the borrower, that larger companies tend to borrow unsecured, and that a banker is more inclined to ask for the added protection of security in making loans to smaller companies. For manufacturing and mining companies the importance of size is striking:

Total Assets	Dollars Loaned Secured
Under $50,000	78.0%
Over $100 million	11.1%

For service companies, the comparison is almost as dramatic: 81.8% of all loans (by amount) to real estate companies are secured, but only 17.8% of loans to sales finance companies and 37.5% of loans to manufacturing and mining companies.

Corporate status may also make a difference. Three-fourths of the volume of business loans to unincorporated businesses was secured, compared with less than half for incorporated businesses. The explanation of this could be that unincorporated businesses tend to be smaller and tend to be concentrated in types of activity where secured lending is more common.

Finally, the survey showed that unsecured loans represent a higher percentage of business loans at larger banks than at small banks, but this too might be explained by the fact that large customers represent a higher percentage of a large bank's loan demand and that more large borrowers tend to borrow unsecured.

[3] *Monthly Review* (Federal Reserve Bank of New York) (June, 1966), p. 162.

Credit Squeezes

In 1966, United States business went through a credit squeeze. The steps that bankers took to respond to the situation serve to illustrate what businessmen can expect when credit squeezes occur in the future. Periods of tight money undoubtedly will occur again; businessmen must understand how to prepare for these situations.

Basically, a credit squeeze is the result of the forces of supply and demand operating in the money market. When a commodity—in this case, loanable funds—is in short supply in relation to demand, we would expect the price to rise. The demand for credit increased in 1966 and interest rates rose. A higher price of money should also increase the supply, since investors would be more willing to save to earn a higher return. But this did not happen to the extent that might be expected in a completely free market.

One reason the supply of credit has not grown as rapidly as demand is monetary policy. The American Bankers Association explained it this way:

The Federal Reserve authorities, charged with the clear duty of protecting the dollar, have had no choice but to permit conditions to tighten markedly as loan demands have mounted rapidly to unprecedented levels. Reflecting these conditions, both interest rates and bank loan-deposit ratios have risen to the highest level since the 1920s.[4]

The fiscal policy of the Federal government is an even more powerful force in influencing the economy. Fiscal policy is outside the scope of this book. It is sufficient to state that monetary policy is a tool for economic regulation that is superimposed on the broader-gauged tool of fiscal policy.

In a credit squeeze, bankers have to respond to the heavy loan demand by limiting their loans to those that will best serve the needs of both their customers and the economy. This means that many loan requests from good customers must be turned down, even though both the credit and the project to be financed are sound. A special subcommittee of the American Bankers Association's Banking and Financing Research Committee has listed ten questions for bankers to ask themselves in rationing the available supply of loanable funds:

First, is the banker certain that the needs for productive credits are being fully met?
Second, is the banker discouraging speculative inventory loans?

---

[4] American Bankers Association, *The Banker's Role in Reinforcing Monetary Policy* (New York: The Association, 1966), p. 2.

Third, is the banker devoting careful and appropriate attention to plant and equipment loans?

Fourth, is the banker discouraging loans for take-over purposes?

Fifth, is the banker carefully screening loans which will affect this nation's balance of international payments?

Sixth, is the banker taking firm action to upgrade the quality of loans that are granted?

Seventh, is the banker actively working to pare down loan requests by "whittling" or deferment?

Eighth, is the banker advising the customer, where feasible and desirable, to shift his borrowing to other channels?

Ninth, is the banker taking care not to overextend his leading operations geographically?

Tenth and finally, is the banker properly screening new applicants for loans?

A company must lay the groundwork well in advance to assure itself of the credit it needs. When faced with a credit squeeze a company must have good credit, maintain a longstanding, mutually profitable relationship with its banks and seek credit only for worthwhile purposes.

TYPES OF BANK CREDIT

Unsecured bank credit is the basic form of lending by commercial banks. It accounts for about half the amount of commercial and industrial loans at banks across the nation. Unsecured loans are unsecured in a legal sense only. The credit standards required for unsecured loans are higher than for any other type of loan. The banker's knowledge of the worth and integrity of the borrower is his security.

Unsecured loans may be on a demand basis (with no set maturity, but callable by the banker "on demand") or on a time basis, typically with a fixed maturity of 90 days, six months, or one year. Time notes are somewhat more common for loans to companies, but they are usually made with the understanding that the loan will be renewed on maturity if the borrower wishes. Very unusual circumstances or a dramatic change in a company's credit would be required before a banker would suddenly call a demand loan or refuse to renew a time note. However, requests for reductions in the amount of a loan are not uncommon.

Both demand and time loans are frequently made under lines of credit that assure the customer of his ability to borrow up to a fixed amount any time during the year. A line of credit is an informal

[5] *Ibid.,* pp. 4–7.

commitment that a banker makes without charge, but the customer is expected to keep balances on deposit in some relation to the amount of credit he has available. A revolving credit is a more formal commitment for which the borrower pays a fee. Under a revolving credit, he is legally entitled to borrow up to the full amount of the credit any time until it expires, so long as he continues to fulfill the terms of the agreement.

Personal loans of the sort made by small loan companies are not included in this discussion of unsecured loans. These loans may be unsecured (or signature) loans, but borrowers do not have to meet very high credit standards. The rates charged for these loans are high enough to offset the statistical average of expected defaults and still earn a good profit.

Proper Use of Unsecured Bank Credit in a Company's Financing Program

Unsecured bank credit is one source of the short-term funds that a company requires. These loans should be self-liquidating—that is, the cash necessary to repay them should be generated in the normal course of business. The most obvious examples are loans to finance seasonal peaks of inventory or receivables. A company making electric trains starts to borrow from its bank in the summer to purchase materials used in manufacturing. When the trains are made, they are sold to retail outlets for the Christmas season, but the terms of sale do not call for payment until January. After the retailer sells the trains, he uses the cash to pay the manufacturer who in turn retires his bank loan. The cash that was originally borrowed became raw materials, finished product, receivables, and finally cash again. The transaction is self-liquidating if all goes well.

Another proper use of unsecured bank credit is to help a company to finance efficiently. An electric utility is constantly growing and raising new long-term capital at regular intervals. If, for example, expansion plans call for new capital investment of $10,000,000 during the next 18 months and the company had to raise the full amount at the beginning of the period, it would have idle funds for a time and would be unable to choose the best time to do its permanent financing. The use of bank loans permits the company to sell long-term debt or equity at the best time. The proceeds of the sale will retire the bank loans. Of course, this type of loan is only self-liquidating if the permanent financing actually takes place. Therefore, the banker must be confident of the company's ability to finance according to plan.

Bankers are reluctant to make unsecured loans to business when the means of repayment are not clear in advance. Loans that depend for repayment on the future earnings of the business or on cash throw off from depreciation are really supplying long-term capital to the business. Banks do make unsecured term loans to be repaid from these sources, but that type of loan is not the subject of this chapter.

Unsecured Loans vs. Other Types of Bank Credit

A commercial bank is sometimes described as a department store of finance. As such, it supplies credit and services of many kinds to a variety of organizations and individuals. Much of this activity is outside the scope of this chapter; some will be dealt with in later chapters. First, we exclude all financing for individuals (except when acting as proprietors) and all financing of organizations other than domestic companies engaged in manufacturing, commerce, or non-financial services. Foreign and import-export financing is a field in itself and includes letters of credit, acceptance financing, and financing secured by warehouse receipts and trust receipts. Financial institutions also require specialized types of financing such as the sale of Federal funds to banks, day loans and call loans to brokers and dealers, and loans to finance companies and leasing companies.

Lest too much significance be attached to the classification of unsecured bank credit, it is useful to compare this with various other forms of credit supplied by banks and to set forth the critical differences.

Loans Secured by Receivables or Inventory. Other things being equal, a banker would prefer to loan to a company unsecured to finance receivables or inventory rather than to take a direct assignment of collateral. The overriding reason for this preference is one of relative costs: It is far easier to execute a simple note than to prepare the additional documents necessary for securing the transaction and then police it to see that the security remains intact until the loan is paid. The primary reason these loans are frequently made on a secured basis is that the company's credit is not sufficiently strong to warrant unsecured loans of the required amount.

Term Loans. Term loans may be secured or unsecured; their distinguishing feature is their maturity of more than one year. Term loans provide a portion of a company's long-term capital, which is used primarily for capital assets and working capital.

Installment Loans. Installment loans to businesses are usually secured and are repaid on a regular pre-determined schedule rather than in a lump sum. Conditional sales contracts are one form of installment loan used for the purchase of capital equipment. Rates on this type of financing from a bank are relatively high to cover the costs of the work involved in preparing the agreement and making regular collections and to compensate for the higher risk which is usually the reason for making a loan in this form. The purpose of installment loans is to provide long-term capital, but an unsecured bank loan might be used instead for interim financing.

Leasing. Recently, many commercial banks have been given authority to compete in the leasing business. From a financial viewpoint, a net lease (one in which the lessee pays all expenses and receives no services) is purely and simply a form of debt. It is used to provide capital assets.

Real Estate Financing. Because the relatively high unit value of most real property and because real property usually represents tangible collateral that can easily be identified, secured transactions are the custom in this field. However, large companies with strong credit and a great deal of real property may prefer to finance the company with general obligations such as debentures.

CREDIT STANDARDS AND CREDIT AVAILABILITY

Businessmen are naturally concerned with obtaining the financing for current operations and future growth. To what extent can they expect their banks to make unsecured loans? A sufficiently high credit standing is an obvious requirement for a company seeking credit of any kind, and we have said that the required standard for unsecured loans is higher than for other forms of borrowing. But good credit is not enough. Many companies with satisfactory credit have found bankers nevertheless unwilling to lend them the money they seek. Some of the reasons will be discussed shortly.

Credit Analysis—A Negative Art

A manual prepared for analysts at the Irving Trust Company states, "We are ultimately concerned with the company's continued ability to meet its credit obligations." Stated another way, the analyst's job is to identify and reject proposed loans to all companies where this ability is in some doubt. At times, when the demand for loans is slack, banks may solicit opportunities to lend money, but even when they do, their proposals are ultimately subjected to scrutiny by credit analysts.

Generally speaking, a loan proposal either meets acceptable credit standards or it does not. A rate of interest is assigned that is commensurate with the nature and risk of the loan and with the company's banking relationship. There is little chance of changing a negative decision by applying a higher rate of interest or by adding collateral or guarantees. Banks are distinctly reluctant to rely on collateral or guarantees to liquidate a loan. A banker may ask for them as added protection, but if he expects that he will have to use them, he probably will not make the loan in the first place.

Key Factors in Credit Analysis

The discussion that follows is intended to give the reader some idea of the scope of a credit analysis and the information a prospective borrower should make available in order to receive favorable consideration.

Amount and Purpose of Loan. Bankers prefer to make loans that will contribute to the growth or profitability of a business. The loan must be large enough to do the job for which it is intended, but not so large as to jeopardize the company's ability to repay it as agreed. There have been occasions when a banker refused a small loan when he would have made a larger one because he did not believe the smaller amount was sufficient to accomplish its purpose. An example would be a company that was not allowing sufficient time to collect its receivables and consequently could run short of the cash needed to conduct its business properly.

Method of Repayment. No loan is made without the method of repayment clearly understood in advance. Loans that depend on future success of the business are riskier than self-liquidating loans. Basically, unsecured loans are restricted to companies with a strong financial condition that have a proved ability to pay them on schedule from normal business operations.

Quality of Management. Credit analysis can be divided into personal, financial, and economic factors. It is difficult to judge the character and ability of prospective borrowers, but analysts are agreed that this problem is the most important and challenging part of their job. As expressed in the Irving Trust Company's manual:

> If the management aspect is favorable, that is, if it has the "know-how" and is thoroughly trustworthy—special arrangements for a loan will sometimes be made when other factors, financial and economic, are not altogether favorable. On the other hand, given favorable financial and economic conditions, but management of a questionable character, a bank is likely to be reluctant to extend credit.[6]

A company whose management is not already well known to a bank should spare no effort to remedy this situation. The analyst will research this subject carefully and check with numerous sources. The company can help by supplying biographical information on its key men and by giving the banker the opportunity to meet as many of them as possible.

Financial Statements. Accurate, adequate, up-to-date records are essential to good business management and the primary evidence of it. In the long run, a company's financial statements will demonstrate the success or failure of management. The statements are the corporate track record. They are used along with statements of comparable companies in assessing how well the company is doing and as a base for predicting future performance.

The quality of these statements is crucial. They should be prepared by a reputable certified public accountant. If the accountant is not known to the banker, he will be checked. If statements do not receive an unqualified certificate, the auditor's exceptions will be carefully analyzed. Basic financial statements are the balance sheet, the income statement, and an analysis of changes in capital and retained earnings. Usually the banker will want to see statements for a number of years and may ask for supplementary data as well. This could include such information as:

1. A description of the company's present debt obligations including repayment schedules and full information on terms that restrict the company in any significant way
2. Full information on long-term leases and any other significant financial commitments or guarantees
3. Explanatory comments on unusual fluctuations in financial statistics such as abrupt increases in receivables or inventory with-

---

[6] Domestic Credit Department, Irving Trust Co., *Credit Analysis* (New York: Irving Trust Co., 1964), p. 102.

out a similar change in sales, unexplained changes in net worth, and so on
4. Plans or forecasts of future operations such as capital expenditures or sales projections (These data might be incorporated into a cash flow projection for some period of time.)

Historical and Economic Data. In addition to facts about the loan proposal and knowledge of the company's management and financial data, the analyst needs information to put the company in perspective. This includes

1. History of and background on the company and its operation
2. Data on the company's industry
3. General economic data for both the country and the area in which the company operates

In order to obtain this information, the analyst may use a number of sources. He will consult the published data available from credit agencies, manuals and rating books, newspapers, magazines, trade journals, and other publications. In addition, there are numerous public records available such as data from the S.E.C., stock exchanges, and government sources.

To supplement the basic data from published sources, banks frequently contact other sources of information. One of the most important is other banks. The banking fraternity is continually exchanging information about customers and follows a strict code of ethics in the process. Other financial institutions such as investment bankers and commercial financing companies also participate in this information exchange. And on occasion, a banker may solicit information from a company's customers, suppliers, and competitors as well.

Importance of Ratio Analysis. The intelligent use of ratios can be of great value in financial statement analysis. Ratios serve as warning signs or indicators that may be helpful in discovering existing or potential trouble spots, especially when a year-to-year trend is noted.

Ratios will probably be used in most credit analysis, but their importance should not be overemphasized. Ratios can serve to reinforce an analyst in his judgment or to point his way to further investigation. A set of "satisfactory ratios" does not in itself assure a company of strong credit, nor will some questionable ratios necessarily cause a loan to be rejected. In fact, undue concern with ratios could cause a company to take action that is contrary to its best interests. For example, some years ago one large railroad improved its cash management and reduced its need for cash, but it continued to keep the same amount on hand solely to maintain its current ratio.

Ratios are not used in a vacuum. They help the analyst to compare a company with other firms and with itself over time. The trend of ratios from one period to the next is as revealing as their absolute level. Interpretation of financial ratios requires experienced judgment and cannot be discussed intelligently in abstraction.

Similar financial ratios tend to be used in analyzing various companies, but ratio standards and the relative importance of the ratios that are used will differ depending on the nature of the business. For example, inventory turnover is important in retailing, but not for a utility. Fixed charge coverage is more important to a real estate firm than to an equipment manufacturer. The following is a list of some of the most commonly used financial ratios.

BALANCE SHEET RATIOS. These ratios are taken from a statement at a given point in time. They will vary with seasonal and short-term changes in the balance sheet.

1. *Current ratio—current assets divided by current liabilities.* A current ratio of 2 to 1 is often considered to be normal for a manufacturing company, but such a standard has very limited utility.

2. *Quick ratio—quick assets divided by current liabilities.* Quick assets are all assets that can be converted to cash in short order including readily marketable securities and receivables, but not inventory.

These two ratios are rough measures of a company's ability to convert its assets into cash to meet its current obligations.

3. *Inventory as a percentage of working capital.* (Working capital is found by subtracting current liabilities from current assets. It measures the amount of assets that are financed with long-term capital.) If this figure is greater than 100%, an inventory reliance exists.

4. *Inventory reliance—the percentage of inventory that will make up any negative difference between quick assets and current liabilities.* The immediate sale value of a company's inventory will determine the reliability of inventory as a source of funds.

Inventory is frequently a critical asset to analysts when it represents a company's stock in trade. The two ratios immediately preceding help to show how much attention must be paid to inventory on hand in analyzing a company's ability to generate cash.

5. Various balance sheet figures such as total liabilities, long term debt, or net fixed assets may be compared with net worth (or equity).
6. *Capital structure.* This divides long-term capital into its components: senior debt, subordinated debt, preferred stock, and common equity.

These last two types of ratio help the analyst compare the owners' stake in their business with the funds provided by others. They are measures of vulnerability in the long run.

TURNOVER RATIOS. Turnover ratios measure the rate at which dollars flow through various balance sheet accounts:

1. *Receivables turnover—net credit sales divided by receivables.* An average collection period makes a similar comparison in terms of days—average receivables divided by a daily average of net credit sales. This figure can be compared with a company's terms of sale.
2. *Inventory turnover—cost of sales divided by inventory.* Days' inventory on hand expresses the same thing by taking inventory divided by a daily average cost of sales.
3. *Working capital turnover—net sales divided by working capital.*

These ratios help the analyst to evaluate the company's basic operating efficiency. They are all interrelated and inseparable from the company's individual methods of doing business. For this reason, trends are easier to use than comparisons between companies.

OPERATING RATIOS. These ratios reflect income statement performance.

1. *Sales volume expressed in dollars of sales per dollar of (a) fixed assets, (b) working capital, (c) long term capital, (d) net worth, and (e) total assets.* These ratios help to relate a company's sales to its level of investment in various categories. They are a measure of efficiency.
2. *Gross profit as a percentage of sales.* This can reflect pricing policies or production and purchasing efficiency.
3. *Net income as a percentage of (a) sales and (b) net worth.*
4. *Times interest charges earned.* This is a measure of a company's ability to meet its fixed interest charges and thus to carry debt. It is computed as follows: Net income (before or after taxes) plus interest, all divided by interest.
5. *Fixed charge coverage.* This can be a key measure of a company's ability to meet its fixed commitments. There are numerous ways to calculate this ratio. An example of one method follows:

Net income before tax
plus   Depreciation and other non-cash charges
plus   Interest on long-term debt
plus   Minimum rental payments under leases

divided by

Interest on long-term debt
plus   Current funded debt and sinking fund requirements
plus   Minimum rental payments under leases

Other Influences on Credit Availability

We have already stated that credit considerations are of primary importance, but a good credit rating does not automatically assure a company of available bank credit. Companies should be interested in some of the non-credit factors that influence their access to loans.

Maintenance of Demand Deposits. Loans are an important source of bank income, but the banker's ability to make loans or any other profitable investments depends upon his ability to attract and maintain deposits. Therefore, a banker is likely to be concerned first with the needs of his large depositors. When money is plentiful, he may be willing to loan to all qualified applicants. When money is tight, he becomes more selective. Therefore, a business man desiring to assure himself of credit availability at all times should maintain adequate demand deposits in relation to the amount of credit he may want. An average figure of 20% is not unreasonable. This means that a company that may need $500,000 in credit should keep at least $100,000 on deposit on the average. These deposits are not frozen; they can be used for business needs and can compensate the bank for other services.

Stability of Banking Relationship. A good customer is proved by time. Bankers, like other businessmen, invest their time and money in developing new business with the hope that, many years later, that customer will still be a source of profitable business. Naturally, he becomes a favored customer. Companies should avoid carrying their business from bank to bank in search of a slightly better interest rate or a few dollars more. This is not to suggest that a company should never change banks or compare services. It says only that banking relationships tend to be relatively stable over the years and that every bank has a roster of good, favored customers. A company should weigh what it has to gain from a change of banks against the need to become seasoned in a new location.

Form and Completeness of Request for Credit. Finally, the manner in which a credit request is presented can often influence the outcome. Businessmen should remember that bankers, like other busy people, try to make their jobs as easy as possible. The company that seeks a loan with its data in good order will be more welcome than the company that requires the banker to ask for each piece of information. And any attempt to withhold information from a banker without sound reasons can arouse suspicion and prejudice the conclusion.

3

Financing Accounts

Monroe R. Lazere

ACCOUNTS RECEIVABLE AS COLLATERAL

Frequently, the required financial accommodation for a business enterprise exceeds the amount available via unsecured bank credit. Rapidly expanding volume indicates a need for larger amounts for longer periods than unsecured credit may make available. Conversely, a weak financial condition or the presence of operational losses reduce the borrower's probable capacity to repay an unsecured loan within a short period, for the anticipated reversal of trend may require some time. Additionally, a new enterprise may lack sufficient history to indicate its capacity to repay an unsecured loan. In such cases, operating cash may be obtained by supporting a loan with a pledge of collateral. Accounts receivable represent one such type of collateral. Since accounts receivable revolve as a result of shipment and collection in continuous cycles, an accounts receivable loan also revolves. In fact, it constitutes a revolving loan secured by the pledge of a revolving current asset. Its value has been amply proved for new enterprise, for growth situations, and for periods of a borrower's financial stringency.

Accounts receivable are generated by a business enterprise when it sells merchandise or performs services and extends normal trade terms (other than C.O.D.) to its customers. By granting such normal trade credit, the enterprise is creating reciprocal debts running to it from its customers. These debts are not evidenced by any instruments but appear on the books of the vendor as accounts receivable and on the books of the purchasers as accounts payable. Such book accounts are current assets of the vendor and may be pledged to

35

a lender to obtain immediate operating cash. Some contractual contractual restrictions on assignability were legally possible prior to the advent of the Uniform Commercial Code. The wide adoption of the Code, however, has rendered (in most states) accounts receivable freely assignable. To conform to modern legal terminology, such book accounts receivable shall hereafter be referred to as accounts.

Cost and Benefit of Financing Accounts

The advantage to the borrower of pledging accounts is that it accelerates his cash flow. It frees his capital from the waiting period required by normal trade terms. In effect, the financer does the waiting (for the payment by the account debtors) and the borrower's capital can be more profitably re-employed for other purposes. The increased rate of turn-over of the borrower's capital enhances the leverage of that capital and should produce increased profits. More specifically, the accelerated cash flow can result in any combination of tangible results such as increased volume, earning of trade discounts on purchases from suppliers, or development of ability to make more advantageous purchases by having available cash.

Credit men now increasingly recognize the affirmative results of the acceleration of cash flow via financing accounts. Accordingly, they are now inclined to accept such financing and no longer find it stigmatizing. Time was when suppliers frowned upon such financing as the creation of a "hidden lien" detrimental to their interests. Patently, however, the borrower could achieve the same acceleration by offering very attractive discounts for anticipation by his account debtors. It is now recognized that the key inquiry is whether the accelerated cash flow thus created is properly utilized rather than improperly diverted. Not surprisingly, therefore, the annual volume of the major types of commercial financing (approximately $25 billion in 1966) continues to increase rapidly, nothwithstanding the almost unanimous adoption of the Uniform Commercial Code with its requirement of a public filing of notice of such financing.

All three of the possibilities that are mentioned above are aptly illustrated by a specific, hypothetical case history. Two young men with a limited capital of $2,500 entered the business of wholesaling electronic tubes. Tubes were in extremely short supply at the time and they could literally sell instantly any tube they could find. Fortunately, they also had located some excellent sources of supply. They lacked only capital or other operating cash. For example, they could buy for cash $2,400 worth of tubes and re-sell their entire inventory for $3,000 almost within the same day. Unfortunately, they were required to give normal trade terms of thirty days and so would be out of operation for thirty days. After collection of the accounts, they could repeat the performance once every thirty days for a total annual volume of $36,000 and annual gross profit $7,200. But by financing their accounts they could repeat the process several times a week.

Assuming that they could repeat the performance three times a week, or do $9,000 in sales a week, they could do a gross volume of $468,000 ($9,000 × 52). Since their gross profit was 20% it would amount to approximately $93,600 per year. If their average turnover is assumed to be 30 days, their average outstanding accounts would be one month's sales or approximately $36,000 with an average cash advance of 80% or $28,800. Assuming a rate of $\frac{1}{24}$ of 1% per day on the cash daily balances, their cost of financing would be approximately $4,320. Hence for a financing cost of $4,320 they could achieve a gross profit of $93,600. Obviously the overly simplified situation here described is not typical. The theory has, however, proved itself in countless actual situations with variations from this idealized case history.

Financers also enter into drop shipment arrangements with borrowers having limited capital and no manufacturing and/or shipping facilities. This method of financing is discussed in connection with factoring (see page 75). The administrative techniques for drop shipment arrangements are similar for factoring and financing accounts. Since the financer, unlike the factor, does not assume responsibility for the credit worthiness of the borrower's customers, this difference is reflected in the respective agreements and procedures.

In short, financing of accounts will assist in handling additional volume. If the operation is unprofitable, however, financing may not necessarily cure the problem. In some instances financing will cure an unprofitable trend. That occurs where lack of cash flow is constricting the operation. On the other hand, if the profits realized as a result of financing exceed the cost of the use of the cash, then the financing is certainly worthwhile. And in determining the cost of the financing, emphasis should be placed on dollar cost, not rate. Financing of accounts, as will appear, requires much more administration by the lender than does unsecured credit. The additional administration is, in fact, the very element that makes possible this type of accommodation, for the administration permits much greater accommodation than could be available on an unsecured basis in the same situation. This increased cost of administration and increased exposure of the lender is reflected in an increased rate. The rate is a lender's method of quoting prices, just as a landlord quotes in dollars per square foot. But the tenant computes his rental cost as total dollars. The same approach is suggested on the cost of financing.

Financing Accounts and Unsecured Loans Compared. An essential difference in the mode of computation of the cost of money here should be noted. In financing of accounts, the lender's charge is a per diem rate on the daily cash loan balance. In unsecured lending the annual interest charge is computed for the period of the note and that amount is deducted from the cash advanced. A dramatic illustration of the difference between rate and cost may be derived from the following illustration developed by Walter S. Seidman, but modified to conform to more recent practice.

In this case, A, a manufacturer, needs a peak loan of $80,000 about the 10th of each month in order to discount his accounts payable. He discusses an unsecured loan with his bank, and it is willing to extend the necessary credit. Since, in this type of loan, the bank requires a compensating balance of 20%, he must borrow $100,000 to have $80,000 net in cash available. The bank will not permit him to borrow and repay the money daily as he needs it, but makes the loan on a 90-day basis at an interest rate of 6% per annum. Therefore the total cost to A financing on this basis is $1,500 for each 90-day period.

A discusses the matter with a secured financer (who may also be a bank). The latter agrees to make advances against accounts receivable under a plan whereby A would only have to borrow as he needs money, and collections on the accounts assigned would be credited against the loan daily. The rate would be $\frac{1}{30}$th of 1% per day on the cash balances, or at the rate of 12% per annum. Offhand, it would seem that the cost to A would be twice the amount he would have to pay the bank unsecured. The fallaciousness of this conclusion is demonstrated in the accompanying table (page 39) summarizing the transactions between A and the secured financer.

The average of daily loan balances due from A to the secured financer in the example given is $36,800. Therefore, the charge for the month at $\frac{1}{30}$th of 1% per day, would be $368.00 Assuming this same pattern were repeated for 90 days, the total cost to A would be $1,104 against the unsecured bank charge of $1,500, or a saving

Summary of Transaction with Secured Financer

Date	Accounts Assigned	Cash Advanced	Cash Collected	Equity Remitted	Collateral Balance	Loan Balance
11/1	$10,000	$8,000	–	–	$ 10,000	$ 8,000
11/2	10,000	8,000	–	–	20,000	16,000
11/3	10,000	8,000	–	–	30,000	24,000
11/4	10,000	8,000	–	–	40,000	32,000
11/5	10,000	8,000	–	–	50,000	40,000
11/6	10,000	8,000	–	–	60,000	48,000
11/7	10,000	8,000	–	–	70,000	56,000
11/8	10,000	8,000	–	–	80,000	64,000
11/9	10,000	8,000	–	–	90,000	72,000
11/10	10,000	8,000	–	–	100,000	80,000
11/11	–	–	–	–	100,000	80,000
11/12	–	–	$10,000	$2,000	90,000	72,000
11/13	–	–	10,000	2,000	80,000	64,000
11/14	–	–	10,000	2,000	70,000	56,000
11/15	–	–	10,000	2,000	60,000	48,000
11/16	–	–	10,000	2,000	50,000	40,000
11/17	–	–	10,000	2,000	40,000	32,000
11/18	–	–	10,000	2,000	30,000	24,000
11/19	–	–	10,000	2,000	20,000	16,000
11/20	–	–	10,000	2,000	10,000	8,000
11/21	–	–	–	–	10,000	8,000
11/22	–	–	–	–	10,000	8,000
11/23	–	–	–	–	10,000	8,000
11/24	10,000	8,000	–	–	20,000	16,000
11/25	10,000	8,000	–	–	30,000	24,000
11/26	10,000	8,000	–	–	40,000	32,000
11/27	–	–	–	–	40,000	32,000
11/28	–	–	–	–	40,000	32,000
11/29	–	–	–	–	40,000	32,000
11/30	–	–	–	–	40,000	32,000

of $396, even though the unsecured bank rate was 6% per annum as compared to a secured financer's rate of 12% per annum.

This is not, to say, of course, that consideration of rate is to be eliminated altogether. It does serve to compare rates as between lenders. But this use of rate should not be confused with the sometimes uneasy feeling that payment of interest above 6% per annum has social or economic consequences per se.

Determination of Financer's Rate

The determination of the rate to be charged by the financer involves a legal consideration. Almost every state has a statute regulating the interest that may be charged for various types of loans.

Frequently, a maximum permissible rate is set for individual or partnership borrowers and a different and higher one for corporations. These laws are distinct from the laws governing the perfection of the security interest. Most security agreements utilized by financers of accounts provide that the law governing the interpretation of the agreement, and the transactions thereunder, shall be the law of the state in which the financer has his office. Since accounts have no physical existence and advances usually are made from the financer's office, this is simple enough. Utilizing fixed assets and/or inventory as collateral, however, complicates this question. The security agreement may provide for domiciling the transactions in the state of either the financer or the borrower, both of which may be different from the state in which the physical collateral is located. Hence the law governing the conflicts of laws must be consulted. In any event, the determination of the operative state law on this question obviously is an important aspect of the financer's investigation and security agreement.

It should be noted that attempts to disguise a charge for the use of funds by labeling it something else, have uniformly been struck down. Nor does it matter that the language of the contract talks in terms of purchase of receivables rather than assignment of receivables. The governing test is whether the financer's compensation is measured by the time during which the cash is outstanding. Additionally, where the collateral is accounts (as opposed to negotiable notes) the provision for full recourse to the borrower buttresses the legal conclusion that the transaction is a loan bearing an interest charge and secured by collateral.

Sales Must Be Unconditional

If accounts are utilized to support a loan, then it becomes necessary for the lender to determine when they arise and how they are to be evaluated. For purposes of financing, an account arises when under the terms of sale, the account debtor's obligation becomes unconditional. In merchandise sales, an account usually arises when title to the merchandise passes. If services are involved, then the account arises when performance has been satisfactorily completed.

Some sales are made subject to specified conditions, which are distinct from normal merchandise warranties or normal warranties of satisfactory performance. The effect of warranties is discussed below. Examples of conditions attached to sales are found in consignment or memorandum sales in which title passes to the purchaser only upon his resale of the merchandise. Guaranteed sales are subject to a condition subsequent. Here title passes, but the purchaser has an absolute right of return if he fails to resell the merchandise.

In any particular transaction, these critical points are determined by the terms of the vendor's offer, the purchase order, the applicable law governing sales, and/or the custom and usage of the trade. Obviously, accounts created under a conditional arrangement cannot be acceptable as collateral to support a loan.

ANALYSIS AND INVESTIGATION OF PROSPECTIVE LOAN

Background of Borrower

Every analysis of a prospective loan starts with the character and background of the borrower. Sometimes, of course, the borrower is well known to the lender and this element is not emphasized. But let there be no doubt about it, this consideration is basic. Where the prospect is a stranger, credit agency reports are available. In addition to the general credit agencies such as Dun and Bradstreet, Bishop, Proudfoot, and Hooper Holmes, certain specialized credit agencies are available in particular fields. For example, National Credit Office specializes in textiles, Lyons in furniture. The Lumberman's Credit Association and the Jewelers Board of Trade are self-descriptive. Trade and bank references can be requested of the prospect and checked. The Uniform Commercial Code has provided another essential step in checking a new prospect. Before undertaking the financing of accounts (or any other form of secured lending) the lender should check the record in the appropriate state office to ascertain whether any other lender has filed a financing statement covering the same collateral. This search can be accomplished easily by a special form UCC 11 (see Chapter 9, pp. 214, 215). Additionally, there are services that provide such reports within hours for a fee.

Occasionally it is said that if the collateral is adequate, the background of the borrower becomes unimportant. No prudent lender subscribes to such a philosophy. In a recently publicized king-sized fraud, the proffered collateral seemingly made the loan riskless. Warehouse receipts of a peerless warehouse company representing a staple commodity were offered as collateral. Most lenders involved in the transaction were unaware of the business entity originally offering the receipts. Some lenders were aware of that business entity and of some questionable background material in the credit agency report. But those lenders felt that the collateral was like money in the bank, and the background material was overlooked. Subsequently, it turned out that the receipts were forged or improperly issued and were created gigantically in excess of the actual amount of the commodity on hand. This case certainly underscores the paramount principle of sound lending—character precedes collateral and may, in fact, condition the collateral.

Initial Investigation: Evaluation or Appraisal of Accounts

Figures available in the financial statement, including a report on operations, enable the lender to analyze financial strength and operating trends. This data assists in probing some fundamental questions: (a) Will the loan aid the borrower? and (b) In the case of an unsecured loan or a secured and amortizing loan, can the repayment schedule be met? Where the loan is secured, the appraisal of the collateral that secures the loan is important. Since the amount of the loan is measured by the collateral, the value of the collateral is obviously a fundamental consideration. The method of appraising the collateral naturally varies with the type of collateral utilized. Real estate and equipment appraisals usually are made by real estate and equipment specialists familiar with their respective markets. For accounts financing, the appraisal takes the form of an initial investigation.

After the preliminary background credit investigation has been completed as above described, the financer of accounts conducts an initial investigation of the prospect's books and records underlying the balance sheet and statement of operations. This examination usually takes place at the premises of the borrower and is performed by a person trained to read such records—usually an accountant. This is not to be construed as a reflection on the financial statement prepared by the prospect's accountant. Normally, his statement consists of a summary of figures as they appear on the books and records of his client. However, it is the detail of the ebb and flow of the component parts of these figures that interests a financer. In short, the orientation is very different, and this initial investigation fleshes out the statement in areas that are extremely significant for the financer.

Two of the key components of such an investigation are (1) careful appraisal of the nature (and value) of the accounts—the collateral for the loan and (2) an estimate of the creditor pressure to which the prospect is being subjected.

Industry Practices. Several elements comprise the appraisal of the collateral value of the accounts. Obviously the accounts cannot be accepted at face or gross value. The first element in the appraisal of accounts requires a knowledge of the nature of and practices in the prospect's industry. Certain industries present unique problems which must be carefully analyzed. Occasionally, for example, the acceptability and price of the borrower's services revolves about rather subjective reactions. This would be true in the case of commercial artwork. Here documentation 'of agreements on price and the account debtor's approval of the work would be necessary. Failing such documentation, the accounts thus created might be of doubtful value.

Another example is the dress market in which the manufacturer is traditionally forced to preserve his customer relationship by accepting returns of styles that do not sell well and at the end of a particular season, the returns of such merchandise may be very heavy. In another typical field, machined parts of low tolerances requiring extreme accuracy also result in receivables that may give rise to excessive returns. This could develop as a result of one poor run through the manufacturer's production line.

Another relationship that could create difficulty is the situation in which the prospect processes the customer's merchandise. A dyer of textiles is a typical case. Here an error damaging the customer's merchandise could result in an offset exceeding the amount of the account receivable. Similarly, an extruder may be supplied with special plastic powder by his customer. The potential claim for unused or misused powder could create an offset. All of the above considerations must be analyzed and evaluated at the time of the initial investigation.

The second consideration is the possibility of normal trade discounts, and, here again, a knowledge of the trade or industry is essential. A popular trade discount in some apparel industries is 8%. This means that an invoice of $100 is paid at $92. Hence the trade discount offered (either expressly or by custom and usage) is the first adjustment. This could be additionally modified by the particular applicant. For example, the applicant may be offering a discount of 1% for payment in 10 days (described as 1% 10 days, net 30). Other examples might be 2% 10 days, 5% 60 days, etc. Further, it can be anticipated that some percentage of the borrower's total billing

will be adjusted for returns of merchandise because the merchandise
was unsatisfactory to the purchaser, because of late delivery, etc.   To
protect against the above types of dilution of the accounts, the lender
must analyze the past experience record as reflected by the applicant's
books of account and particularly the accounts receivable ledgers.

In certain industries, vendors' warranties play an important role.
In sales of machinery, for example, the vendor may issue a warranty
for thirty days, or a year.   Depending on the complexity of the equipment, such warranties may portend serious collection difficulties unless
the vendor maintains a large service organization.   If the vendor
becomes bankrupt, however, the financer relying on such collateral
may find himself in an uncollectible morass.   The cost of establishing
a servicing operation to induce account debtors' payments may be
prohibitive.

Another appraisal problem arises from co-operative advertising arrangements which a supplier sometimes makes with a retail store.
Under such an arrangement the retail store will advertise the product
of the supplier and is permitted to deduct up to an agreed percentage
of the gross invoice in payment for the advertising.   Such arrangements must be studied to gauge adequately the proper percentage
of advance.

Concentrations in Accounts.   Although the financer (as distinguished from the factor) is not guaranteeing the credit worthiness
of the accounts, he must obviously consider the possibility of concentrations in the accounts.   The potential insolvency of an account
debtor representing 50% of the borrower's outstandings, for example,
would easily result in a shortage of accounts to cover the loan.   Additionally, a borrower's bad run of merchandise concentrated in one
account debtor could result in a single substantial return.   A bad
run spread over many account debtors leaves open the possibility
of making adjusting arrangements.   Hence the evaluation procedure
necessarily includes a study of concentrations.   Credit loss experience
is studied for the obvious reason.

Account Aging.   Another indispensable element in appraising the
collateral of accounts is the preparation of an aging of the accounts.
This consists of the listing of all the borrower's accounts in columns
indicating the time period of the maturity of the accounts: those
shipped within thirty days of date of the analysis, sixty days, ninety
days, etc.   This enables the examiner to determine how much of
the outstanding accounts may be stale and therefore should not be
eligible for cash advance.

Contra Accounts. Further, the possibility of contra accounts must be examined. Such an account arises when the borrower buys from as well as sells to a particular customer. The sale will appear in the receivables ledger of the borrower, while the purchase by the borrower will appear in his payables ledger. The unknowing financer may advance on the receivable, giving it full value. Upon a liquidation, however, the account debtor could properly offset the amount due him from the borrower, since patently the borrower could not assign a greater right than he himself had. Hence the financer may find himself unsecured for the difference.

Incomplete Performance. Accounts that require further performance by the borrower must be carefully examined. Progress billing may develop where a contractor or subcontractor is permitted to requisition for payment upon completion of agreed percentages of the contract. A failure to complete the balance of the contract could result in offsets or counterclaims wiping out the amount of the requisition utilized as collateral. Hence, if the borrower becomes bankrupt before completion of the contract, the financer, resorting to the collateral, may find that it has disappeared.

A similar problem may arise where the borrower has contracted to deliver a quantity of merchandise over a period of time. Partial shipment and invoicing may be permitted. But if bankruptcy ensues before complete delivery, the oustanding invoices utilized as collateral may dissolve by virtue of offsets and damage claims for non-delivery of the balance of the merchandise. Some contracts for such periodic deliveries expressly spell out items of the purchaser's damage.

Estimating Creditor Pressure on Prospect. Estimating the financial stress of a prospective borrower is another vital part of the initial investigation. The need for this estimate is quite apparent, for fraud is the greatest risk run in financing of accounts. Of all losses incurred by accounts financers only a very small percentage stem from frauds perpetrated by the pre-planned activity of a dishonest person. The large bulk of such losses develop as a result of the manipulations of normally and formerly honest businessmen under heavy financial pressure. The normal sequence is to commit a few irregularities to obtain funds with which to meet a payroll, pay a pressing bill, etc. The most common types of such irregularities are the presentation of invoices or accounts where the merchandise has not been shipped (or services not performed) or only partially shipped (or performed), the failure to report returns or credits, and the surreptitious depositing of remittances belonging to the lender. The borrower's intention, of course, is to straighten out the entire matter the following week. Unfortunately he finds that the following week he cannot cure the irregularities but must commit further irregularities to meet the new payroll or other obligations. As the process snowballs, the irregularities mount. The analysis of financial stress is therefore a form of preventive hygiene.

Financial pressure can lead to serious problems other than fraud. If the condition of the prospect indicates a strong possibility of an imminent insolvency, then all the hazards are magnified. The borrower's urgency to create shipments may lead to the delivery of shoddy merchandise and therefore potentially higher returns. The bankruptcy of the supplier encourages the account debtors to delay payment and, indeed to seek real or imaginary reasons to avoid payment. The financer may be involved in legal expense of defending the validity of his security interest against the attack of general creditors. He will incur the administrative cost of effecting collection of widely dispersed accounts. And finally, the desperate borrower may borrow from his customers and thus create contra accounts offsetting a good portion of the collateral. Such loans may be bona fide or, in fact, on-account payments more conveniently labeled. Either way, however, the financer's jeopardy is the same.

INDICES OF FINANCIAL STRESS. Certain indices of financial stress should be examined during the initial investigation. An aging of payables will reveal the extent to which the injection of loaned funds will relieve creditor pressure. The loan and exchange account will reveal the extent of the prospect's juggling of funds. Occasionally the examination of this account will dramatically alter the analysis. A harmless entry may appear on a balance sheet: "exchange payable X thousand dollars." Upon examination of the ledger account, the investigator finds that that amount has been exchanged—in and out—with great velocity. This usually indicates a financial tightness and the possibility of some serious juggling or kiting of funds. And finally, the examination of the surplus account may reveal a net worth fattened by a questionable reappraisal of fixed assets.

WITHHOLDING-TAX LIABILITY AND THE FEDERAL TAX LIEN ACT. Another key element in the analysis of pressure is a determination of the mounting liability of the prospect for witholding taxes. If the accumulation of such taxes is mounting rapidly, then there may be an imminent possibility of a tax lien being filed against the prospect. In such a case, the auditor should determine whether the advances to be made by the financer would be sufficient to offset or eliminate this possibility. Once the tax lien is in fact filed, it is superior to any future assignments of accounts or any additional pledge of collateral. Thus, continuing to make advances against additional collateral after the filing of the lien, would be subject to a possible attack by the Internal Revenue Service.

The problem of Federal tax liens has been greatly modified by the passage of the Federal Tax Lien Act of 1966. It, therefore, may be worthwhile to discuss it at this juncture, both as to initial and interim audits of the borrower, originally a prospect. Affirmatively, the 1966 Act adopts the language of the Uniform Commercial Code defining a security interest in collateral. Thus it eliminates the former occasional problem of determining whether a secured creditor under local state law was so considered under the old Federal statutory language. Further, it eliminates the inchoateness doctrine which formerly plagued secured creditors whose collateral by agreement covered charges and disbursements accrued subsequent to default. Additionally, it provides a secured creditor with legal remedies against the Federal government in those occasional situations in which the Internal Revenue Service executes upon the debtor's property in derogation of the rights of such creditor's prior perfected security interest. In such event, recovery of damages is now available against the United States, or more immediate (and therefore more effective) injunctive relief now can be obtained. Further, advances made pursuant to a revolving financing arrangement within forty-five days after the filing of the Federal tax lien are protected, provided the financer's security interest had been perfected prior to the tax lien filing—and provided further, that the financer had no knowledge of the tax lien filing within the forty-five day period.

Knowledge on the part of the financer or imputation of knowledge to the financer, however, can present difficulties under the new legislation. Hence all routine procedures for checking on tax lien filings should be pursued with the utmost diligence. The forty-five day period should not be utilized to relax procedures, even though it appears to be designed to obviate extraordinary investigative procedures, at least for distant borrowers.

Another difficulty with the new legislation arises from Section 105 thereof, which enacted new Section 3505 of the Internal Revenue Code. This section seems to impose some responsibility for the debtor's unpaid withholding taxes upon sureties and lenders who advance funds specifically for payroll, if the provider of such funds was aware of the debtor's lack of intent, or inability, to pay the withholding taxes related to such payrolls. Since the legislation is new, construction of several of its key terms must await both the regulations of the Internal Revenue Service and future court decisions. Let it suffice here to note the problem and its possible future course of development, with the caveat that advances directly into the borrower's payroll account should be avoided, whenever possible.

Setting Amount of Advance

Experience has indicated that an average reserve of from 20 to 25% of net receivables is an adequate provision for normal dilutions. Hence the financer's usual advance against accounts is approximately 75 to 80% of net accounts, after deducting trade discounts, eliminating delinquent accounts and contra accounts, and adjusting for undue concentrations. The profit margin of the borrower must also be considered in setting this percentage. It is obviously desirable not to advance a percentage on the accounts that exceeds the borrower's cost of creating them. He should be required to await the collection of the receivables before realizing his profit. His continued investment in the accounts tends to assure his conservatism in the selection of and collection from his customers.

BASIC MECHANICS

Financing of accounts may be conducted under a notification or non-notification arrangement. The difference lies in whether the account debtor (the borrower's customer) is advised by a legend on the invoices and statements that the accounts have been assigned and are payable to the financer. As indicated above, in the early days of non-notification financing of accounts, credit men feared it as a hidden lien. The merits and weaknesses of this position have become academic, in view of the adoption of the Uniform Commercial Code in most states. The Code requires the filing of a financing statement thus giving creditors public notice that the borrower has undertaken an arrangement to finance his accounts. Notwithstanding such public notice, however, most borrowers prefer non-notification financing. They prefer to avoid repetitively advising their customers of their financing arrangements. Additionally, they prefer to avoid such customer resistance as may arise from the resultant complication of their customers' bookkeeping.

Procedure Before and After the Uniform Commercial Code

The operational techniques and procedures of financing accounts were developed prior to the widespread adoption of the Uniform Commercial Code. The procedures involved the execution of a basic contract between borrower and financer and thereafter the periodic (daily, weekly, or, rarely, monthly) assignment of receivables by the borrower. Advances by the financer were made against such assignments. Remittances received by the borrower were turned over to the financer in the form in which they were received by the borrower. The financer would then credit the borrower's account for the amount of such checks and deposit them in the financer's bank account. To avoid the use of the financer's name on the endorsement of such checks, a coded endorsement was utilized.

The then governing law required that the financer exercise dominion over and control of the receivables in order to maintain his lien thereon. It has been properly argued that the then governing law did not technically require that the remittances received by the borrower be turned over in kind to the lender. Other devices for requiring the borrower to account would have been legally valid and would have maintained the lien. But when an operation becomes geared to an accelerated cash flow resulting from financing of accounts, the lender's control of the flow should be built into the flow of the accounts. Otherwise the borrower may miscalculate his ability to account for collections and repay the loan. Additionally, the physical checks and the pay statements usually thereon constitute a verification of the bona fides of the original accounts assigned.

In conformity with this philosophy, therefore, the above described procedures were developed. Although the Uniform Commercial Code dispenses with the requirement of dominion and control, most financers insist on retaining most of the old procedures. The reason is obvious. Although the Code simplifies the methods of perfecting liens for various security devices, the experienced financer recognizes that the existence of a legal lien does not insure the existence, quality, or quantity of the collateral. Finally, although the Code permits the blanket assignment of present and future accounts, most financers prefer detailed scheduling. This provides them (in the language of the schedule form) with a specific warranty of bona fides, non-offset, etc., for the accounts particularized. Hence the passing of the collateral through the financer's office remains a sound method of operation.

Over the years, the handling procedures of the financers have become more streamlined. Bulk, rather than detailed, assignments can be made. Microfilming, bookkeeping machines, and data processing equipment are utilized to reduce the amount of clerical work involved in the finance operation. But certain cardinal requirements remain. Within a limited number of hours the financer must be able to reconstruct, update, and reproduce the borrower's accounts receivable ledger. If he is required to liquidate his loan by pursuing his collateral, the financer obviously must possess current and complete records of that collateral.

Perfecting Security Interest

The legal requirement of perfecting the lien on the accounts is also basic. The several methods of doing so under pre-Code law as well as the present method under the Code will be discussed more fully in later chapters. It must be recalled that the secured financer is advancing funds to a borrower whose financial condition does not warrant an unsecured loan in the same amount. Hence in the event of an insolvency the financer must be in a position to assert his legal right to the collateral against general creditors. It is therefore essential that the financer so perfect his lien on the accounts as to avoid having his right to the accounts set aside as preferential transfers under Section 60A of the Bankruptcy Act. The perfection of the lien, however, is governed by applicable state law. As above stated, most states have enacted the Uniform Commercial Code, and therefore a security interest in accounts must be perfected thereunder.

United States Government as Account Debtor. In addition to perfecting his security interest under the Code, the financer of accounts on which the United States government is the account debtor must observe another precaution.

Since the Federal government through its many agencies is a major customer for many small businesses, consideration should be given to the handling of such accounts. Prior to 1940 no claim against the government could be assigned without its consent. Although such an assignment was good between the parties, the government was not required to recognize such assignment. In order to facilitate the financing of small suppliers, legislation was enacted in 1940 and amended in 1951.

This legislation, known as the Assignment of Claims Act of 1940, permits the assignment of accounts on which the Federal government or any of its agencies is the account debtor with certain conditions: The amount of the total contract (or order) must exceed $1,000; the assignment must be to a bank or other financial institution; and notice of the assignment must be given to the contracting officer, the disbursing officer, and the surety, if any. During national emergencies any procurement agency may insert a no-offset clause in its contract. Such a provision removes the possibility of having the indebtedness of one agency of the government to a borrower reduced by the borrower's obligation to another agency of the government (the Internal Revenue Service, for example).

THE OPERATIONAL RELATIONSHIP

After the initial investigation has been concluded satisfactorily, the contract is executed. For a typical contract, see Fig. 3–6, page 66 et seq. This underlying contractual relationship is necessary to formalize the rights and obligations of the parties, since the arrangement contemplates an on-going relationship of revolving collateral and cash advances and repayments thereof. For the lender-borrower relationship herein described, it also constitutes one of the three fundamental elements required under the Code to perfect a security interest in accounts. These elements are a security agreement, the advance of cash thereunder, and the filing of a financing statement.

In connection with the closing of the contract, a resolution of the borrower's board of directors is required, authorizing the contract and permitting the lender's bank to credit to the account of the lender checks and notes made payable to the borrower. This is accomplished by a coded endorsement and thus effectuates the non-notification arrangement. A secretarial certificate of resolutions appears as Fig. 3–1, page 52.

Financer's Discretionary Rights

An examination of the contract immediately reveals that the financer has considerable discretion in the determination of acceptable collateral and in the exercise of certain rights. This reservation of discretion is an unavoidable requirement. Obviously the lender would be foolhardy to commit himself to make loans in the unforeseen and unforseeable future. The changes in circumstances and condition of the borrower that might vitally affect the safety of the loan are too difficult to enumerate. Hence the lender perforce must reserve the discretionary power. The reputation of the lender is the borrower's assurance that this discretion will not be abused.

CERTIFICATE OF RESOLUTIONS
of

....

I, ... , do hereby certify that I am , ... Secretary of .... , a corporation, and that the following is a true copy of resolutions duly adopted by the Board of Directors of said Corporation at a meeting thereof duly called and held on the .... day of .... 19 :

"RESOLVED: That it is to the best interests of this Corporation to enter into arrangements with XYZ FINANCIAL CORPORATION , herein designated as "Secured Party", providing for financing or factoring accommodation to be extended to this Corporation by said Secured Party and for the creation of security interests in favor of Secured Party upon this Corporation's present and future tangible or intangible property; and further

RESOLVED: That the President or any Vice President of this Corporation is hereby authorized and empowered to make, execute, and deliver in the name of this Corporation a security agreement or agreements with Secured Party, and any amendments or modifications thereof, and that each of the officers of this Corporation, and any person whom this Corporation or any officer thereof may from time to time designate, is hereby authorized and empowered to make, execute and deliver to Secured Party in the name of this Corporation any and all such assignments, pledges, endorsements, transfers, and other documents and instruments, and to do all such acts, as may be appropriate to consummate transactions between this Corporation and Secured Party pursuant to such security agreement or agreements; and further

RESOLVED: That all acts and transactions of the officers of this Corporation and of any such designees, done in execution or performance of any such security agreement and of transactions thereunder, are hereby ratified and approved; and further

RESOLVED: That any officer, agent or nominee of Secured Party is hereby authorized and empowered to endorse the name of this Corporation to any and all checks, drafts and other instruments or orders for the payment of money, payable to this Corporation or its order, and to deposit the same in any account of Secured Party with any bank, banker or trust company, and to deal with any and all such instruments and the proceeds thereof as the property of Secured Party; and further

RESOLVED: That any bank, banker or trust company is hereby authorized and requested to receive for deposit to the credit of Secured Party, without further inquiry, all such checks, drafts and other instruments or orders for the payment of money, payable to this Corporation or its order, without responsibility or liability to this Corporation for the disposition which Secured Party may or shall make of the same or the proceeds thereof."

I further certify that the location of the office of said Corporation, as specified in its Certificate of Incorporation, is the .... of .... , State of .... , and that its principal and only place of business is located at ....,
(Street Address)
.... , ...
(City, Town or Village)   (State)

I further certify that the Certificate of Incorporation and By-Laws of said Corporation contain no provision requiring a vote or consent of stockholders to authorize the action of the Board of Directors set forth in the foregoing resolutions, and that said resolutions are and remain in full force and effect.

IN WITNESS WHEREOF, I have hereunto set my hand as .... Secretary of said Corporation, and impressed its corporate seal hereon, by order of the Board of Directors, this .... day of .... , 19

The foregoing is hereby approved and confirmed:

.... Secretary

[Corporate Seal]

....

....

....

....
Directors

STATE OF   )
           : ss.:
COUNTY OF   )

.... , being duly sworn, deposes and says that he is Secretary of .... , a .... corporation, and that the persons who have signed the foregoing approval and confirmation constitute together all the directors of said corporation and the holders of more than two thirds of the issued and outstanding shares of said corporation.

Sworn to before me this

.... day of .... 19 .

....

....
Notary Public

Fig. 3–1. Certificate of Resolutions

The same analysis applies to the provision indicating that the financer will lend "up to" a stated percentage of acceptable accounts. Patently, the credit loss and return experience, as determined by the initial investigation, will set the general viable range of the percentage of advance. But developments subsequent to the execution of the contract may alter the analysis. Hence it is reasonable for the lender to provide a reservation of the discretionary right to modify the percentage downward. Obviously, except in special situations (such as a court order under Chapter XI of the Bankruptcy Act) the lender is free to make an overadvance beyond the stated percentage.

Rate of Compensation

The current prevailing practice is to fix the rate at a fraction of one per cent per day on the cash daily balances. This assures the borrower that he is charged in direct proportion to the assistance received. To gear the charge to the accounts could penalize a borrower who does not require his full availability. Similarly, it would unfairly burden a borrower whose deteriorating financial condition justified the lender's reduction of the percentage of advance.

The current range of per diem rates varies from $\frac{1}{15}$th of 1% on small and more marginal accounts to $\frac{1}{40}$th of 1% on larger and secured but bankable accounts. For very large accounts the last rate could be even lower.

Documentation

The contract also requires the borrower to turn over to the lender the checks from his customers in the form in which they are received. The reasons for this provision have already been discussed (see page 49).

The borrower also is usually required to supply the lender with copies of invoices and the documentary evidence of shipment. Such evidence may be (rarely) the customer's own receipt but is more usually bills of lading or parcel post receipts. Receipts of local truckers who deliver to the over-the-road carrier may also be utilized, but here care should be exercised. Their records frequently are rather informal. The documentation requirement serves a double function. First, it provides the lender with complete and detailed records of the collateral supporting the loan. In the event of a liquidation in which the lender must proceed on his collateral he is in a position to prove the specific obligations of the account debtors.

Second, this requirement serves as a brake on a dishonest borrower. The presentation of such documentary evidence would, if false, involve forgery and thus eliminate the excuse of an honest mistake. Notwithstanding these advantages certain lenders dispense with the requirement of documentation of shipment in an effort to cut handling costs.

Obviously, however, a bona fide bill of lading does not assure the lender that a bona fide account has been created. For the cartons or boxes properly signed for by the trucker may contain sawdust or an incomplete shipment of merchandise. The right of the lender to verify the accounts is therefore vital. The implementation of this provision is discussed below (page 61).

Returned Merchandise

In normal operation, a certain limited amount of merchandise returns may be anticipated. Since the financer's security interest extends to such merchandise, it should be segregated for identification. Normally, however, the reporting of such returns results in an adjustment of the control and detailed ledgers. Such adjustment should be effected in the same manner as the adjustment for delinquent accounts discussed below (page 61). Should insolvency ensue before such adjustment is completed, however, the identifiable returns should be available to assist in the liquidation of the loan balance.

Personal Guaranty of Borrower's Principals

Finally, the personal guarantee of the principals of the borrower is normally required. The financial strength of the guarantors is not the key element here. The requirement is made to assure the lender that the managing principals undertake a personal responsibility to see that the accounts will be of sufficient quantity and quality to retire the loan. It also serves as insurance of the principals' co-operation in liquidating the loan, if that becomes necessary.

FINANCER'S INTERNAL PROCEDURES

Control Ledgers

For each borrower, the financer maintains a control ledger. A sample is shown in Fig. 3–2, pp. 56–57. For each type of account (collateral and cash) the ledger shows the amount assigned or advanced, the amount remitted, and the balance at the conclusion of each day. Accumulation of the daily cash balances may be thrown off by the bookkeeping machine to assist in the computation of charges. The control ledger thus enables the financer to determine quickly whether the cash is in proper relationship to the borrower's collateral. If the cash exceeds the agreed percentage of collateral, the account is overadvanced. If, as a result of remittances, the cash is below the agreed percentage, then cash may be released to the borrower. Such "equity" releases normally are made periodically (most often weekly).

Detailed Ledgers

The financer maintains some form of detailed ledger of accounts for each borrower. For small and marginal accounts this may be hand posted and result in a duplication of the accounts receivable ledger of the borrower. The posting media utilized for this ledger would be the Schedule of Collateral constituting the specific assignment by the borrower (see Fig. 3-3, pp. 58-59) and the Remittance & Credit Report used in transmittal of collections (see Fig. 3-4, page 60). It is the detailed ledger, of course, that contains the heart of the lender's collateral position.

In order to reduce mechanical labor and operational costs, some of these procedures have been streamlined. Assignments may be made merely by reference to a sequence of numbered invoices. As previously indicated, microfilm is sometimes used to assign in bulk an entire ledger, and sometimes copies of the borrower's monthly statements to its customers are utilized as a detailed accounts ledger by the lender. These procedures save considerable labor and time. In recent years the use of computers has enabled financers to detail a large volume of such transactions rapidly and expeditiously. Regardless of the system utilized, however, extreme caution must be exercised to insure that a reproducible, updated list of accounts is available to the lender on very short notice.

Credit report information and credit limits may be marked on such ledgers to avoid concentration and overextensions of credit to weak account debtors.

Aging of the borrower's accounts must be undertaken periodically by the financer or provided by the borrower. The aging should also indicate skipped invoices. A skipped invoice is an invoice remaining unpaid after the account debtor has paid a subsequent invoice, and may signal unreported returns or unadjusted claims. Reserves for delinquent accounts and skipped invoices must be created

XYZ FINANCIAL CORPORATION

CLIENT: _____

DATE	REFERENCE	COLLATERAL		CASH			
		ASSIGNED	REMITTED	ADVANCED	REF.	REMITTED	COLL

TOTALS

FOLIO REFERENCES:
EC – ERROR CORRECTION   TR – TRANSFER TO RESERVE   R.T. – RETURNED CHECK
BC – BANK CHARGE   DC – DOCUMENTS CHARGE ON L/C   PO – POSTAGE
SC – SERVICE CHARGE   EQ – EQUITY   ◇ – REVERSAL ENTRY

Fig. 3–2. Contr

RESERVE FOR PAST DUES	
DATE	AMOUNT
SVCE. CHGE.-PRIOR MO.	
PAID	

_____ % ADVANCE

_____ RATE

_____ CLEARANCE

NTH OF_____

BALANCES		ACCUMULATIONS			
AL	CASH	DAILY CASH BALANCES	CASH REMITTANCES	COLLATERAL ASSIGNED	PROOF

ABOVE FIGURES OMIT RECEIVABLES IN
RESERVE FOR DELINQUENCY, ETC. ALL
PAYMENTS ON SUCH ITEMS BELONG TO LFC

ger Page

ORIGINAL

XYZ FINANCIAL CORPORATION

SCHEDULE OF ACCOUNTS PLEDGED

The undersigned hereby certifies that the customers listed below are indebted to the undersigned, in the amounts and upon the terms herein set forth, for goods sold, delivered and accepted or for work, labor and services rendered and accepted.

NAME OF DEBTOR	ADDRESS	INVOICE NO.	DATE OF INVOICE	TERMS	GROSS AMOUNT OF INVOICE	LEAVE BLANK	
						RATING	AMOUNT OWING
——— AMOUNT BROUGHT FORWARD ———							

TOTALS OR AMOUNTS
BROUGHT FORWARD

Dated this _____ day of _____ 19 ____

For value received, and in accordance with the underlying security agreement between the undersigned and XYZ FINANCIAL CORPORATION (hereinafter referred to as "secured party"), the undersigned hereby pledges, assigns, transfers and sets over unto secured party, its successors and assigns, and vests secured party with a security interest in all property, rights to property, title and interest in and to the foregoing accounts and the merchandise represented thereby and the proceeds due or to become due thereon, together with all rights, securities and guarantees possessed by the undersigned with respect thereto, including the right of stoppage in transit. All the covenants, warranties, guarantees, and stipulations of the undersigned, contained in the aforesaid security agreement between the undersigned and secured party, are hereby repeated and shall apply to each account above listed, and to the said merchandise and proceeds. Without limiting the generality of the foregoing, the undersigned warrants that it is solvent, that this schedule correctly sets forth undisputed accounts and contract rights now owing to the undersigned for work, labor, and services actually rendered, or for bona fide sales and deliveries (not consignment shipments or guaranteed sales) in accordance with specifications of the above buyers, of merchandise which was the sole and unconditional property of the undersigned prior to its sale; that the above accounts will be paid in full and that there are no defenses, offsets, contra-accounts or counterclaims of any nature whatsoever against any of them; that the correct maturities of said accounts have been set forth; that proper entries have been made on its books disclosing the transfer thereof to secured party; that all rejections, returns, or resale of merchandise and all collections received or credits allowed by it upon any and all accounts previously pledged to secured party have been duly, properly and regularly entered to the credit of the respective customers on the books and records usually used for such purpose, and that prompt report and payment thereof has been forwarded to secured party; that none of said accounts have been pledged, sold or assigned to any other party; and that said accounts are free and clear of all liens or claims of any nature whatsoever.

Accepted by XYZ FINANCIAL CORPORATION   Firm Name _____

at New York, N. Y., on _____   By _____

(Date)   (Title)

Schedule No. _____

Signature O. K.	Shipping receipts examined	Checked Schedule with Invoices	Additions Checked	Entered in Clients Ledger

Fig. 3–3.   Schedule of Collateral

ORIGINAL

⬤   ⬤

REMITTANCE & CREDIT REPORT

NO._____

_____19____

FROM
NAME_____

To   XYZ FINANCIAL CORPORATION:

The following remittances were this day received, have been found correct, and are enclosed herewith in their original form.

NAME OF DEBTOR	DATE OF BILL	GROSS AMOUNT OF BILLS	RETURNS AND ALLOWANCES	AMOUNT OF DISCOUNT	AMOUNT OF CHECK	LEAVE BLANK
TOTAL						

IMPORTANT

1. Send your Customer's Pay Statement to us together with the original check.

2. If any part of same is for bills not assigned to us, the excess will be returned.

3. Report all returns, allowances, and bankrupt accounts to us daily.

4. Any merchandise returned to you by accounts assigned to us shall be set aside and marked "Property of XYZ FINANCIAL CORPORATION".

CERTIFICATION

Regarding accounts previously assigned to you, we hereby certify that all returns, allowances, credits and claims of our customers -- whether or not we dispute them -- which we have received *or are aware of*, have been reported to you on this or prior remittance reports.

Dated_____

Firm Name_____

By_____
(Title)

Fig. 3–4. Remittance & Credit Report

to insure that the cash account is supported by fresh and current collateral. Normally, a delinquency formula for each borrower is established. This usually is thirty or sixty days past due under the borrower's normal terms of sale. Reserving for delinquent accounts and skipped invoices obviously alters the relationship between the cash balance and the current collateral balance in the borrower's control account. This is adjusted by the retention of the "equity" arising from collections. If, within a short period, normal collections do not bring the cash account into proper relationship with the current collateral account, future schedules of accounts should be underadvanced to expedite the adjustment.

Verification

The major portion of the internal operations of the financer is directed toward processing and testing the collateral. Notwithstanding the mountains of paperwork involved in these procedures, the simplest and surest test of bona fides of an account is to inquire of the account debtor whether he owes the money and to have him respond affirmatively. If the non-notification arrangement is to be maintained, however, this must be done discreetly. The usual method is to utilize an accountant's verification (see Fig. 3–5 page 62) addressed to the account debtor and requesting confirmation of the indebtedness. A certain percentage of each borrower's accounts should be verified monthly. One labor-saving device is to require each borrower to submit to the financer a portion of his monthly statements to customers. The financer then utilizes the statements for purposes of verification of balances. Chain stores usually do not require such statements but make payments on a voucher system. In such cases, telephone verification or shipping and receipt verifications are possible. Here the confirmation of specific details is requested. It must be recognized that only a small percentage of requests for verification will result in an affirmative response, but responses showing discrepancies will signal the advisability of heavier probing in this direction.

Processing Remittances

The staff of the financer processing remittance checks must be alert to utilize the information produced by the borrower's physically

Accountant and Auditor

Date...

....

....

....

Gentlemen:

We are auditing the books of ....

....

and desire confirmation of the following indebtedness: ....

....

... ,..

....

....

....

We would thank you to verify promptly, indicating contra account, if any. Kindly call attention to any offsets, returns, consigned or guaranteed sales, payments or notes sent us and not shown hereon.

Enclosed is self-addressed envelope for your reply.

Very truly yours,

Please sign below if the figures indicated are correct.   If incorrect indicate differences in remarks space.

Signed..

Remarks...

....

....

....

....

....

....

Fig. 3–5.   Accountant's Verification

turning over the account debtors' checks. The requirement of the physical checks makes it difficult for the borrower to substitute new fictitious accounts for fictitious accounts that appear to be delinquent. By insisting upon pursuing the accounts to their ultimate disposition, the financer prevents a possible kiting of fictitious accounts. The drawer of the check should have exactly the same name as the account debtor. Similarity of names that could lead to confusion must be carefully watched. It may indicate that the borrower is seeking deliberately to becloud a situation. For example, the alleged account debtor could be well known and have a very strong credit rating, while the payment is received from a worthless but similar name. (e.g., High Grade Steel Corp. is listed as account debtor and is very acceptable, but payments may be received from Hygrade Steel Products Co.).

The pay statements and vouchers appearing on the checks are another form of verification. They indicate the account debtor's record of the transaction and may indicate a description different from that presented by the borrower's assignment (e.g., the borrower assigned an invoice dated February 1, but the account debtor is paying an invoice dated February 10). In this connection the skipping of invoices of an account debtor may be significant. It may indicate an unreported return or some similar problem in the account.

Financer's Canceled Checks

As part of its internal controls, the financer examines the endorsements on all its canceled checks issued as advances to borrowers. If the endorsements indicate that the checks were not deposited in the borrower's account but were cashed or diverted elsewhere, extreme tightness in the borrower's cash flow is indicated and further investigation should be undertaken.

Interim Audits

The initial investigation, as previously indicated, is designed to determine the quality of the accounts and the viability of the borrower. This investigation supplements the financial statement. The interim audit is designed to again supplement the financial statements periodically submitted by the borrower. It also provides an external control procedure to supplement the internal control procedures conducted in the office of the lender. Interim audits should be conducted regularly during the life of the account on a thirty- or sixty-day cycle.

Most financers have detailed audit programs with specific questions to be answered by the field auditor. Again the alertness of the auditor plays an important role in the examination. Some obvious considerations may be visually determined. Does the plant activity seem to be commensurate with the volume of accounts generated? Does the physical inventory seem adequate to the ongoing activity of the borrower, or is his credit being reduced as evidenced by a reduced flow of incoming merchandise?

It is important that the borrower's books of account be posted up to date. Sloppy bookkeeping on the part of the borrower or an unwarranted lag in posting is in itself an indication of danger and deterioration. If the lender maintains a duplicate ledger of the borrower's accounts, then a comparison of the ledgers is important. This establishes whether the paper work is being properly handled and whether fictitious invoices have been submitted to the financer and not recorded on the books of the borrower. Such an examination would also reveal the possibility of the borrower's depositing customers' checks belonging to the financer. A review of the borrower's shipping procedures will indicate whether the shipping evidence being submitted to the financer is in conformity with actual shipments made.

The auditor's emphasis must be upon the borrower's records of original entry. For example, the details of the borrower's deposits into its own account should be examined. The source of these deposits may reveal the improper deposit of checks which should have been transmitted to the financer. In addition, cash receipts journals may reveal cash received but posted as returns to the accounts receivable ledger. In another area, returned merchandise which is repaired and re-shipped may be reflected in receiving and shipping records, but not reflected as credits and re-charges in the receivables ledger. Such a situation would indicate that at any given moment the financer's collateral may be somewhat, or perhaps substantially, less than the financer knows.

Further, payroll and withholding records probably reflect an accurate count of the employees available to produce and/or ship the merchandise, or perform the services underlying the borrower's accounts receivable. Obviously a realistic ratio of employees to accounts created must be maintained and should be noted. Further, the exchange account should be regularly and carefully reviewed. Abnormal activity here may indicate an increasing tightness of cash and a possible kiting of funds.   Finally, the withholding tax liability should be carefully noted.   The complications inherent therein have been discussed above (see page 46).

Taking off a trial balance and comparing it with prior trial balances will indicate whether the operation is progressing or retrogressing. Again the aging of payables will indicate the measure of creditor pressure experienced by the borrower.   Where the borrower's situation has badly deteriorated the realistic financer may find it best to call a halt to the financing operations.   Such decisions are frequently difficult to make but must be faced before extreme deterioration results in unwarranted over-exposure on the part of the financer.

As is generally true in commercial financing, no checklist can be complete or substitute for the alertness and intuition of the financer's staff.   The information developed in the financer's office, the nature of the borrower's industry, the borrower's financial condition, the financer's "feel" of the situation—all these may suggest further reviews and tests.   Clearly, however, routinely copying book figures or ticking off items on the auditor's report will not provide the information required for executive decision. Imagination, practical business acumen, seasoning, and realism are the key elements in sound accounts financing.

SECURITY AGREEMENT

(Accounts, Contract Rights, Chattel Paper, Instruments, and Goods pertaining thereto.)

BETWEEN

NAME _____

ADDRESS _____

AND

XYZ FINANCIAL CORPORATION
FIFTH AVENUE
NEW YORK, N. Y.

XYZ FINANCIAL CORPORATION
New York, N. Y.

Gentlemen:

The following is the security agreement between us:

1. You will from time to time make advances to us or for our account, upon the security of accounts receivable and other choses in action, all of which, whether secured or unsecured and whether or not evidenced by instruments or other writings, together with the proceeds thereof and the merchandise pertaining thereto, are herein called "collateral".

2. You will advance to us up to   per cent (%) of the net amounts of acceptable collateral, and will pay the remainder (less your compensation specified in Paragraph 5, plus any overpayments by account-debtors, and less deductions by account-debtors and any unpaid compensation, charges or expenses due to you) after your actual receipt of collections upon the collateral and at such times as you may determine. No payment of such remainder need be made by you if we shall be in default hereunder or shall be otherwise indebted to you; in any of which events you may retain and apply such remainder upon any indebtedness then or thereafter owed to you by us. "Net amount" of receivables collateral means the gross amount less returns, discounts, credits and allowances of any nature.

3. We shall be privileged to collect the proceeds of collateral for you at our expense, but such privilege may be terminated by you at any time in your discretion, and shall automatically terminate upon the happening of an event of default as hereinafter defined. We will receive in trust and deliver to you, in original form and on the day of receipt, all checks, drafts, notes, acceptances, cash, and other evidences of payment applicable to any collateral. You shall not be required to take any affirmative steps to collect collateral or to preserve rights against prior parties to any instruments or chattel paper.

4. All the collateral will arise from the bona fide sale and delivery of goods or the due performance of services by us, and will be for a liquidated amount subject to no offset, deduction, counterclaim, discount, condition, or conflicting security interest. We shall deliver to you such invoices, shipping or other receipts, and other papers and instruments as you may require.

5. Your compensation shall be an amount equal to one   of one per cent (1/   of 1%) per day on the cash daily balances due you from us. Your minimum monthly compensation shall be $, but in no event shall your total compensation for any month exceed the maximum permitted by the laws of New York applicable to loans to corporations. Your compensation and other charges (if any) are due and payable to you at the close of each month, and payment thereof shall be secured by all collateral. All checks received by you shall be subject to collection and to bank clearance of five days, which is hereby agreed to be a reasonable period. You will account to us monthly, and each such account shall be binding on us unless we notify you in writing to the contrary within thirty days.

Fig. 3–6. Security Agreement (Accounts)

6. During the effective term of this agreement and thereafter until all our obligations to you are duly and fully paid and discharged, you shall have a continuing security interest in all present and future collateral, whether or not specifically assigned or pledged to you, and none thereof, and no part of our inventory, will be or become subject to any security interest except in your favor. All collateral, and any other property or money of ours which may in any manner come into your possession or become subject to a security interest in your favor, shall secure and may be applied by you upon any obligations which we may at any time owe to you, whether arising or acquired under this agreement or otherwise. With respect to all present and future collateral, we will make appropriate entries in our books, and execute and deliver all papers and instruments, and do all things, necessary to evidence and effectuate your prime security interest therein.

7. You shall be vested with, and may exercise in your name or ours, all our rights, security interests, insurance, and guarantees with respect to all collateral, including the rights of stoppage in transit, seller's lien, reclamation, and resale. If any account-debtor shall reject or return any goods represented by collateral, we will forthwith deliver the same to you, or notify you and hold the same segregated in trust for you and subject to your order; and you may take and sell the same, crediting to us the net proceeds after expenses. In case of resale, the collateral thereby created shall be subject to your security interest. You are authorized and empowered to compromise or extend the time for payment of any collateral, upon such terms as you may reasonably determine, and to accept the return of goods, without notice to or consent by us, and we shall remain liable to you for any loss or deficiency so arising.

8. We warrant that all collateral will be paid in full at maturity. If any account is not paid within _____ days

it may be charged back to us and we shall pay you the full amount remaining unpaid thereon or, at your option, such amount may be charged against and deducted from any payment then or thereafter due from you; but such collateral may nevertheless be retained by you as security. If an account-debtor becomes the subject of proceedings under the Bankruptcy Act or any insolvency statute or is placed in receivership or assigns for the benefit of creditors or becomes insolvent or suspends business, all the accounts owed by such account-debtor shall thereupon become subject to the foregoing provisions of this paragraph.

9. We warrant that we are solvent and will so remain, and recognize that we induce you to make advances hereunder upon our written representations concerning our financial condition and the results of our operations, which we shall deliver to you upon reasonable request from time to time. We will make due and timely payment or deposit of all Federal, state, and local taxes, assessments or contributions required by law, and will execute and deliver to you, on demand, appropriate certificates attesting to such payment or deposit. Your auditors shall have the right at any time during business hours to inspect our premises and to audit, check and make extracts from our books, accounts, records, orders, correspondence, and all other papers.

10. We hereby constitute you and each of your officers and agents as our attorney-in-fact, with power to endorse our name upon any instruments or other form of payment or evidences of security interest that may come into your possession; to sign our name on any invoice, bill of lading, warehouse receipt, or other documents relating to collateral, on drafts against account-debtors, assignments and verifications of collateral, and notices to account-debtors; to receive, open, and dispose of mail addressed to us; to execute and file financing statements and other instruments or documents; and to do all other acts and things necessary to carry out this agreement and perfect and protect your security interest. All acts of said attorneys-in-fact are hereby ratified and approved, and they shall not be liable for any acts of commission or omission, nor for any error of judgment or mistake of fact or law. This power, being coupled with an interest, is irrevocable while we shall remain indebted to you.

11. The breach or violation of any warranty, covenant, or undertaking on our part (whether caused by our act or default or that of any other person); or our default in making payment of any sum at any time due and owing by us to you; or the filing by or against us of any petition under the Bankruptcy Act or proceeding for receivership or under any insolvency, dissolution or conservation statute; or our suspension of business, commencement of liquidation, assignment for benefit of creditors, or offer of extension or composition; or the appointment of a creditors' committee or liquidating agent for us; or the issuance of an attachment, injunction, or execution, or filing of a judgment or other lien, against us or any of our property, shall each constitute an event of default hereunder. Upon the happening of any such or other event of default, all our indebtedness to you shall accelerate and become due, and you shall become entitled to recover from us, and the collateral shall secure the payment of, the damages sustained by you, including but not limited to all attorneys' fees, court costs, collection charges, travel, legal and other expenses, which may be incurred by you to collect the indebtedness or to establish your security interest in and protect, enforce and realize upon the collateral, either as against account-debtors, ourselves, guarantors, or other persons, or in the prosecution or defense of any action or proceeding related to the subject matter of this agreement.

12. We represent and covenant that our chief place of business, and the office where our records concerning accounts and contract rights

are kept, is at _____ , and
       (Street and Number)   (City, Town or Village)   (County)   (State)

that you may rely upon the foregoing until you have received written notice to the contrary.

13. Our obligations to you hereunder shall be payable on thirty days written demand, and your prior recourse to collateral shall not constitute a condition of such demand. All your rights and remedies shall be cumulative and may be exercised concurrently or seriatim. Your express or implied waiver of a particular breach of any covenant or warranty on our part, or your failure at any particular time to exercise a right or remedy available to you, shall not be or constitute or be deemed to be a waiver of any subsequent breach or of such or any other right or remedy. We waive presentment, demand, protest, and notice thereof as to any instrument, as well as all other notices to which we might otherwise be entitled. In case of termination or expiration of this agreement, rights and obligations arising out of transactions having a prior inception shall not be affected, and the provisions hereof shall continue in effect until all prior transactions, rights and obligations shall have been fully concluded and discharged. We waive the right to trial by jury in any litigation over any matter connected with this agreement. Neither party shall be bound by any matter not expressed herein or in other writings between them, nor shall this agreement be modified, or any waiver of any provision hereof be effective, except in writing signed by the parties. We shall not, and shall not have the power to, pledge your credit for any purpose or commit you to any obligation or undertaking.

Fig. 3–6. Security Agreement—Continued

14. This agreement shall remain in effect for a period of one year from the date hereof, and shall be deemed automatically renewed for successive periods of like duration; subject, however, to the right of either party to terminate it, as at the end of the first or any succeeding period, upon at least sixty days' written notice. You shall have the right to terminate this agreement at any time, if an event of default on our part shall occur as above set forth.

15. This agreement is entered into for the benefit of, and shall be binding upon, the parties hereto and their successors and assigns. It shall become effective as of the date of your acceptance below. Inasmuch as this agreement is to be accepted by you at your office in New York and the transactions hereunder will take place at your office, this agreement and all transactions, assignments and transfers hereunder, and all rights of the parties, shall be governed as to validity, construction, enforcement and in all other respects by the laws of the State of New York.

Dated: _____ 19____

By _____
President

Attest:

_____
Secretary

[SEAL]

Accepted at New York, New York

on _____ 19____

XYZ FINANCIAL CORPORATION

By _____

GUARANTY

To

XYZ FINANCIAL CORPORATION

In order to induce you to enter into the within and foregoing agreement with

(hereinafter referred to as the "client") and/or to continue under or to refrain at this time from terminating your present arrangement with the client, and in consideration of your so doing, the undersigned (and each of them if more than one) jointly and severally guarantee to you, without deduction by reason of setoff, defense or counterclaim of the client, the due performance of all the client's contracts and agreements with you, both present and future and any and all renewals, continuations, modifications, supplements and amendments thereof, and the due payment to you of any and all sums which may be presently due and owing or which shall in the future become due and owing to you from the client. This is a guaranty of payment and not of collection, and shall include but not be limited to any and all amounts charged or chargeable to the account of the client and any and all obligations incurred and sums due or to become due to you, whether by way of overdraft or otherwise, under the aforementioned agreement and any other contract or agreement and any renewals, continuations, modifications, supplements and amendments thereof, as well as any and all other obligations incurred and other sums due or to become due to you whether or not such obligations or indebtedness shall arise under any contract or agreement or shall be represented by instruments of indebtedness or shall be acquired by you from any third party; and in addition the undersigned shall be liable to you for attorneys' fees equal to 15% of such indebtedness and obligations, if any claim hereunder is referred to an attorney for collection. You shall be entitled to hold all sums at any time to the credit of the undersigned and any property of the undersigned at any time in your possession, as security for any and all of the undersigned's obligations to you, no matter how or when arising and whether under this or any other instrument, agreement or otherwise. Any and all present and future debts and obligations of client to the undersigned are hereby waived and postponed in favor of, and subordinated to, the payment and performance of all present and future debts and obligations of client to you, and are hereby assigned to you. The undersigned hereby waive notice of acceptance hereof, notice of creation or acquisition of the obligations hereby guaranteed, and all notices and demands of any kind to which the undersigned may be entitled, including without limitation all demands of payment and notices of non-payment, protest and dishonor to the undersigned, or the client, or the makers or endorsers of any notes or other instruments for which the undersigned are or may be liable hereunder. The undersigned waive notice of and hereby consent to any agreements or arrangements whatever with the client or anyone else, including without limitation agreements and arrangements for modification, payment, extension, subordination, composition, arrangement, discharge or release of the whole or any part of said obligations or indebtedness, contracts or agreements, or other guarantors, or for the change or surrender of any or all security, or for compromise, whether by way of acceptance of part payment or of returns of merchandise or of dividends or in any other way, and the same shall in no way impair the undersigned's liability hereunder. The undersigned shall have no right of subrogation, reimbursement or indemnity whatsoever and no right of recourse to or with respect to any assets or property of the client or to any collateral for the debts and obligations of the client to you,

Fig. 3-6. Security Agreement—Continued

unless and until all said debts and obligations shall have been paid in full. Nothing shall discharge or satisfy the liability of the undersigned hereunder except the full performance and payment of said obligations and indebtedness with interest. The undersigned agree that if the client or any of the undersigned should at any time become insolvent, or make a general assignment, or if a petition in bankruptcy or any insolvency or reorganization proceeding shall be commenced by, against or in respect of the client or any of the undersigned, any and all obligations of the undersigned shall, at your option, forthwith become due and payable without notice. Your books and records showing the account between you and the client shall be admissible in evidence in any action or proceeding, shall be binding upon the undersigned for the purpose of establishing the items therein set forth, and shall constitute prima facie proof thereof. This instrument is a continuing guaranty and shall continue in full force and effect until terminated by the actual receipt by you by registered mail of written notice of termination from the undersigned or from the legal representative of any deceased undersigned; such termination shall be applicable only to transactions having their inception thereafter, and rights and obligations arising out of transactions having their inception prior to such termination shall not be affected. The death of any one or more of the undersigned shall not effect a termination of this instrument as to such deceased or any of the surviving undersigned, nor shall termination by any one or more of the undersigned affect the continuing liability hereunder of such of the undersigned as do not give notice of termination. You may enforce your rights hereunder without first resorting to any other right, remedy or security. The undersigned waive all right to a trial by jury in any action or proceeding based hereon. This instrument cannot be changed or terminated orally, shall be interpreted according to the laws of the State of New York, shall be binding upon the heirs, executors, administrators, successors and assigns of the undersigned, and shall enure to the benefit of your successors and assigns.

Witness: _____

_____ (L.S.)
(Signature of Guarantor)

Dated: _____, 19____

_____
(Address)

Witness: _____

_____ (L.S.)
(Signature of Guarantor)

Dated: _____, 19____

_____
(Address)

Fig. 3-6.   Security Agreement—Continued

4

Factoring

Robert Martin
Partner, Coleman and Company

CHARACTERISTICS OF FACTORING

Historically traceable to Roman times, factoring arose as a merchandising rather than financial service. More modernly a commission merchant in the local market for the distant mill, the factor relieved the mill of the selling, styling, and credit responsibilities for that local market. Additionally, he assumed the financial burden of carrying the mill's inventory for local sale. This evolutionary process is described in Chapter 1 (see page 10).

"The Old-Line" Factor

Although factoring in America began with textile mills, clients are now factored in a variety of industries. The distinctive service of accepting responsibility for the credit worthiness of the client's customers remains the major function of the modern "old-line" factor. The term *old-line factor* is commonly employed in the field of commercial financing to refer to the institutions dealing primarily with the credit function. The term distinguishes such factors from other institutions financing receivables, who are sometimes inaccurately referred to as "factors."

In technical terms, the distinguishing feature of the old-line factoring (hereinafter called "factoring") arrangement is the purchase by the factor of the receivables of its client without recourse to the factored client for any financial inability of the account debtor to pay. This differs from the financing of accounts which involves a

73

legal assignment of receivables by the client to the financer as collateral for a loan, with full recourse to the client for nonpayment of the invoice by the account debtor.

Types of Factoring

Maturity Factoring. The fundamental factoring function is highlighted by an arrangement described as "maturity factoring." In this contractual relationship, the factor, after prior approval of the credit of the proposed account debtor as to the amount and terms, assumes the credit risk of the account debtor for the amount approved. The factored client does not receive an advance against the receivable but is paid in full by the factor upon the maturity date under the terms of the invoices. For this service, the factor is paid a commission, which is a charge ranging from $3/4$ of 1% to $1\frac{1}{2}\%$ of the volume of the client's sales.

Advance Factoring. Factors, however, also advance money to their clients. The advance arrangement supplements the credit guaranty facility of the factor by enabling the client to draw against the receivables purchased by the factor prior to their maturity. This advance payment will frequently solve most of the client's financing problems. It amounts to the client's selling his customers for cash on delivery. Just as in the administration of any other good accounts payable department, the factor prefers to withhold from the client some amount to cover possible claims, returns, allowances, and similar items. Normally, this is a percentage of the client's outstanding accounts. Such advances are generally made within the framework of accounts purchased by the factor. In many situations, however, the client requires accommodation beyond this framework. In such cases the factor may provide an unsecured overdraft. This is usually related to, although not secured by, the inventory in the possession of the client. The reason for such a measuring rod is that the client's inventory will be converted into sales which will be purchased by the factor to retire the loan. This constitutes no more nor less than payment for accounts receivable prior to their creation. For very substantial overdrafts, or for clients whose credit strength does not justify an overdraft, the factor may take a security interest in the inventory out of which the receivables will be created. Whether secured or not, however, the factor has prepaid for accounts receivable he has contracted to buy and the client has contracted to sell. Hence repayment of such an overdraft is made not by cash but by the factor's crediting to the client's account all or part of the unpaid purchase price of the accounts receivable as created.

Drop Shipment Factoring. Another factoring service is called a "mill agent" or "drop shipment" arrangement. It usually involves a borrower without manufacturing or shipping facilities. Most frequently it entails a new operation, such as a salesman or designer striking out on his own and creating his own enterprise. Such a company submits orders to its vendors through the factor. If the factor approves the credit of the client's account debtor to whom the merchandise will be shipped, it signs a guaranty which may take the following form:

We guarantee the payment of the bill arising from the sale of merchandise referred to herein, provided the merchandise is delivered to and finally accepted by the consignee referred to herein, and provided there are no merchandise disputes, claims, etc. This guarantee does not cover cancellations of any kind and may be terminated in whole or in part by us at any time prior to shipment of the merchandise. Kindly note that all approved bills due mills and/or vendors maturing during any one week will be paid on Friday of that week.

This guarantee to the client's suppliers constitutes the essence of a drop shipment arrangement.

The client buys and sells simultaneously, without taking physical possession of the merchandise. When an order is received from a prospective account debtor, the client immediately makes out a corresponding purchase order to his supplier. The purchase order goes *first* to the factor for credit approval. When the credit of the prospective account debtor is approved by the factor, the client's purchase order, with the aforementioned guarantee, duly signed by the factor, is forwarded to the supplier (and shipper) of the merchandise.

The supplier then ships in the name of the client and sends his invoice and shipping documents to the client and factor. When the client receives his supplier's invoices showing that the merchandise has been shipped, the account debtor is billed. The bill to the account debtor shows the merchandise sold by the client, and the invoice is payable to the factor. Out of the proceeds of the accounts sold to the factor, the factor pays the supplier. Thus, the client's account with the factor will reflect the difference between his sales and his purchases—or his gross profit.

For drop shipment accounts a factor's statement to his client would include two columns marked (1) "client's bills" and (2) "client's credits". Obviously, "client's credits" are for charge backs to the factored client's suppliers. The factored client is using the proceeds of the purchased accounts receivable for his accounts payable, and his own credit is never involved.

This procedure works extremely well for clients who are sales oriented but without a credit base. They usually want merchandise shipped in their name in order to become established in their trade.

CLIENT'S USE OF CREDIT BALANCE. A further variation of the drop shipment arrangement occurs when guaranties are issued by the factor for merchandise to be purchased and added to the client's inventory. When this happens the factored client does not buy and sell simultaneously. Here the factor may have the inventory so purchased pledged to him or he may depend upon the credit standing of the client. In this instance, the client is using his credit balance with the factor (whether already created or to be created out of future sales to guarantee and then pay for merchandise purchased or to be purchased.

Another interesting variation of the use of a factor's credit balance occurs when the factored client is a foreign company. Such a client may be selling in the United States in dollars with the duty, freight, etc., included in the delivered price of the merchandise. The factor buys the total account and pays the duty, freight, etc., out of the proceeds, remitting the balance to the foreign shipper. This arrangement allows a foreign shipper to offer his merchandise to American customers without requiring the purchaser to worry about foreign exchange, duty, ocean freight, etc.

Other Types of Accommodation. Currently functioning as a financial institution, the factor provides other types of financial accommodation. These include secured inventory loans, letters of credit, and the financing of accounts and export shipments. In these areas, the factor functions as any other lender or financer operating in the specified field. The operational techniques and legal structure of the relationship with the client are covered in the chapters dealing with the particular types of loans enumerated.

Accounting Treatment by Factor and Client. The effect of factoring on the client's balance sheet is completely different from that of any other type of financing. Under either a maturity arrangement or an advance arrangement, the factored client normally is not indebted to the factor. The client does not have a liability on his statement at all but rather an asset reflecting the amount due from the factor. Obviously, this has a significant and affirmative effect on current asset/liability ratios. To illustrate, assume the following balance sheet:

Current Assets		Current Liabilities	
Cash	$ 10,000	Accounts payable	$160,000
Accounts receivable	100,000	Net worth	150,000
Merchandise	200,000		$310,000
	$310,000		

This balance sheet is better than average, and shows a ratio of current assets to current liabilities of about two to one. Assume now a factoring arrangement for the operation. The accounts receivable are all sold and the client immediately receives 90% of the amount of receivables. These funds can be used by the client forthwith to reduce his accounts payable. Notice that the client does not incur a debt for the funds received. He was paid for a purchase. He did not borrow. The above balance sheet now becomes:

Current Assets		Current Liabilities	
Cash	$ 10,000	Accounts payable	$ 70,000
Balance due from		Net worth	150,000
factor	10,000		$220,000
Merchandise	200,000		
	$220,000		

Reflecting the factoring arrangement, the balance sheet shows a current ratio of more than three to one. Factoring improved the balance sheet and thus the credit standing also. Indeed, a maturity factoring arrangement may improve the bank relationship of the client.

The accounting treatment of the transactions between factor and client is identical for both maturity and advance arrangements. The factor buys the accounts receivable, crediting the account of the client. Here it is important to emphasize that the factor assumes more than the risk of the account debtor's financial inability to pay. He also, normally, assumes the obligation of making payment at maturity. Thus the client is not only assured that the bills will be paid but he knows precisely *when* they will be paid.

Once the credit balance in favor of the client has been set up on the factor's books, the funds advanced against that credit are, of course, merely charged against this credit balance or, as it is technically called, "client's equity." This is why such funds are considered advances, not loans.

Interest Charges

As stated above, in maturity factoring there are generally no interest charges. In an advance arrangement, the accounting must provide for a periodic charge for interest from the time the money is advanced until the average maturity or due date. There are numerous ways of accomplishing this. They vary from factor to factor, but usually the result is the same. In effect, there is no difference between a factor's advancing funds prior to the average maturity date of the bills and a customer's anticipating his bills and deducting anticipation. In each case, the vendor is paid before maturity and therefore pays interest. The per annum interest rate charged by the factor varies, but it is higher than the prime rate charged by commercial banks in the Federal Reserve District of New York. It must be noted, however, that factored clients pay only for money in use and are not required to maintain compensating balances such as are required by commercial banks.

RELATIONSHIPS BETWEEN FACTOR, CLIENT, AND ACCOUNT DEBTOR

Examination of Prospective Clients. In examining a new prospect, a factor will consider his financial condition and his profit-making potential. The percentage of returns and allowances to total sales will also be important. Then the factor will consider not only the sales volume, but also the credit exposure created by the prospective client's customers, related to the length of terms offered and the quality of accounts sold. The average unit of sales involved will also be considered (i.e., the number of invoices issued monthly). Here the workload is measured, for the factor does all the bookkeeping and collection of accounts receivable. The new business department must also inquire into the possible concentration of large amounts of credit extended to one company, possibly from several different clients. The number of different customers, as distinct from the number of invoices, is an important element. For example, a manufacturer may issue many invoices, giving the appearance of a statistical spread, but all the customers may be part of an inter-connected chain and, thus concentrated, represent a very substantial credit risk.

Diversification of Clients. A factor must also consider the diversification of all its business. Although factoring started with textile mills, today the product is less important than the type of customer. Customers can be divided roughly into two classes, one called "wholesale" and the other called "retail." A client whose customers sell directly to consumers will normally issue many invoices and will have many customers. In the factors' jargon, companies selling to department stores, supermarkets, chain stores, local apparel stores, or any other local stores such as furniture stores, hardware stores, toy stores, or the like are retail companies. On the contrary, wholesale clients will sell to other processors; a spinner of yarn will sell to cloth manufacturers, a weaver or knitter may sell to slack manufacturers, or a lumber merchant may sell to furniture manufacturers. Such companies are wholesale companies. Obviously, a wholesale client has fewer customers and fewer invoices than a retail client. Half retail and half wholesale clients will obviously provide a factor with a very desirable diversification, and within each group (whether wholesale or retail) different products could provide still more diversification. Often, however, different products will not help diversification at all. For example, a lumber merchant, a piece goods weaver, and a metal spring manufacturer often sell to the same furniture manufacturer. The product no longer particularly concerns the new business solicitors. They address themselves to the trades in which the accounts receivable will be created.

The Contract. A sample factoring contract is shown in Fig. 4–4 (page 90). For maturity contracts, a rider is appended (see Fig. 4–1).

A key provision indicates that the factor purchases the account of the client. The client warrants that all his invoices represent bona

---

4. If you request anticipation of payment by us, we may in our sole discretion (but shall not be obliged to) anticipate in whole or in part, at the then current interest rate, any payment to become due to you pursuant to paragraph 5. The amount, if any, which we shall advance to you pursuant to the provisions of this paragraph shall be in our sole discretion. Any debit balance in your account shall be repaid to us on demand, and shall bear interest at the then current interest rate.

5. We will average the due dates of all accounts purchased by us for each month, and ten (10) days after the average due date so figured, we will pay you the amount due you thereon, after making deductions in accordance with this agreement; but in order to protect us against possible returns, claims, allowances, etc., we may in our sole discretion reserve such amount of past sales as in our opinion is necessary to cover such contingencies. The "amount due you" shall be the gross amount of accounts, less returns, allowances, and discounts to customers on the shortest selling terms. We will render you a statement of your account on or about the 15th of each month for the previous month's business. You agree that any statement of account rendered to you is correct and accepted by you and shall be conclusive as between you and us, unless notice to the contrary is received by us within thirty (30) days of mailing of such statement to you.

Fig. 4–1. Factoring Contract Clauses for Maturity Arrangements

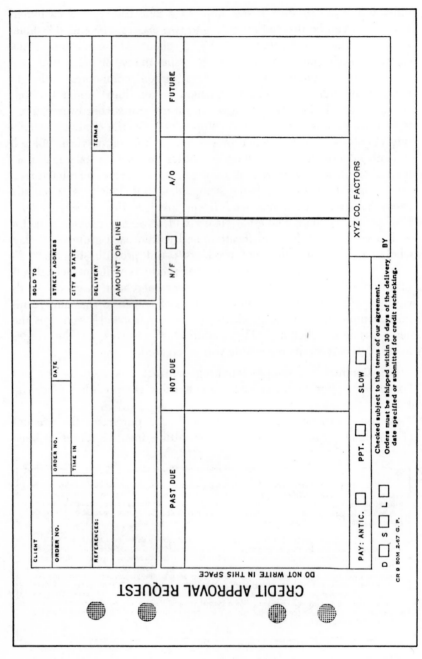

Fig. 4-2. Credit Approval Request

NAME

ADDRESS

RATING

LIMIT

DATE	ACCOUNT NAME	ORDER NO.	JAN.	FEB.	MAR.	APR.	MAY	JUNE	JULY	AUG.	SEPT.	OCT.	NOV.	DEC.

Fig. 4–2. Credit Approval Request—Reverse

fide, existing obligations, without offset or counterclaim. By such warranty, the client continues his normal responsibility for claims made by account debtors for faulty merchandise, late shipment, short shipment, and the like. Thus, the client retains his responsibility for proper performance of the sales contract, and the factor assumes the credit risk. The client may therefore eliminate its credit, collection, and bookkeeping departments.

The factor must buy all accounts receivable arising out of any approved sale. It follows, therefore, that the heart of a factoring organization is a staff of expert credit and collection men. They must be capable of analyzing credit information quickly and accurately. They must also be capable of collecting firmly and politely from slow-paying accounts. Utilizing such a specialized staff enables the businessman to increase his sales with less credit exposure.

The contract further provides that the client obtain the factor's approval prior to consummation of a sale. A form for obtaining such approval is shown in Fig. 4–2. Figure 4–3 is a form for transfer of accounts.

Notification. The account debtor pays the factor directly. Historically, and with very few exceptions, factors have printed on the invoices mailed to the account debtors a "notification" legend substantially similar to the following:

THIS ACCOUNT HAS BEEN ASSIGNED
TO AND IS PAYABLE ONLY TO
XYZ COMPANY, FACTORS
PARK AVENUE
NEW YORK, N.Y. 10016
If this bill is not found to be correct
in all respects, XYZ Company must
be notified at once.

Until the adoption of the Uniform Commercial Code by practically all States, this legend served in most instances to perfect the factor's title to the accounts.[1] The legend still imposes on the account debtors an obligation to pay directly to the factor. In most states, the legal significance of such notice is well settled. Where a notified

[1] Since the advent of the Uniform Commercial Code, factors file thereunder. This results from the inclusion in the definition of "Secured Party" of a person to whom accounts have been sold [Section 9–105(i)], and, with certain exceptions, filing is required to perfect a security interest. Such filing provides the incidental benefit of preserving the factor's security interest in returned merchandise.

account debtor pays a shipper who fails to remit to the factor, the account debtor is liable again to the factor.

In addition to the legal reason for notification, there are operational reasons that are probably paramount. Most important, it facilitates the complete and direct control of collection procedures that is essential to efficient operation of the factor's credit department. Further, notification advises the account debtor that slowness in payment means that he will be dunned by a factor, not by the shipper. Such dunning is obviously unpleasant, and the factor takes the onus off the shipper. This helps the salesmen by providing them with a scapegoat.

TRANSFER OF ACCOUNTS RECEIVABLE

SEE REVERSE SIDE

- Use as many sets as necessary.

- Please enter total only on last page — in space indicated.

- See instruction sheet and sample.

- Attach adding machine tape.

THIS IS TO CERTIFY that the account-debtors named herein are indebted to the undersigned Assignor in the sums and on the terms respectively stated. For value received, we hereby sell, assign, transfer, and set over to COLEMAN & COMPANY (herein called "Assignee"), its successors and assigns, the accounts set forth herein, the proceeds thereof, and our right, title and interest in the merchandise represented thereby, including returned or unaccepted merchandise. We warrant that said accounts truly represent actual indebtedness owed by the account-debtors therein named upon the terms stated; that the same are now outstanding and owing in full for merchandise actually ordered, sold, delivered, and accepted or services actually rendered; that no payments have been made on any thereof; that there are no defenses, deductions, offsets, counterclaims or conditions thereto; that such merchandise was owned by the undersigned at the time of sale, free from liens or encumbrances other than in favor of the Assignee; that the acquisition, manufacture, processing, sale, advertising, delivery, handling, marking, labelling, and invoicing thereof duly complied with applicable Federal, State, and local laws, rules and regulations; and that said accounts are owned by the Assignee free from liens or encumbrances other than in favor of the Assignee. The Assignee shall have a continuing security interest in said accounts and in the merchandise represented thereby and in any credit balances held by the Assignee and in any other tangible or intangible property of the Assignor now or hereafter in the possession or under the control of the Assignee, to secure the payment of all liabilities, absolute or contingent, of the Assignor to the Assignee, due or to become due, now existing or hereafter arising, and whether incurred directly or acquired by the Assignee from others.

We hereby constitute and appoint the Assignee and its designees irrevocably as our attorneys-in-fact, with power and authority in our name or otherwise to sell, assign, transfer, compromise, collect, and discharge the said accounts and merchandise, in whole or in part, and to receive, endorse, and collect all checks and other instruments and evidences of payment pertaining thereto.

(CONTINUED ON THE REVERSE SIDE)

Fig. 4–3. Transfer of Accounts Receivable

TRANSFER OF ACCOUNTS RECEIVABLE
(SEE REVERSE SIDE)

G 0 1 6/66

DATE _____ 196___

PAGE No. _____

STAPLE YOUR TAPE HERE

INVOICE DATE		NAME OF DEBTOR	CITY & STATE	DISC.	TERMS	"AS OF" DATING	GROSS AMOUNT OF INVOICE	INVOICE NUMBER
MONTH	DAY							
1								
2								
3								
4								
5								
6								
7								
8								
9								
10								
11								
12								
13								
14								
15								
16								
17								
18								
19								
20								
21								

DISCOUNT
NET | DISC. DOLLARS
1%
2%
3%
8%

INTEREST ON TERMS OF SALE
10 DAYS
30 "
10 E.O.M
40 DAYS
60 "
70 "

TOTAL (LAST PAGE ONLY)

DATING

ACCEPTED IN ACCORDANCE WITH TERMS OF OUR FACTORING AGREEMENT.

XYZ COMPANY
New York, N. Y.

- CONTINUED FROM REVERSE SIDE -

All the terms and provisions of our existing factoring agreement with the Assignee are incorporated herein, with the same force and effect as though here set forth at length.

Name _____

By _____

84

Frequently, the account debtor becomes aware that the bill will be payable to a factor before receipt of an invoice with a notification legend. The credit departments of all factors routinely write prospective customers of their factored clients requesting various information (e.g., the name of the customer's bank, perhaps an up-to-date financial statement, or even a guaranty of the indebtedness by the principals). Such correspondence, of course, indicates that the bill will be payable to the factor and that the credit risk will be assumed by the factor.

FACTOR'S INTERNAL PROCEDURES

Credit Department

Traditionally a factor's credit department was organized as follows: A credit man approving department stores, discounters, chain or individual apparel or furniture stores, and the like would be in the "retail" division. He would approve credit for diversified stores and would deal with different industries. On the other hand, a credit man approving the credits for a yarn spinner selling to manufacturers of sweaters or for a converter selling piece goods to a manufacturer of mens' pants would be in the "wholesale" division. Such credit men were generally limited to one or two industries and would normally and preferably handle all dealings with any one client and his customers. A factored client having two divisions, one selling directly to retailers and another selling to wholesalers or manufacturers, would probably deal with two different credit men.

Each credit man's authority would usually be limited to a fixed dollar amount. Hence, to approve a credit of more than the limit assigned to him, the credit man requires the approval of either his superior or a credit committee. Typically, the first rung of this credit department "ladder" is a limit of $5,000 except for first grade concerns with capital of over $1 million and with Dun & Bradstreet AaA 1 ratings. Here the limit might be $25,000.

The rise of discount stores and supermarkets often requiring large credit extensions has caused a partial breakdown in the "ladder" system. Requests for large credits (in the retail division) for discounters or chain stores may go directly to a senior credit man specializing in this type of retailer. In short, the factor attempts to develop the relationship between the client and the credit man on a one-to-one basis, but also attempts to have the credit man as familiar as possible with the type of credit extended.

Lines of Credit. Normally, factors prefer to assign a "line of credit" (a maximum amount that the customer can owe) to each customer and only withdraw or lower that "line" when they have adverse information such as a record of slow payments. The factored client (having sold all of his accounts receivable) does not know when bills are paid. This causes a problem in the use of "credit lines." One solution is to apply the line of credit to the terms. If the line of credit be $5,000 and the terms of the factored client are thirty days, the factored client would have approval to ship up to $5,000 in any thirty day period until he was advised to the contrary. Another variation would be to permit any factored client to ship any single amount without prior approval. For example, some factors permit shipments valued at up to $100 to anyone and automatically assume such credit risks. Sometimes lines of credit are assigned in accordance with Dun & Bradstreet ratings. Often, before a complete investigation can be made to set a maximum line of credit, a single order may be submitted and approved. Note, however, that at any time before actual shipment of the merchandise the factor reserves the right to withdraw the "line" or to discontinue further assumption of the credit risk for small shipments. The alternate to "lines of credit" is a procedure requiring each order to be submitted to the factor separately. In very volatile industries, separate submissions of orders are preferable.

All of this is "management by exception," and all of these procedures can be readily programmed for a modern third-generation computer.

Invoice Receiving Department

Each factor has a department generally called an "Invoice Receiving Department." This department will see that: original invoices are properly mailed; duplicate invoices are properly prepared for posting; shipping documents are properly controlled; and the listing of the invoices contains sufficient information to calculate properly the discount and the average due date. The invoices then become the debit to the factor's accounts receivable, and the listing sheet becomes the credit to the client's account (an account payable to the factor).

There are many variations of this procedure. Frequently the factored client will mail his own original invoices and under some conditions will retain the shipping documents. This involves special administrative procedures. If the merchandise has been sold on a "bill and hold" arrangement, there will be no shipping documents, but these invoices must be separately controlled. Patently, care must be exercised here to determine the transfer of title to the merchandise and responsibility for insurance coverage. If the merchandise is sold on alternate terms (for example, 2% if paid in 30 days, net if paid in 60 days), this must be properly noted so that a proper due date will show on the accounts receivable record. Sometimes a different proper average due date may be reflected in the client's account. Where alternate terms are granted, the due date of the invoice to the account debtor may not necessarily correspond with the due date used for computing the average due date applied to the client's account. The factor normally buys the accounts receivable on the basis of the highest discount and calculates the average due date on the basis of the highest discount and the concomitant shortest terms. The account debtor, of course, may elect the lower discount and the longer terms.

Accounts Receivable and Verification

Once the accounts receivable created by the factor's client have been credited to his account on the factor's books, the client no longer has to keep any record of these receivables. He may handle them by exception. Unless he hears from the factor to the contrary, he assumes that the bills are paid and has to take no action. It further follows that the factor may commingle receivables obtained from several clients, for such receivables are all the property of the factor. For the same reason, the factor verifies the receivables as his own. The disguised form of verification utilized by the financer of accounts (see page 61) is neither necessary nor desirable for a factor.

Adjustment Department

Account debtors, however, occasionally make deductions, and therefore all factors have fairly substantial adjustment departments. Perhaps the account debtor will write in and request a change of terms. He may make an improper deduction for discount, or there may be any of a number of variations from the original terms and amount of the invoice. All of these must be straightened out by the factor with the client, and although the factor keeps the records, he follows the instructions of the client with respect to such situations.

It is noteworthy, of course, that the factor assumes no financial responsibility for such deductions. If the disputes are not adjusted and paid for within a reasonable length of time, the factor will charge back the disputed amount to the client. This stems from client's warranty of satisfactory performance previously described (pp. 79, 82). The factor's adjustment department normally originates all the necessary paper work. A notice of each deduction is sent directly to the client.

Collection Department

Accounts not paid at maturity are handled by the collection department. This is normally separate from the credit department which has approved the order. The collection department, of course, works in conjunction with and usually is supervised by the credit men who approved the original credit. They attempt to effect collection with a minimum of offense to the account debtor.

Client's Accounting Department

In a maturity arrangement, payments are made to the client automatically. The client is aware of the amount and time of payment, and the checks are issued at the factor's office routinely.

In an advance account, however, payments are not automatic. When the client requests an advance against his credit balance, the client's accounting department (a department of the factor) must determine whether the advance, if made, is proper. Up-to-date credit balances must be calculated, including transactions that might be in transit. Discounts and other possible charges against this credit balance must also be computed. A minimum of equity must be maintained by the client, and this must be determined.

Note that the factoring agreement provides for a credit balance that must be no lower than a fixed percentage of a given number of days' shipments. Assume that a company ships $50,000 a month on 60-day terms; the usual factoring agreement would require equity of 10% of the previous 70 days' sales. This minimum equity must be calculated by the client's accounting department each time an advance is requested to be sure that the advance is within the terms of this provision of the agreement. This equity provides a reserve to protect the factor against future claims for adjustment by the account debtors.

If the adjustment department or the collection department has been advised by the account debtors of any significant disputes, claims, or allowances pending, the equity must be increased in anticipation thereof. Moreover, if there have been any substantial shipments for which the factor's credit department has not approved the underlying order, this must be noted by the factor's client accounting department. Such sales are known as client's risk sales and are credited as any other. If they are not paid on due date, however, they are charged back against the client's equity or credit balance after a reasonable time.

It is therefore apparent that the client's accounting department must be in close touch with the accounts receivable adjustment department, the collection department, and the credit department. Every factoring organization must be closely knit.

XYZ Company

Factors

Park Avenue

New York, N. Y.

Gentlemen:

We confirm our factoring arrangement with you, pursuant to the following security agreement:

1. You hereby sell to us, and you will sell or assign to no one else, all accounts receivable and contract rights (collectively called "accounts") now existing or hereafter created in your business, the proceeds thereof, and your title in the merchandise creating the same. You agree to execute and deliver to us, in manner and form prescribed by us, formal assignments of each and every such account, satisfactory evidence of shipment, and such other documents as we may from time to time demand, but in the absence of such formal assignment this agreement shall constitute the same. All invoices, bills and notices relating to same shall have printed on their face a notice that the account is assigned and payable only to us, and shall be delivered to us in such form as we may require. Postage for mailing the foregoing shall be paid for by you.

2. If the sale of merchandise or services creating an account sold to us by you has been approved in writing by our credit department and such approval has not been withdrawn by us prior to the final acceptance of said merchandise or services by the customer free from claim or dispute, we shall, in accordance with paragraph 5, credit you with the net face value of said account as if paid. If the standing of any customer becomes unsatisfactory to us or if there be any claim or dispute with the customer, we may withdraw our approval of sales to that customer provided the merchandise or services involved have not already been finally accepted by the customer free from claim or dispute. Such withdrawal shall not entail any liability on our part to you or any other person.

3. We shall have no recourse against you for nonpayment of any such approved account due solely to inability of the customer to pay. If any invoice is not paid when due because the merchandise or services were not finally received and accepted or because of claims or disputes or for any other reason except inability of the customer to pay, we shall have the right to charge back to you all invoices of such customer, and you will pay us therefor on demand. You or your selling agent will promptly advise us of all claims and disputes and promptly adjust the same, at your expense but subject to our approval. You will be charged with and agree to pay us, upon demand, the amount of any liability, loss or expense caused us by any transaction under this agreement, including but not limited to any allowance or deduction resulting from adjustment of any account, except loss incurred by us due solely to inability of the customer to pay. We may inspect your records relating to these transactions at any time during business hours.

4. Interest on your account with us is to be computed at the rate of six (6%) percent per annum on all debit and credit balances. Each month we will charge you interest on the amount of all sales shipped during the month, based upon terms of payment plus ten (10) days additional to cover slow payments and time for clearance of checks.

5. Upon our acceptance of accounts, we will advance to you upon request up to   percent of the net face value of the same and will in the ordinary course of business credit your account each month with the net face value of all accounts purchased during the month. The "net face value" shall be the gross amount, less returns, allowances and discounts to customers on the shortest selling terms. We will render you a statement of your account on or about the 15th of each month for the previous month's business, paying you as requested any amount then due you, after making deductions in accordance with this agreement; but in order to protect us against possible returns, claims, allowances, etc., we will hold as a reserve a sum equal to   percent of the aggregate amount of sales during the   days preceding but in no event less than the reserve held at the end of the preceding month. We may, without responsibility or liability to you, from time to time revise the aforesaid reserve upon written notice to you. We may remit to you any amount due you in excess of such reserve as we deem proper. You agree to pay on demand any debit balance in your account. You agree that any statement of account rendered to you is correct and accepted by you and shall be conclusive as between you and us, unless notice to the contrary is received by us within thirty days of mailing of such statement to you.

Fig. 4–4.   Factoring Contract

6. If you decide to ship accounts which our credit department has not approved in writing, you shall nevertheless assign the same to us and receive advances thereon in such amounts as are satisfactory to us. Said accounts will be recorded and collected by us as are all others, except that we will assume no responsibility for ultimate payment and we may charge back any or all such accounts to you at any time.

7. For our services you agree to pay and be charged monthly with commission on the aggregate sales price set forth in all your accounts (less discounts on the shortest selling terms) as follows:

8. We shall have a continuing security interest in all your present and future accounts, the proceeds thereof, the merchandise represented thereby, the products or proceeds of resale thereof, any and all credit balances held by us for your account, and any and all other property of yours now or hereafter in our possession or under our control, as collateral for the payment of any liability or liabilities, absolute or contingent, due from you to us and of all claims by us against you, due or to become due, whether now existing or hereafter arising, and whether incurred directly, under this agreement or otherwise, or acquired by us from others. All advances made by us to you shall be repaid to us at our office in New York City, New York. If you make any misrepresentation concerning any account or any other matter pertaining to or arising out of this agreement, or if you violate any of the terms or provisions of this agreement, or if any indebtedness from you to us is not paid when due, or if in our sole and exclusive judgment there shall have been an adverse change in your financial standing, or if a petition is filed by or against you under any bankruptcy or insolvency statute, or if you become insolvent or commit any act of bankruptcy, then in any of such events we may forthwith terminate this agreement. If this agreement be terminated for any reason, your indebtedness to us shall immediately become due and payable and we shall have the right to liquidate your account and shall not be obligated to make further advances or to pay you any equities pending the complete liquidation of your account, you to remain liable for any deficiency. All accounts charged back to you for any reason shall be retained by us as further security, and we will credit you only with the amounts collected thereon.

9. In the event of any disputes, chargebacks or returns, or in the event of the liquidation of your account, and even after the termination of this agreement, we shall retain title to any rejected or returned merchandise, or any merchandise upon which we have a lien, and we may take possession of the same at any time and dispose of it upon five (5) days notice at public or private sale, and if it be at public sale, we may be the purchasers thereof; we are further authorized with respect to any rejected or returned merchandise to make adjustments or allowances with the customers, and such adjustments or allowances shall be binding upon you or your assignees, receivers or trustees in bankruptcy, unless you have paid to us the full amount of the invoice within five (5) days after mailing by us to you of notice of such proposed adjustment or allowance. In the event that any returned merchandise shall come into your possession, you agree to segregate and hold such merchandise in trust for us or, if we so elect, you will deliver such merchandise to us or our designee, on demand. We shall have the rights of an unpaid seller, including the rights of replevin, reclamation and stoppage in transit, and any merchandise so recovered shall be considered between us as returned merchandise. We shall not be liable to you or any other person for exercising any of our rights under this agreement. You agree that all checks and other instruments received by you in payment of accounts sold by you to us, whether drawn to your order or our order, shall be turned over to us forthwith, and if drawn to your order, the same shall be duly endorsed by you to our order. You hereby constitute us your attorney-in-fact for the purpose of endorsing your name on all checks and other instruments.

10. If we should be required to pay or withhold any taxes or other levies imposed by any governmental authority, whether related to sales or merchandise, the amount thereof may be charged to you, or if we elect, shall be paid by you.

11. Our failure to exercise any right, privilege or remedy shall not be construed as a waiver of said right, privilege or remedy with respect to the circumstance which gave rise thereto, or with respect to any future or similar circumstance. This agreement shall not be modified orally nor by any course of conduct of the parties nor in any manner other than by written agreement signed by the parties. All notices shall be in writing, sent by regular mail to each of us at the last known address which one of us has from time to time furnished to the other in writing.

12. You certify to us that below are the names and residence addresses of your officers, partners or agents:

Name	Title	Address

Fig. 4–4.　Factoring Contract—Continued

Specimen signature cards for these persons are enclosed, and it is understood that we may rely upon the signatures of them or any of them until receipt by us of written notice to the contrary.

13.　You certify to us that your address as set forth at the head of this agreement is your mailing address, your chief place of business, and your office in which your records concerning accounts are kept and maintained. We shall be entitled to rely upon this certification until we have received written notice to the contrary, and you shall not effectuate any change without first giving us such notice.

14.　You authorize us to execute and file any financing statements, notices and other instruments, and to do all acts, necessary to carry out this security agreement and perfect and protect our security interest.

15.　This agreement is consummated and will be performed in, and shall be construed, interpreted, and enforced in accordance with the laws of, the State of New York. It shall continue from the effective date hereof for one year, and thereafter from year to year, but may be terminated during either the original one year term or any renewal by either party, upon at least　　　　days written notice to the other by registered or certified mail.

The effective date of this agreement is 19

Witness:	Very truly yours,
	XYZ COMPANY
....	By: ....
	Executed at New York, N. Y.
	on the.........day of 19
	Read and Agreed to:
Witness:	....
....	By: ....

EXTRACT OF THE MINUTES of a meeting of the Board of Directors of ....
.... duly held at the office of the Company on the ....day of ....
19 . All the directors were personally present. The following resolution was unanimously adopted:

> RESOLVED, that any officer be and he hereby is authorized and empowered to enter into, execute, deliver and modify from time to time, in the name of and on behalf of this Company, an agreement or contract in writing with　　　XYZ Company, and such other papers necessary to effectuate such agreement or contract providing for factoring transactions between the Company and said　　　XYZ Company, upon such terms and conditions as he may deem fit and proper, and that any officer is hereby authorized to execute and deliver to　　　XYZ Company transfers and assignments of accounts.

I, ..., Secretary of .... do hereby certify that I have compared the preceding with the resolution duly adopted at the aforesaid meeting of the Board of Directors of said Company, and that the same is a correct transcript of said resolution and of the whole thereof.

WITNESS my hand and the corporate seal:

....	(CORP
Secretary	SEAL)

Fig. 4—4. Factoring Contract—Continued

In order to induce   XYZ   COMPANY (herein referred to as "Factor") to enter into the foregoing Agreement and to engage in transactions thereunder, and in consideration thereof, we hereby jointly and severally guarantee to Factor the due payment and perfo mance by

                    (herein referred to as "Client") of all moneys to be paid and all things to be done by Client pursuant to the foregoing Agreement, as well as the due payment by Client of all other obligations which Client may at any time owe to Factor, however arising; and we hereby indemnify Factor, and covenant to hold it harmless, against all obligations, demands, losses, or liabilities (by whomsoever asserted) suffered, incurred or paid by Factor as a result of, or in any way arising out of, or following, or consequential to, transactions under the foregoing Agreement, except losses due solely to inability of an account-debtor to pay where the account was approved by Factor, and such approval was not withdrawn in accordance with said Agreement.

We agree: that this guaranty shall not be impaired by any modification of the foregoing Agreement, nor by any modification, extension, release, compromise, or other alteration of any of the obligations hereby guaranteed or of any security therefor, to all of which we hereby consent; that this is a guaranty of payment and not of collection, and that our liability hereunder is direct and unconditional and may be enforced by Factor without first resorting to any other right, remedy or security; and that this guaranty shall remain in force until revoked, by registered mail, as to subsequent transactions. In furtherance hereof, we hereby assign to Factor, as security, all claims and demands which we now or may hereafter have against Client.

We waive: notice of acceptance hereof; the right to a jury trial in any action hereunder; presentment, demand, protest, and notice thereof as to any instrument; notice of default; and all other notices and demands to which we might otherwise be entitled.

This guaranty and waiver, and the rights and obligations of the parties hereto, shall be governed and construed by the laws and decisions of the State of New York.

WITNESS our hands and seals this   day of   **19**

Witness:

_____   _____(L.S.)
                                      Signature

                                      Address

_____   _____(L.S.)
                                        Signature

                                      Address

Witness:

_____   _____(L.S.)
                                        Signature

                                        Address

Fig. 4–4.   Factoring Contract—Continued

5

Inventory Financing

Monroe R. Lazere

Financing accounts gears the availability of operating cash to the outstanding accounts. As the accounts mount, the requirement of operating cash to carry them mounts. Thus the availability and the cash requirement operate in tandem. In some situations, however, this arrangement is insufficient to meet the borrower's needs. In a seasonal operation, for example, the accounts may be at low ebb and the cash necessary to carry inventory may be high; the borrower may be required to maintain or create a large pre-seasonal inventory in anticipation of a forthcoming selling season. In other situations, too, accommodation beyond the availability on accounts may be required. In such cases the merchandise inventory may be utilized to secure a loan of additional operating cash.

As evidenced in the usual inventory security agreement, financers generally consider inventory financing as supplemental to accounts financing. This view arises from the necessity of following the merchandise collateral into the security interest of accounts in order to effectuate cash repayment. Under the Uniform Commercial Code the security interest in inventory technically may attach, by agreement, to the accounts as proceeds. However, for administrative reasons discussed below, financers prefer a full-fledged accounts security agreement and all of the procedural techniques provided thereunder. It follows, therefore, that a financer normally does not advance against inventory unless he is also financing the accounts of the borrower.

Although a current asset, inventory is not self-liquidating, as are accounts. To reduce inventory to cash requires a sale of the merchandise, involving time and expense. It is therefore subject to a market risk, and a default by the borrower may result in expensive liquidation procedures for the financer. Evaluation of the inventory for loan purposes is therefore a prime consideration for the financer.

INVENTORY SUITABLE AS COLLATERAL

Within a given business operation, the merchandise inventory may consist of different elements requiring different treatment and analysis. The inventory supporting the loan may be raw material or component parts, work is process in a manufacturing operation or finished goods. The nature of the merchandise is of course a matter of paramount importance. Highly styled items would obviously be extremely hazardous since their value would be subject to rapidly changing market conditions. Examples are dresses, ladies hats, shoes, etc. The same consideration applies to novelty items that may be only a passing fad. Hula hoops and Daniel Boone caps are illustrations. Perishable merchandise is obviously a special problem. Non-perishable merchandise may present other problems. Technological obsolescence, highly specialized component parts, and the length of shelf life of the merchandise all must be considered. Graded merchandise dictates caution as to grade used.

The financer usually prefers to limit himself to loans on merchandise that is fairly staple and requires little or no additional fabrication for resale. Finished goods and component parts are obviously more acceptable than work in process. The staple nature of the merchandise permits a reasonably predictable future value. The more staple the merchandise (e.g., a standard commodity) the more readily available is price information from Exchanges and current publications. The absence of additional processing insures against requiring a financer to enter the fabricating field in order to realize on his collateral. Non-staple and incompletely fabricated inventory of course can and frequently do serve as collateral for financing. But greater care and more frequent reviews of the status of the borrower and the inventory must then be undertaken. Retaining of specialized merchandise appraisers is a worthwhile precaution.

Restrictions on Sale

Another consideration is the possibility of legal or contractual restrictions on sale of the merchandise. Gold, for example, may be sold only by federally licensed vendors. The sale of alcoholic beverages is regulated in many states. Some items are subject to price agreements under the Robinson Patman Act. Such problems should be discovered before, not after, the loan is concluded. Arrangements to overcome such problems frequently may be made, given sufficient time. To seek to resolve them under the pressure of a liquidation can be very costly to the financer.

Storage Facilities

Finally, the storage facilities should suit the merchandise. Frozen shrimp in a greenhouse, for example, will never do. The facilities should be well maintained and free of unwarranted fire hazards. Proper housekeeping by the borrower may protect the collateral against contamination, deterioration, shoddiness, and unreasonable exposure to pilferage, fire, etc.

Merchandise Turnover

The inventory loan requires a very careful analysis of the inventory turn-over. Does the pledged merchandise turn over in the regular course of business? Or is the merchandise collateral stale and non-moving although theoretically valuable? A segment of inventory may have had a high acquisition cost value but is not moving and therefore has little or no liquidation value. The study of the flow of sales of specific inventory items is therefore essential.

In short, if merchandise is to be accepted as collateral for a loan, the financer would be well advised to become very familiar with the nature of, marketability of and legal restrictions on sale of the merchandise. The practical business acumen of the lender is vital, for no attempted list of possible difficulties and variations could be complete.

BORROWER'S BACKGROUND AND FINANCIAL CONDITION

Assuming that the merchandise can qualify under appropriate administrative arrangements, the analysis of the borrower's background and financial condition becomes the next order of business. Much of this analysis has been covered in Chapter 3. Since, however, the collateral of merchandise is much less liquid than the collateral of accounts, the viability of the borrower is even more vital here. If the borrower is too weak financially, the possibility of an imminent liquidation presents even greater problems than does a loan secured by accounts. Hence the standards of financial strength may justifiably be higher for this type of loan.

Having determined that the borrower and the merchandise to be pledged are satisfactory, the lender now examines the security devices available.

USE OF WAREHOUSE FACILITIES

The simplest inventory financing arrangement was known as the common law pledge. It was and is the familiar device utilized by pawnbrokers. These lenders take physical custody of the item and make a loan secured by the value thereof. In order to redeem the pledge and regain possession of the item, the borrower must repay the loan. The adoption of the Uniform Commercial Code supersedes the common law and therefore eliminates the common law pledge, but the Code provides an analogue. Article 9, Section 305, provides for perfection of a security interest on goods and instruments and negotiable documents by the lender's (secured party's) taking possession thereof without the requirement of filing a financing statement. Manifestly, however, this simple expedient would be impractical in most mercantile operations.

Public Warehouses

One possible alternative would be to place the merchandise in the lender's name in a public warehouse Such a warehouse is generally defined to be an enterprise lawfully engaged in providing storage facilities for hire to the general public. The financer, of course, should check the financial stability of the warehouse chosen. Possession by the bailee (provided he has not issued negotiable receipts for the goods) is deemed to be possession by the secured party upon the bailee's receipt of notice of the secured party's interest (Article 9, Section 305). As will be developed later, non-negotiable receipts have great advantages in utilizing warehousing in the financing of inventory. In the arrangement just described, the filing of a financing statement is not required, for obviously the warehouse would be fully aware of the interest of the secured party (lender).

In many situations the use of a public warehouse facility would be impractical, for the cost of transporting the merchandise to and from the borrower's premises usually would be prohibitive. In a manufacturing operation, the need for immediate access to raw material and/or component parts to maintain a smooth production flow creates obvious difficulties. Occasionally, however, in a wholesale operation, where shipments to customers can be arranged directly from the public warehouse, such an arrangement is feasible.

The warehouse charges are usually a fraction of one per cent of the value of the merchandise handled in and out. Such charges are the responsibility of the borrower and are superior in lien to the financer's security interest. Hence the financer must be alert to any undue accumulation of unpaid charges.

Field Warehouses

In most cases a field warehousing arrangement is more manageable. These are usually established by one of several well recognized and highly regarded warehouse companies specializing in such arrangements. Among such warehouse companies are Lawrence Warehouse Company, Douglas-Guardian Warehouse Corporation, New York Terminal Warehouse Company, and St. Louis Terminal Warehouse Company. The field warehouse may be created on a divided portion inside the borrower's premises or outside in a field yard. The most common illustration of the latter arrangement is the field warehousing of lumber in a lumber yard. Whether indoors or outdoors, the technical features of the field warehouse are the same. The space utilized for the warehouse is leased by the warehouse company from the borrower. It must be fenced off as an identifiable area with limited access. A sign must be posted indicating the warehouseman's complete control of that portion of the premises. The purpose of the sign is to prevent giving a visiting creditor an erroneous impression of the borrower's affluence. The warehouseman's sign puts such a creditor on notice that the debtor does not have unencumbered title to the merchandise in the enclosure.

As in the public warehouse arrangement, the borrower is responsible for the warehouseman's fee, here normally consisting of a setting up charge plus a fraction of one per cent of the value of the merchandise handled. Here also, the lien for the warehouseman's charges is superior to the security interest of the financer, and again the financer must be alert to any undue accumulation of unpaid charges.

Customarily, one or more employees of the borrower are detached from the borrower's payroll and technically become employees of the warehouse thus acting as custodians. The word "technically" must be emphasized. They are paid by the warehouseman who is reimbursed by agreement with the borrower. More significantly, however, their new technical status may not alter their loyalty to the borrower with whom they frequently have had a long relationship and from whom they have been accustomed to take orders. The financer should recognize such possible conflict of interest, despite the issuance of a fidelity bond and despite the responsibility of the warehouseman. Preventive operational reviews and safeguards are obviously preferable to legal entanglements.

The pledged merchandise is placed in the field warehouse under the control of the custodian. After an initial inventory is taken, warehouse receipts are issued for the opening inventory. Merchandise thereafter added will result in new receipts. Merchandise removed in accordance with the arrangement results in the ultimate cancelling of prior receipts. Here again, the filing of a financing statement under the Code is obviated. The warehouse company is a bailee of goods belonging to the borrower and is aware of the secured party's (lender's) interest. Hence the possession of the bailee is deemed the possession of the secured party under Article 9, Section 305, and no filing is required. This provision follows pre-Code theory under which the bailee's possession was constructively the possession of the lender and hence tantamount to a common law pledge.

Warehouse Receipts

Warehousemen may issue either negotiable or non-negotiable receipts. This subject was governed by the widely adopted Uniform Warehouse Receipt Act which now has been superseded by the even more widely adopted Article 7 of the Uniform Commercial Code. Although some highly technical changes thereby were effected in legal language, the law remains, for practical purposes, the same. The negotiable receipt is in terms negotiable. The legal incidents thereof are designed to preserve such negotiability. For example, the negotiable receipt limits the warehouseman's lien for charges to the actual charges arising out of the merchandise underlying the particular receipt. Secondly, merchandise may not be released without surrender of the receipt. Indeed, the warehouseman is criminally as well as civilly liable to the receipt holder if he makes such a release without obtaining the receipt. The negotiation of the receipt transfers good title to the receipt to the innocent purchaser for value, even though title to the underlying merchandise may be subject to attack. This of course may result in having good title to an instrument that evidences merchandise from which the title has been pulled away. This could occur if the depositor's title to the merchandise is successfully attacked.

The financer, however, normally is more interested in ease of administration than negotiability of the receipt. For an on-going financing operation, the difficulties in the use of a negotiable receipt are obvious. The administrative problems of effecting releases are increased, since the physical receipts must be surrendered with each release. Hence in the vast majority of such financing operations, the financer prefers utilizing the non-negotiable receipt, which is so designated across its face. This permits partial releases by duly authorized letter or other written instruction and hence creates considerably greater flexibility in the operation. Further, the loss of a negotiable receipt results in the requirement of posting of a bond and a court order to obtain a duplicate receipt. Lost non-negotiable receipts, on the other hand, may be reissued after an exchange of written agreements between the parties.

Responsibility of Warehouseman

Primarily the warehouseman is liable for damages arising from the non-existence of the goods for which the receipt has been issued or for failure of the goods to correspond to the description contained in the receipt. In short, he must be able to re-deliver the goods represented by the receipt. Care, however, must be exercised in examining the receipt. If the receipt is for containers or cartons of certain markings or "said to contain" certain merchandise, then the warehouseman's liability has obviously been limited. He is then responsible by the terms of receipt only for the containers. As to the contents, he may rightfully assume them to be as represented by the depositor (borrower). It also is vital to note that the warehouseman properly can and usually does accept the dollar value placed upon the merchandise by the depositor.

Further, and very importantly, in the usual financing arrangement, the warehouseman is required to exercise such care as a reasonably prudent owner would exercise in preserving the merchandise. Casualty risks are normal hazards which may result in loss notwithstanding such care. Hence the prudent financer makes certain that the merchandise underlying the receipts is amply insured in his favor. The types of insurance to cover the financer should include at the very least fire, flood, burglary, pilferage, sprinkler damage, etc. Reliable insurance advice should be sought and heeded.

Security Agreement

The usual arrangement involving warehouse receipts loans includes an underlying agreement between the borrower and lender (see Fig. 5-1), and a corporate resolution authorizing the agreement (see Fig.

INVENTORY SECURITY AGREEMENT

(WAREHOUSE)

XYZ Corporation
Park Avenue
New York, New York

Gentlemen:

This is a supplement to the financing agreement between us dated _____
_____, 19___:

1. For all your loans and advances to or for the account of the undersigned, together with interest thereon, and also for the commissions, obligations, indebtedness, charges and expenses properly chargeable against or due from the undersigned, and for the amount due upon any notes or other obligations given to or acquired by you for or upon account of any such loans or advances, interest, commissions, obligations, indebtedness, charges and expenses or otherwise (all of which, no matter how or when arising or acquired and whether under the financing agreement as hereby supplemented, or otherwise, are hereinafter referred to as "Obligations"), you shall be secured by a pledge to you of goods and merchandise deposited in public or field warehouses acceptable to you, under agreements between the undersigned and such warehouses pursuant to which negotiable or non-negotiable warehouse receipts for such goods and merchandise shall be issued by such warehouses. All such goods, merchandise and warehouse receipts are hereinafter referred to as "Security". You shall have the sole discretion as to the amount of any such Obligations, the relation thereof to the value of the Security, and the period during which any such Obligations shall remain outstanding.

2. The undersigned will perform any and all steps requested by you to create and maintain a valid pledge of all Security. Warehouse receipts in form acceptable to you shall be issued in your name or negotiated to you, and if you so request the undersigned will by separate instrument assign to you all of its right, title and interest in all Security. A physical inventory of all Security shall be taken by or at the direction of the undersigned at least every three (3) months or at more frequent intervals if you so request, and a copy of each inventory so taken shall be signed and supplied to you. You may examine and inspect the Security at any time. All Security shall be completely and separately identified and described in writing and shall be in such quantities and at such stated valuations as shall be acceptable to you. At the request of the undersigned you shall instruct the warehouse companies from time to time to release Security to the order of the undersigned upon payment to you of the accepted stated valuation of the Security to be released or upon payment of such lesser valuation as shall be acceptable to you or upon the substitution and pledge pursuant hereto of other Security acceptable to you. No Security shall be removed from warehouse without your consent in writing.

3. The undersigned warrants and covenants that all Security is and will at all times be the sole property of the undersigned, free and clear of any and all liens except your lien thereon, and the undersigned will pay and discharge all costs and expenses of acquisition, maintenance, storage, and handling of the Security. The undersigned will insure the Security for your benefit against loss or damage by fire, theft, burglary, pilferage, loss in transportation and also, where requested by you, against other hazards, in companies, in amounts and under policies acceptable to you, and all premiums thereon shall be paid by the undersigned and the policies delivered to you; and in the event of failure of the undersigned so to do, you may procure such insurance and charge the cost thereof to the undersigned.

4. Your lien shall continue in full force and effect, and you shall at all times have the right to take possession of and to hold all Security, until payment in full of all Obligations and until the liquidation of all accounts receivable assigned to you.

Fig. 5—1. Inventory Security Agreement (Warehouse)

5. In the event of any breach by the undersigned of any provision of the financing agreement as hereby supplemented, or upon failure of the undersigned to pay any of the Obligations when due, or upon the termination of the financing agreement as hereby supplemented, the undersigned will pay all Obligations forthwith upon demand. Upon default, you shall have the sole right and power, then or at any time or times thereafter, to sell and dispose of all of the Security without advertisement and upon reasonable notice to the undersigned, either at public or private sale or sales, for such prices and upon such terms and in such quantities as you may deem advisable, and you may be the purchaser of all or any part thereof; Upon such sale you shall have the right to apply the proceeds thereof first toward the payment of the expenses of taking, moving, storage, and sale (including reasonable counsel fees), and then toward the payment of all Obligations; you shall account to the undersigned for any surplus and the undersigned will continue liable to you for any deficiency. You shall not, however, at any time be required to have recourse to the Security.

6. You shall be deemed to have exercised reasonable care in the custody or preservation of any Security in your possession if you take such action for such purpose which we shall reasonably request; but no omission to do any act not requested by us shall be deemed a failure to exercise reasonable care, and no omission to comply with any such request shall of itself be deemed a failure to exercise reasonable care.

7. On all loans and advances made hereunder, your charge, which the undersigned agrees to pay, shall be at the rate of one _____ of one per cent per day on the cash daily balances due you from date of advances and until repaid, payable monthly.

8. This supplement is incorporated in and shall have a term concurrent with the financing agreement. This supplement is made in the State of New York and shall be interpreted according to the laws of said State; is entered into for the benefit of the parties hereto, their successors and assigns; cannot be changed orally; and shall be deemed dated as of the date of your acceptance below.

ATTEST:

By_____
                 President

_____
      Secretary

(SEAL)

ACCEPTED AT NEW YORK, NEW YORK

on_____, 19_____

XYZ CORPORATION

By_____

Fig. 5–1.   Inventory Security Agreement (Warehouse)—Continued

SECRETARY'S CERTIFICATE

of

_____

"RESOLVED, that the President, Secretary, Treasurer or
other officer or any agent of this corporation, or any one or more of
them, be and they are hereby authorized and empowered to enter into
and execute on behalf of the corporation an Inventory Security Agreement with XYZ Corporation relating to the creation of a security
interest in any goods, merchandise or other property now or hereafter
belonging to or acquired by the corporation, and the proceeds thereof,
in favor of XYZ Corporation, and from time to time to modify or
supplement said agreement and to make and modify or supplement
arrangements with said XYZ Corporation as to the terms or conditions on which such security interest shall be effectuated, and they are
hereby further authorized and empowered from time to time to con-
sign, pledge, mortgage or otherwise hypothecate to or with XYZ
Corporation goods, merchandise or other property now or hereafter
belonging to or acquired by the corporation, and for said purposes
to execute and deliver any and all consignments, schedules, mortgages,
agreements, warehouse receipts, endorsements, instruments of
pledge and /or other instruments in respect thereof, and to do and
perform all such other acts and things deemed by such officer or agent
necessary, convenient or proper to carry out, supplement or modify
any such agreement and arrangements made with XYZ Corporation,
hereby ratifying, approving and confirming all that any said officers
or agents have done or may do in the premises."

I, _____, do hereby certify that I am the

Secretary of _____ a corporation organized and

existing under and by virtue of the laws of the State of _____,

having its principal place of business in the City of _____;

that I am the keeper of the corporate records and the seal of said corpora-

tion; that the foregoing is a true and correct copy of a resolution duly

adopted at a meeting of the Board of Directors of said corporation duly con-

vened and held in accordance with its by-laws and the laws of said State, at

the office of said corporation in the City of _____, State

of _____, on the ____ day of _____,

19____, as taken and transcribed by me from the minutes of said meeting and

Fig. 5–2. Certificate of Resolution

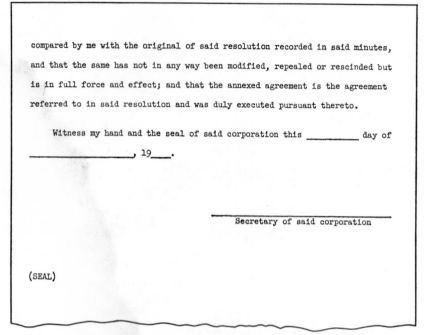

compared by me with the original of said resolution recorded in said minutes, and that the same has not in any way been modified, repealed or rescinded but is in full force and effect; and that the annexed agreement is the agreement referred to in said resolution and was duly executed pursuant thereto.

Witness my hand and the seal of said corporation this _____ day of _____, 19____.

_____
Secretary of said corporation

(SEAL)

Fig. 5–2. Certificate of Resolution—Continued

5–2). Since the inventory loan is supplemental to the financing of accounts, the agreements for such financing are also simultaneously executed. Frequently, however, the agreements for financing accounts are already operative. It will be observed that the financer has reserved a discretionary right to require full payment upon demand and to apply all the collateral to repayment of the indebtedness. In this connection, it should be noted that security agreements normally define the indebtedness to include all obligations to the financer, however created. As with all such discretionary rights (see page 51) the reputation of the financer is the borrower's best protection. As has been indicated, this right is vital to the financer in the event of unforseen financial deterioration of the borrower or some other unforeseeable difficulty.

INVENTORY SECURITY INTEREST FILED UNDER CODE

Where the use of warehouse facilities is not practicable, a second type of security interest in inventory may be obtained. To perfect this security interest a financing statement must be filed under the

Code. The mechanics of such filing are described in Chapter 9. Administratively, however, this arrangement is similar to the pre-Code factor's lien, and the security interest extends to all inventory on the borrower's described premises. This similarity extends to permitting the security agreement to provide that collateral, whenever acquired in the ordinary course of business, shall secure all obligations covered by the security agreement.

To effect such a security interest under the Code three basic elements are necessary: A financing agreement, the filing of a financing statement, and consideration—i.e., an advance of funds under the arrangement. A security agreement different from one contemplating warehousing is in Fig. 5–3 (pp. 118–9). The corporate resolution (Fig. 5–2) is the same and should be executed simultaneously. As with warehousing, insurance endorsed to the financer, as his interest may appear, must be obtained and maintained in force for the life of the loan.

As in the security agreement contemplating warehousing, the security interest perfected by filing under the Code reserves for the financer a discretionary right to require full payment upon demand and to apply all the collateral to repayment of the indebtedness. The reasons for this requirement have already been discussed (see page 51). Subject to such right, however, the mode of operation of the financing is agreed upon by the parties.

While perfecting a legal security interest is relatively simple, the existence of a security interest does not of itself assure the existence, quality, or quantity of the collateral. Hence, careful administrative procedures are vital to insure that sufficient readily saleable merchandise is available to support and liquidate the loan. Operational safeguards must be followed even more scrupulously in this arrangement than in a warehouse arrangement.

OPERATIONAL PROCEDURES AND SAFEGUARDS

Advances and Repayments

Under both major security devices described above, the administration of the inventory loan is similar. The similarities and differences therefore may be discussed conveniently together. Where no warehouseman controls the inventory, the checking procedures patently must be more intensive.

An inventory loan may be a revolving loan similar to a loan on accounts. That is, it may fluctuate upward or downward as the merchandise inventory is increased or decreased and whether or not such merchandise is represented by warehouse receipts. Or it may be a paydown loan (requiring scheduled reductions) after a specific opening advance. For either method, however, the financer must carefully follow the trend of the borrower's financial operations to ascertain the capacity of the borrower to repay the loan or eliminate, within a reasonable time, the revolving loan. If the borrower exhibits a losing trend, then the financer risks the unhappy prospect of being locked into an inventory loan. The loan may be required indefinitely as part of the borrower's capital structure, or alternatively, the financer may be required to liquidate the inventory himself.

The paydown inventory loan can be reduced by allocating an agreed percentage of sales or an agreed percentage of the normal advance on accounts toward that purpose. To arrive at a workable formula, the cost of merchandise as a percentage of sales price must be determined. Cash advanced as a percentage of the total inventory pledge must also be considered. Thus a formula may be developed that is both prudent for the financer and manageable for the borrower. This type of administration is more frequent when the advance is made pursuant to an inventory security interest filed under the Code.

If the inventory collateral is not generating regular sales but is drawn upon intermittently, then the paydown should be related to the original advance. This method is more frequently established where warehouse receipts are utilized. Preferably, the earlier releases should be repaid at a higher percentage than the percentage advanced. For example, if the original advance is 60% of the value, the repayments might be at 65% of value in the earlier stages. This increases the collateral margin of the financer and also increases the interest of the borrower in the remaining merchandise. It also provides protection for the financer against shrinkage of the merchandise values resulting from broken lots, deterioration, and the possibility that merchandise remaining toward the end of the financing period will be slower moving and less saleable

The measurement of the original advance warrants some comment. Generally it is a percentage of borrower's cost. The agreed percentage should be modest enough to provide for the normal dilution of value through spoilage, shrinkage, broken lots, pilferage, etc. It should also be pegged to include liquidation costs. Depending on the merchandise involved the acceptable range is from 50% to 75% of borrower's cost.

Records

As with accounts financing, a control ledger should be maintained for inventory. Indeed the same form of control ledger may be utilized. Daily, it should reflect cash in, cash out and balance as well as inventory in, inventory out, and balance. This should be reconciled periodically to the detailed records.

Where warehouse receipts are utilized, they can serve effectively as a detailed ledger. Merchandise in should be on such a receipt. It should be reflected also on tally sheets executed by the borrower. These should include the warranty and representation of the borrower regarding the nature and value of the inventory. The warehouse receipts alone do not include such warranty or representation by the borrower, and, as above indicated, the warehouseman usually makes none. Merchandise out should be released on standardized forms that can serve as a posting medium.

In the absence of a warehouse arrangement, a summary of weekly withdrawals can be required of the borrower. Usually this is practicable only as to finished goods. The summary can be checked by determining the percentage of sales that represents the cost of merchandise. This will provide an approximation of the outflow of goods, since all sales are being funnelled through the financer's control records. Again, the borrower should be required to certify weekly or periodically as to increases in inventory. Further, the borrower's periodic presentation of receiving-clerk tally sheets can provide an approximation of the inflow of newly acquired merchandise.

It becomes evident that in a non-warehouse arrangement the record keeping is looser. Further, the control of merchandise by the financer is also reduced. However, the use of the merchandise by the borrower is simplified since there is an easier flow of merchandise through his plant. Additionally, the warehouseman's charges are eliminated.

On a paydown loan, the initial advance is frequently substantially less than the advance for a revolving loan on the same collateral. Hence the inflow may not be followed as closely as otherwise. Periodic certifications should then be required of the borrower describing existing inventory on the premises and the values thereof.

Audits

It is important to recognize that all of the above procedures involve paper records. The relationship of the paper records to the physical reality is therefore a paramount consideration. Periodic certifications of a physical inventory should be required of the warehouseman, if present. This can be further tested by the financer's physical inspection and spot checking of the major items at regular intervals. Since most financers couple inventory loans with loans on accounts, the interim audit (see Chapter 3, page 63) should include this physical inspection. It is important that such inspection be made with a full-time representative of the warehouse company. The financer must avoid raising a question as to whether he relied on his own physical examination or upon the supervision of the warehouse company. The legal responsibility of the warehouse company is an important element in the transaction and must not be weakened.

Where the services of a warehouseman are not utilized, the financer's physical inspection becomes even more vital and should be more frequent. Where the inventory consists of a large number of varying items (styles, colors, and patterns) maintaining an exact perpetual inventory may be cumbersome. The audit program therefore should particularly include physical spot checks of the major items and an examination of the perpetual inventory records of the borrower. A major focus of all of these procedures is to determine whether some of the merchandise supporting the loan is becoming slow moving and therefore stale. Frequently the borrower, in order to maintain a well-rounded supply of merchandise for his customers, is required to keep in stock some slow-moving inventory. This enables him to fill all orders promptly. Such slow moving inventory should, however, be down-valued for purposes of calculating the proper advance on the merchandise. For administrative convenience and to facilitate more rapid spot checking of the major items constituting the collateral, orderly and systematic placement of the merchandise on the borrower's premises is highly desirable. Usually a well-managed borrower would accomplish this in any event.

Certain additional items must be checked. First it must be ascertained that all sales are flowing through the financer. The loss of inventory through cash sales unreported to the financer can result in a reduction of inventory not evidenced by the financer's internal controls. Further, the sales-cost analysis figures of the borrower must be rechecked to make certain that the outflow inventory figure being utilized by the financer still properly reflects the actual event.

Control of Proceeds

As above stated, the normal arrangement combines an inventory loan with accounts financing. Although theoretically the security interest in inventory flows into a security interest in accounts as proceeds of the inventory, the normal accounts financing procedures should be used. This enables the financer to maintain reproducible records on the accounts. It also enables him to utilize the advances on receivables to effectuate the repayment schedule on the inventory loan. This can be accomplished by breaking the advance on accounts into two checks and redepositing one of them for credit to the borrower's inventory account.

Liquidation

The standard for financial health of the borrower must understandably be higher when an inventory loan is involved. If the borrower's financial health is deteriorating, then the financer must be careful about not remaining in too heavy an inventory position. This frequently involves a very delicate decision. If the financer reduces his inventory position too rapidly, he may precipitate the very problem he fears—the insolvency of the borrower. On the other hand, a declining borrower may mean a difficult inventory liquidation. Hence very refined judgment and precise balance may be required. In the event, however, that the financer is required to liquidate the inventory to effect repayment, care must be exercised to utilize brokers and salesmen. The news that a lender holds the inventory usually results in a low and slow market. Effective disguise may be difficult where a financing statement has been filed against the borrower. Nevertheless, an orderly liquidation through normal trade channels should be attempted.

TEMPORARILY PERFECTED SECURITY INTEREST—DELIVERY OF GOODS OR DOCUMENTS OF TITLE TO DEBTOR

A third major inventory security device formerly utilized by secured lenders was the Trust Receipt. Prior to the widespread adoption of the Uniform Commercial Code, a majority of states, including New York, operated under the Uniform Trust Receipts Act. This act provided for the perfection of a temporary security interest in goods, documents of title, and negotiable instruments. It also was utilized for longer periods in automobile financing and the floor planning (see page 140) of appliances on dealers' premises.

The legal aspects of pre-Code Trust Receipt financing are more fully discussed in Chapter 8, treating the perfection of liens under pre-Code law. A modified analogue of the Uniform Trust Receipts

Act is found in Article 9, Section 304, subsections (4) and (5), of the Uniform Commercial Code. While the phrase "Trust Receipt" does not appear there, the section provides for temporarily perfected security interests upon delivery to a debtor of goods, negotiable instruments or documents of title. Normal business prudence dictates that such a delivery be evidenced by a receipt. In practice such receipts are in fact utilized. For ease of recognition of the nature of the transaction, such a receipt may be considered a trust receipt (without initial capitals) although, under the Code, the term is no longer a phrase of art (having specific legal meaning). Indeed, some financial institutions have continued to utilize their old forms in these situations while their supplies last.

Former Function of Trust Receipts

Primarily, the old Trust Receipt served to create or maintain a lien (now a security interest) on inventory during movements to effectuate a change of location and/or physical character of the merchandise. It was also the only device that could be utilized in the release of documents and negotiable instruments and therefore was frequently employed in import-export financing. In that context, its function was to enable the lender to deliver to the borrower the documents of title that had been presented under the letter of credit. The lender having paid or guaranteed the amount thus drawn down under the letter of credit—usually through the lender's bank that had opened the letter of credit—now had possession of the documents representing the merchandise. But the borrower needed possession of the merchandise in order to process it and/or re-ship it, thus creating the receivables that would ultimately repay the amount paid or guaranteed by the lender. The lender, therefore, delivered the documents of title (most frequently bills of lading) to the borrower. The documents were usually endorsed by the lender to the borrower, who presented them, usually through his forwarding agent, to the carrier, thereby obtaining possession of the merchandise. To maintain his security interest in the merchandise, the lender released the documents under a Trust Receipt and usually filed a Statement of Trust Receipt Financing.

Assume the following situation. Financer F has a security agreement with importer I. The agreement provides for the financing of accounts and the guaranteeing of letters of credit by F on behalf of I. Since only a bank can open a letter of credit, F guarantees the B bank, which opens the letter of credit for I. For simplicity's sake, assume that the letter of credit provides for a sight draft and no acceptances are created thereunder. I's foreign supplier ships the required merchandise and presents to the foreign bank the bill of lading plus other documents required under the terms of the letter of credit. It should be noted, of course, that the terms of the letter of credit are established by importer I with the advice and counsel of F and F's bank. The documents are made in favor of B, the opening bank (F's bank). Upon such presentation through bank channels to B, it debits F's account for the amount involved and endorses the documents to F's order. F now endorses them to the order of I and delivers them to I, who executes a Trust Receipt therefor. Utilizing the documents, I obtains possession of the goods (via his freight forwarder) and uses them to create accounts receivable. The lien of the Trust Receipt attaches by operation of law to the accounts receivable thus created as proceeds of the sale of merchandise represented by the documents of title subject to the Trust Receipt. Normally, however, F requires I to execute a separate assignment or pledge of the receivables. F would of course file a Statement of Trust Receipt Financing to perfect his lien under the Uniform Trust Receipts Act.

Temporary Security Interests Under the Code

The Uniform Commercial Code eliminated the "Trust Receipt" but provided for a similar temporary security interest. The requirement for and general mode of filing of financing statements under the Code are fully set forth in Chapter 9. The present discussion will center upon the perfection of a security interest for a temporary period, without filing, under Article 9, sections 304(4) and 304(5). Temporary perfection of a security interest is thereunder permitted, without filing or possession by the secured party (or bailee) in order to facilitate the handling, for short periods, of instruments, documents, or goods. A security interest in negotiable instruments can be perfected only by the secured party's taking possession thereof with two exceptions. One is where the secured party delivers the instrument to the debtor for sale, exchange, presentation, collection, renewal, or registration of transfer. The other is where the security interest arises for new value under a written security agreement. Each exception is valid for only twenty-one days.

Release of Import Financing Documents. But the emphasis here is on goods or documents of title representing goods. Two distinct methods of operation were envisioned and covered by the drafters of the Code. First is the situation in which a security agreement exists between the parties. In such event, there is a regular and on-going relationship. The most common transaction of this kind is import financing, described above. Here the financer pays or guarantees payment for documents presented under a letter of credit.

Assume the same financing relationship between F and I as was described above. The transaction proceeds in exactly the same manner under the Code. However, no Trust Receipt is required of I by F. The security interest of F remains valid for a period of twenty-one days. However, F would get a receipt for the documents from I. Section 9-304(4) provides that, new value having been given by the financer under the security agreement, a security interest attaches to the negotiable documents and is valid for twenty-one days. In this case, Section 9-304(5) produces the same result. Presumably, payment to F should be effected within that period. Such payment may be in cash or as an adjustment of advances under the accounts financing arrangement.

Removal of Goods from Warehouse. The second typical transaction arises when the financer advances against goods in a field warehouse, for which non-negotiable warehouse receipts have been issued in the name of the financer. Section 9-304(3) provides that possession by the warehouseman bailee who has issued non-negotiable warehouse receipts to the financer perfects the security interest of the financer without filing. Normally, in such a transaction, the financer permits the withdrawal from the warehouse of goods (to an agreed dollar amount) without immediate payment by the borrower. This is sometimes described as a permissible "float." Section 9-304(5)(a) provides that the security interest shall remain perfected after the release of such merchandise for a period of twenty-one days. Presumably, payment to the financer for the released merchandise would be made within that period. Operationally, this provision permits an easier flow of the transactions. The merchandise removed from a public or field warehouse for processing and sale is no longer subject to the security interest that was perfected by possession of the bailee. To avoid a hiatus, a temporary security interest is continued in the merchandise until a receivable is generated to which another security interest attaches in favor of the financer pursuant to the financing arrangement for accounts.

An illustration of this type of transaction is as follows. Financer F advances to vendor V on goods in a public or field warehouse, pursuant to a security agreement for inventory financing. V is a

wholesaler of vinyl floor tiles. The advance is 60% of V's cost of
goods, and non-negotiable receipts in favor of F have been issued
by the warehouse company W. As V obtains sales orders for quantities of tiles, he must remove them from the warehouse for shipment.
If V were required to pay F for the advance on the quantity of
goods removed, V usually would experience some difficulty in so
doing. Hence the normal arrangement provides for a permissible
float. Warehouse W is here permitted to release to V up to $10,000
worth of goods at cost, without a cash payment to F. This permits
a smoother flow of goods for V. Effectively, it enables him to utilize
the goods removed from the warehouse to create receivables against
which advances are received to repay the inventory advances on the
goods thus removed. V sells $10,000 worth of merchandise (at his
cost) for $12,000 at his sales price. Against $12,000 in receivables
(created on the same day as the removal of the goods from the
warehouse) V receives 80% thereof or $9,600 from F under the receiv-
ables financing arrangement. Of this, F may apply $6,000 to inven-
tory loan for the goods removed under the "float." The balance of
$3,600 is advanced to V to be used for operating expenses. F is
thus repaid for the released goods and the "float" is reinstated. Since
the goods are in W's possession as bailee, no Uniform Commercial
Code filing was required of F in connection with his security interest
in the goods. Upon removal of the goods from the warehouse, F's
security interest is continued under section 9-304(5) without filing.
This temporary security interest, however, is valid only for twenty-one
days.

Expiration of Temporary Security Interest

It becomes obvious that the drafters of the Code inserted sub-sec-
tions (4) and (5) in section 9-304 to make possible a perfected security interest upon delivery of goods, instruments or documents to
the debtor in situations where the flow of the transaction required
such delivery. This is, of course, the same type of transaction formerly covered by Trust Receipt Financing. In each case the prudent
lender would obviously require a receipt from the debtor to complete
the records of the transaction. Where merchandise is released from
a public warehouse to the borrower, a receipt is normally required.
In the case of a release to the borrower from a field warehouse,
such receipt is usually not required, but the warehouse records clearly
reflect the release. Hence in most situations, the old Trust Receipt

is now a trust receipt and the perfection of the security interest (trust) is created or continued (but only for a period of twenty-one days) by operation of this section. Thus, the avoidance of the time gap in the perfected security interest presents a theoretical neatness and symmetry.

In practice, however, the time lag can actually exceed a period of twenty-one days. For example, documents presented under a letter of credit and released under section 9-304(4) could relate to merchandise on a ship that has been delayed in transit, or a dock strike or similar delay may develop. Such a delay could easily extend the time gap beyond twenty-one days. Or shipment could be delayed for any one of many reasons in a transaction releasing goods from a warehouse under section 9-304(5). But as has been above indicated, most financing dealing with this type of transaction is coordinated with a regularized financing arrangement for accounts and/or inventory. It is therefore a very simple matter to include a clause covering negotiable documents in the financing statement filed for accounts and/or inventory. The danger of running over the twenty-one day limitation would thereby be avoided. Such filing would of course be equivalent to the filing of a Statement of Trust Receipt Financing under pre-Code law, thus completing the analogy. In the case of the warehouse "float," an inventory financing statement would solve the time-element problem. The borrower, however, may be unhappy about the filing.

Conflicting Security Interests

In the above-described situations, there is another and perhaps even more compelling reason for filing a financing statement covering documents and goods. Disputes on priorities between conflicting security interests could very easily become a major problem. If one financer is financing accounts and another the goods in a field warehouse, a dispute could arise as to the accounts generated by the goods released for the "float" pursuant to section 9-304(5)(a). At the moment of conflict, the inventory financer may not have been paid for the amount of the "float." The goods have now been shipped. Twenty-one days have not expired since the release from the warehouse. Does the temporarily perfected lien under section 9-304(5)(a) follow the proceeds? But the accounts are subject to the security interest of the accounts financer. Here one financer's proceeds are another financer's collateral.

The inventory financer did not file, since he relied on the bailee's possession under section 9-304(3). He released the goods under a temporary security interest pursuant to section 9-304(5)(a). Neither of these provisions requires filing. Hence in the determination of priorities (section 9-312) the first-to-file rule is inapplicable. The first-to-perfect rule thereupon becomes operative, but does not help. The security interests of both financers attach simultaneously—when the receivable is created. The question of which financer prevails, therefore, becomes rather murky.

Unfortunately, in such a situation, the filing of a financing statement by the inventory financer does not resolve the priority problem. For in such event, the inventory financer possibly may elect to disregard his filing and claim under section 9-304(3) and section 9-304(5)(a). Filing does, however, publicly announce the inventory financer's relationship, and thus affords the two financers an opportunity of becoming aware of each other's existence and of working out a mutually satisfactory arrangement on the priorities. The need for such communication and accommodation between two financers of the same debtor points up a basic principle of secured lending. Normally a financer secured by current assets should be completely in control of all loans against current assets. For this purpose a letter of credit financing arrangement is considered an inventory loan and thus a current asset financing arrangement. Obviously, this principle does not apply if the financer is secured only by fixed assets.

Usually an inventory financer will insist on control of the accounts to enable him to follow and regulate the flow of inventory into accounts and then into cash repayment. On the other hand, an accounts financer who has searched the appropriate filing office prior to advancing cannot rest on that search. After filing and commencing the financing relationship, such a financer must be wary of a subsequent inventory financer. Nor does the borrower's covenant in the security agreement not to finance his inventory with a third party provide sufficient assurance to the accounts financer. A cash-hungry borrower may find a reckless and/or unsophisticated lender, and the priority problem may thereupon arise. An action against an insolvent borrower for breach of the above described covenant will not be helpful to an accounts financer thus entangled. The most reliable line of defense against such an entanglement is the periodic audit of the borrower's books by the accounts financer. Early discovery of the prohibited practice frequently enables the accounts financer to take the steps necessary to protect his position. Such steps may range from discontinuing the financing of the accounts to working out a mutually satisfactory arrangement with the inventory financer.

Sale of Merchandise and Negotiation of Instruments

It should be noted that the Code expressly provides that a buyer of goods in the ordinary course of business, a holder in due course of a negotiable instrument and a holder to whom a document of title has been negotiated—all take free of any other perfected security interest. In short, such items may continue to move freely in the commercial world.

SECURITY AGREEMENT

[Inventory]

....

New York, N. Y.   ...., 19........

Gentlemen:

This letter, when accepted by you, will become a security agreement supplementing and forming part of the Security Agreement [Accounts, Contract Rights, etc.] between us dated ...., 19........:

1. We hereby grant a continuing Security Interest in your favor upon all of our present and hereafter-acquired Inventory, and the products and proceeds thereof. The term "Inventory" includes all our present raw materials, components, work in process, finished merchandise, and packing and shipping materials, wherever located; and all such chattels hereafter acquired by us by way of substitution, replacement, return, repossession or otherwise; and all additions and accessions thereto, and the resulting product or mass; and any documents of title representing any thereof. Your Security Interest shall attach to all of the foregoing without further act on your or our part. Upon your request, we will from time to time at our expense pledge and deliver such Inventory to you or to a third party as your bailee; or hold the same in trust for your account; or store the same in warehouse in your name; or deliver to you documents of title representing the same; or evidence your Security Interest in some other acceptable manner. The advances made and to be made hereunder are primarily to enable us to purchase raw materials and defray the cost of labor and similar manufacturing expenses which add to the value and marketability of the finished product manufactured, processed, or otherwise dealt in by us; and since such advances will be used for the foregoing purposes, your Security Interest shall be deemed to be a Purchase Money Security Interest.

2. Your said Security Interest shall secure (a) any advances which you may make hereunder, and (b) any other indebtedness which we may from time to time owe to you, fixed or contingent, whether arising under the aforesaid Security Agreement or after the termination thereof, or otherwise arising or acquired by you, and (c) all interest, charges, commissions, expenses (including attorneys' fees and legal expenses) and other items chargeable against us by reason of any of the foregoing. The term "advances" means moneys paid to us or to others for our account, or obligations to third parties incurred by you at our request.

3. We agree that the making of Inventory advances is always wholly discretionary on your part, and that you shall be the sole judge of the amount of such advances and of the total of such advances to be outstanding at any particular time. All such advances shall be repayable on demand, and shall bear interest at the same rate as specified in the aforesaid Security Agreement.

Fig. 5–3. Inventory Security Agreement (Non-Warehouse)

4. We warrant, covenant, and agree that:

(a) All Inventory is and shall remain free from all purchase-money or other liens or incumbrances except such as are held by you.

(b) You shall have the right at all times to immediate possession of all Inventory and its products and proceeds, and to inspect the Inventory and our records pertaining thereto.

(c) We shall insure and keep insured all Inventory for full value, with such coverage and in such companies as you may approve, at our expense, and the policies shall be duly endorsed in your favor and delivered to you. If we default in this regard, you shall have the right to insure and charge the cost to us. You assume no risk or responsibility in connection with the payment or non-payment of losses, your only responsibility being to credit us with any insurance payments received on account of losses.

(d) All excise, floor, sales and any other taxes that may be assessed upon or paid by you with respect to any of the Inventory shall be charged to and paid by us, and we agree to indemnify you against loss by reason of any such taxes. We will make due and timely payment or deposit of all Federal, State, and local taxes, assessments or contributions required of us by law, and will execute and deliver to you, on demand, appropriate Certificates attesting to the payment or deposit thereof.

(e) None of the Inventory shall be removed or disposed of without your written consent, except to bona fide purchasers thereof in the ordinary course of our business and on orders approved by you in writing. All our sales shall be promptly reported to you, and the accounts or other proceeds thereof shall be subject to your security interest in accordance with the aforesaid Security Agreement.

(f) You shall not be liable or responsible in any way for the safekeeping of any of the Inventory, or for any loss or damage thereto or for any diminution in the value thereof, or for any act or default of warehousemen or of any carrier, forwarding agency, or other person whomsoever, or for the collection of any proceeds, but the same shall be at our sole risk at all times.

(g) You shall have the right (but shall not be obliged) to pay and to charge as an advance to us hereunder any dyeing, finishing, processing, or warehousing charges, landlord's bills, or other claims against or liens upon the Inventory.

5. Our default in the payment or performance of any obligation or undertaking on our part hereunder, or the happening of any event specified as an event of default in the aforesaid Security Agreement, shall be an event of default hereunder. Upon the happening of such or any other event of default, you shall have, in addition to all rights and remedies of a Secured Party under the Uniform Commercial Code or other applicable statute or rule, the following rights and remedies:

(a) You may peaceably by your own means or with judicial assistance enter our or any other premises and take possession of the Inventory, and remove or dispose of it on our premises, and we will not resist or interfere with such action.

(b) You may require us to assemble all or any part of the Inventory and make it available to you at any place designated by you and reasonably convenient to both parties.

(c) We agree that a notice sent to us at least 5 days before the date of any intended public sale or the date after which any private sale or other intended disposition of the Inventory is to be made, shall be deemed to be reasonable notice of such sale or other disposition. All notice is waived if the Inventory is perishable or threatens to decline speedily in value or is of a type customarily sold on a recognized market.

(d) In the event of any such public or private sale or other disposition, we will pay to you on demand any deficiency remaining after crediting the net proceeds of sale, less all expenses of taking, handling, and sale, including reasonable counsel fee. All rights of redemption are waived. You shall account to us for any surplus.

6. Until we shall notify you in writing to the contrary, you shall be justified in assuming that our Inventory is and will continue to be principally kept at our address specified below.

Very truly yours,

....
(Name of Debtor)

by X ....
(signature)

....
(typed or printed name of signatory)

....
(title of signatory)

....
(Address of Debtor)

Accepted at New York, N. Y.:

....
(Name of Secured Party)

by X ....
(signature)

....
(typed or printed name of signatory)

....
(title of signatory)

Fig. 5–3. Inventory Security Agreement (Non-Warehouse)—Continued

6

Financing Consumer Installment Sales

Philip Cohen
Vice President, Leumi Financial Corporation

NATURE OF CONSUMER INSTALLMENT CREDIT

Scope of the Field

Finance companies and banks have been engaged in consumer installment financing for many years. This field is very wide, with varying degrees of strength in the paper taken as collateral. Similarly broad variations are found in the consumer's investment or equity in the purchase underlying the installment paper.

At one end of the scale there is automobile paper and at the other personal loans. These account for approximately 70% of all installment credit outstanding. Between these extremes the major categories of merchandise financed in the spread of consumer installment activity are: appliances, furniture, television and radio, encyclopedias, ready-to-wear merchandise, and household goods.

Growth of Consumer Installment Credit

The growth of consumer installment credit has been phenomenal. After an average expansion of installment debt outstanding of $4.3 billion a year for the four years 1961–1964, a record expansion of between $7 and $8 billion took place in 1965. By the first third of 1966, installment credit outstanding neared the $70 billion mark.

Non-installment credit, which includes retail charge accounts, credit card plans, and single payment loans, also continues to expand.

This development has been responsible for the rapid growth of many of our large industries. Certainly the flood of credit (consumer and corporate) has helped produce the economic growth of the 1960's. "You're not going to have a ten million car year if you don't have consumer credit," the president of a large finance company has said.

The growth of installment debt has been the result of several basic economic factors. An increase in the number of households of almost 20% in the last ten years has provided an expanding market. A more potent force has been the almost 60% growth in the median income per family in the last decade, giving a rapidly expanding capacity to borrow in anticipation of needs. Moreover, for most families in times of adversity, incomes are better maintained than formerly because of unemployment benefits and other welfare programs. Further, the presence of more than one worker in many families as well as the governmental efforts to stabilize employment have had an effect.

These elements have strengthened the repayment ability of borrowers and thus increased their willingness and ability to borrow. Other stimulants to the demand for credit have been longer repayment periods and the wider availability of credit in the purchase of more products and services.

From the standpoint of the consumer, it is no longer considered a stigma to buy on time. Consumer credit has been responsible, in a great measure, for a standard of living for our laboring and middle classes unequalled elsewhere in the world. It also has established for retailers and dealers a service and technique that has increased their sales measurably.

Methods of Collection

Although a good part of the financing of this type of consumer credit is handled by banks and finance companies on a direct collection basis with or without recourse to the dealer, the emphasis in this chapter is on indirect collection, with full recourse to the dealer or retailer generating the paper, under a loan agreement.

Direct Collection. Direct collection means that the financer has agreed to purchase the retail installment contract from the dealer after having approved the retail purchaser's credit and sends the purchaser its own coupon payment book (covering the number of payments called for in the retail installment contract) with instructions to make the payments directly to the bank or finance company. "With recourse" means that the dealer has to repurchase from the financer the equipment or merchandise on any contract on which the purchaser has defaulted in his payments. "Without recourse" means that the financer, having purchased the contract, owns it and therefore must liquidate it.

Indirect Collection. Consumer installment financing handled on an indirect collection basis is very similar to non-notification, full-recourse commercial receivables financing. Indirect collection may be defined as the arrangement under which the dealer or retailer collects the installment payments of his customers in his place of business and then remits these payments to the financer's office or deposits them in the financer's bank account at a branch of the bank near the retailer's place of business. A fundamental difference between the direct collection operation and the indirect collection operation is that the former often involves a large network of branch offices, whereas the latter is similar to the centralized operation in commercial receivables financing.

FINANCER'S CRITERIA FOR ACCEPTING PROSPECT

Suitability of Merchandise

The underlying theory and practice of consumer credit have undergone many changes over the last fifty years. The first major growth of financing installment sales occurred in the early 20th century with the automobile. This product still represents the largest area for installment financing and illustrates the characteristics of merchandise suitable for installment selling.

For the suitability of the merchandise is a paramount consideration. In the first place, the automobile is durable. It will last and have a usable value for several years. Hence, even with prolonged credit terms, the consumer is not "paying for a dead horse." The automobile thus illustrates the fundamental principle that the life of the equipment should be longer than the life of the obligation. Second, the automobile is a relatively uniform type of merchandise, the value of which can be readily known or estimated in advance. Further, the consumer is seldom if ever unwilling to keep on paying because he feels that his car has become obsolete. By the same token, the automobile has a substantial resale value related to its original cost, for a wide market exists for used cars. Third, the automobile is just that—mobile. Hence repossession is not difficult and neither is moving the automobile to a locality where the best resale market exists.

No other article sold on installment terms has these features in the same degree. Consumer durables, such as refrigerators and washing machines, have the same original wide acceptance, but there has never been the same wide consumer acceptance of used articles in this field. Further, repossession and shipment to a better resale market of these articles present definite problems with respect to realization value. Furniture has an even poorer resale value. Clothing does not have the durability necessary to make it really suitable as sound collateral for installment financing, and it has almost no resale value or consumer acceptance as used merchandise.

There is another consideration in connection with the suitability of merchandise for installment financing. It is the price of the item. At one end of the scale, the price of automobiles is high enough to make twelve, twenty-four, or even thirty-six monthly payments large enough in amount to warrant the handling and bookkeeping expense involved. At the other end of the scale, small consumers' appliances such as electric irons and toasters, and clothing and furniture do not usually result in large enough individual transactions and large enough monthly installments to warrant handling a transaction on an individual basis. The dealer, however, to avail himself of time-selling as a sales weapon in his merchandising program finds it worthwhile to absorb the bookkeeping and overhead expenses. Thus, while small appliances, furniture and clothing are sold on time, there are dealers who are unable to find a financer who will finance their transactions on a direct collection basis.

Moreover, in the fields of furniture, clothing, jewelry, and small appliances, the dealer is seeking repeat trade and therefore is not interested in direct collection by the financer. The dealer wants the customer returning to the store to make payments because he hopes that the customer will buy something else on the way out. That is why the cashier's cage, in a retail store selling on the installment basis, is always located in the back of the store. It compels the customer to walk through the length of the store and back again when he comes in to make a payment.

Between these extremes of automobiles and small appliances and clothing are the larger consumer appliances, such as refrigerators, washing machines, and television and radio sets. In the early days of installment financing, financers were reluctant to handle installment sales of these types of merchandise on a direct collection, individual-transaction basis. Banks, for example, frowned upon loans that were not for "productive" or "commercial" purposes. Such loans were not regarded as self-liquidating. With regard to financing the consumer, the commercial bank was not equipped to handle credit accounts of individual consumers nor did it have the specialized supervision of a collection department to oversee delinquent purchasers, check losses, and make repossessions. It was unwilling to risk consumer dissatisfaction with durables that seemed to need repairs constantly, leading to consumer reluctance to continue payments. Shortly before World War II, financers were handling the business on direct collection. In 1939, one-half of all consumer installment paper was held by retailers. The other half was sold by retailers to finance companies and banks. Banks had become interested in the remarkable safety and high return of installment paper as a result of their favorable experience with sales finance companies during the depression years. After the war, direct collection plans were resumed. As salaries and other overhead expenses of the finance companies increased, however, even the major appliance business tended to go back to the indirect collection form of financing. About 1956, a portable microfilm machine came on the market, and this piece of equipment has added definite impetus to the financing of consumer installment sales on an indirect collection basis by financers.

Essentially, there has been an abandonment of emphasis on durable goods and the equity of the consumer in such goods in the evolution of the theory and practice of consumer credit. Financers have gone into fields that formerly were considered out of bounds for installment credit. This has resulted from the change in consumer attitudes toward the use of debt over the years. Individuals these days are more willing to commit their future income to debt repayment than they were thirty to fifty years ago. Rising incomes and employment and the increasing security of both jobs and incomes have encouraged consumers to take on additional debt. At the same time, financers and retailers have actively promoted consumer credit and have adopted new and more flexible credit plans to facilitate credit purchases. For example, there are various types of revolving credit plans with lines of credit used according to the consumer's needs and repaid over a period of months. These credit plans have extended installment credit to the financing of soft goods and services.

Nature of Retailer

After having evaluated the merchandise on which the installment sale is based, the financer turns to a consideration of the nature and quality of the "Retailer," who, in appliances, furniture, and other fields is also called a "Dealer" or "Seller." Financial strength is important. There is a big difference in desirability of the prospect between the retailer that is a fairly well capitalized, or even modestly capitalized, department store and the retailer that operates a credit jewelry store or sells books or encyclopedias on a door-to-door basis. Three qualitative differences that should be emphasized here are (1) the financial stability of the retailer, (2) the kind of merchandise sold, and (3) the method of selling.

Financial Stability. Using a form entitled "Retail Accounts Preliminary Audit Investigation" (see Fig. 6–4, pp. 143–6), the financer's auditor or examiner obtains information regarding a retailer prospect. This information will enable the credit committee to evaluate and pass on the merits of the prospect's installment sales, or "consumer paper."

On the first page of the form, the examiner is asked to obtain information on capitalization, net worth or capital, financial statement of recent date, Dun & Bradstreet report on prospect, the business history and moral risk aspect, and names and addresses of banks. This helps to determine the financial stability of the retailer prospect. Further on, information is sought on any previous record of financing. If there has been some, the previous financer will be contacted for its experience with the prospect.

Information is also obtained on the condition of accounts payable and on the names of the active creditors. One of the pertinent questions is whether the retailer is too heavily indebted in relation to the amount of merchandise inventory on hand.

The relative financial stability of the retailer is an important and basic factor in determining whether the financer will be faced with a liquidation at some future time. Balance sheets of retailers doing an installment business should provide a reserve for deferred income or for unrealized gross profit. Unrealized gross profit refers to the profit on the sale of a piece of merchandise on an installment basis that is deferred over the number of months of the retail installment contract and earned or "realized" on the basis of the amount of payments received from the customer. Deferred income refers to the finance charge based on the term of the installment contract which is deferred over the number of months the contract has to run and taken into income for the particular periods involved on the basis of the amount of credit still outstanding during these periods.

Regardless of designation, this reserve is required to cover the collection and liquidation expense inherent in carrying accounts receivable that remain outstanding for extended periods. In all cases, there will also be a reserve for bad debts.

Credit Policy and Collection Experience. The evaluation will also include an analysis of the credit worthiness of the prospect's customers; his collection experience which involves also a review of his collection procedures; an extended review of delinquency analyses; and a survey of repossessions, accounts turned over for legal action, and bad-debt writeoffs. The Preliminary Audit Investigation should be exhaustive in these matters.

In analyzing customers' credit worthiness, it is important to review the credit applications received by the retailer and the standards utilized for employment, income, residence, and credit record. In this connection, a case history may be cited that involves the rediscounting or refinancing of a portfolio of accounts of a smaller financer that was in the business of buying at a discount, without recourse, home improvement paper from dealers in home improvements and repairs.

The term of the paper was five years, and the average installment contract was about $3,000. In these sales there is no chattel security in the goods. As security the financer took a second mortgage, and in some cases a third mortgage, on the homes of the individual customers for whom the improvements or repairs had been made. A review of the customers' credit applications and credit files, including litigation reports, in the office of the finance company indicated that the financer was buying paper on very marginal accounts with reported incomes that could just about support the mortgage payments. There were also records of judgments against them. The financer relied, in many cases, on the customer's alleged equity in his home to rationalize its purchase of the home improvement contract. The rediscounting financer did not wish to be a party to foreclosure actions in order to obtain repayment of loans and believed that the customers did not appear to be worthy of the amounts of the loans being extended to them. The account was declined.

Aside from the general consideration of credit worthiness of customers for the amount of credit extended to them, it is important to consider the geographical distribution of the customers in anticipation of a possible liquidation. The expense involved in a liquidation can be extremely high if the customers are spread all over the country. Of course, this does not apply to department store operations, but it does appear in certain other types of retail distribution, for example in the selling of encyclopedias.

Merchandising Policies. Other questions that the examiner must answer are designed to provide information on the method of selling and the kinds of merchandise sold. For example, is the retailer selling name-brand merchandise or, in the case of furniture, is this a "borax" operation? "Borax" refers to a cheap grade of furniture that is marked up two, three, or four times on cost. Specifically, the form covers:

1. How sales originate: canvass, door to door, newspaper advertisements, radio and television advertising
2. Breakdown of sales: per cent furniture, appliances, television, miscellaneous
3. Down payments and terms
4. Lines carried: furniture, appliances, television, soft goods, musical

PRICING. The kinds of merchandise sold, and the related consideration of the prices charged for such merchandise, are significant. To the degree that the merchandise is non-durable, non-essential, and even frivolous, so runs the danger of non-payment. For when the customer awakens from the salesman's spell and realizes what he has bought and at what price, he often rebels. Hence, if the price of the merchandise sold bears no reasonable relationship to the intrinsic value thereof or to the price at which it can be bought for cash, the quality of the installment receivables is seriously impaired. Price gouging is as insidious as unconscionable finance charges. The latter have been regulated by legislative action in many states. The former is not susceptible of such regulation.

TERMS OF SALE. Terms of sale, including down payments and finance charges, are of prime importance. A tendency on the part of retailers to extend longer terms on appliances and furniture should be viewed with a jaundiced eye by financers. There have been established, within a relatively small range, reasonable finance charges and reasonable down payments.

In recent years, down payments have been increasingly overlooked by retailers in order to stimulate sales. To satisfy financers, retailers have, from time to time, resorted to misrepresenting the down payment or to actually making a so-called down payment in order to validate the sale. This latter element tends to come up more frequently on the part of salesmen in a door-to-door operation. They will invest a relatively small down payment for the customer with the expectation that the sale will stick and they will earn a much larger commission. Such a practice leads to customer repudiation and no end of trouble in collections.

Thus the consideration of terms becomes an integral part of the total evaluation of the retailers for financing of his paper.

Selling Techniques. A further matter, the method of selling, is equally important. Legitimate and traditional selling methods used in a department store are certainly more apt to create a sound receivable than is the foot-in-the-door technique of door-to-door salesmen. This does not mean that sales originating in the latter manner cannot be considered for financing, but they certainly require close scrutiny. In between the department-store kind of selling and the so-called foot-in-the-door selling lies a variety of selling techniques. In each case, it is very important to know the techniques used and the terms given in the consummation of a sale.

The following are two very successful case histories of financing consumer installment sales. Two different companies, one located in Pennsylvania, the other in New Jersey, are in the business of selling china, stemware, and cookware to young brides or engaged girls. The sales are made on the so-called "club plan" or "party plan" basis and involve a type of door-to-door or "in-the home" selling. The Pennsylvania company had sales representatives covering the entire country. The average sale was about $250.00 and terms averaged fifteen months. Outstanding installment receivables were $1.5 million and the quality of the receivables may be noted from the fact that there was only a 7% delinquency covering accounts more than thirty days past due on an installment payment. The star sales person, a woman located in the Midwest, earned $52,000 in commissions one year. After several years, the company was able to secure bank financing.

The New Jersey company sells in a number of the nearby Eastern states. Similarly, the average sale is $260.00 and the average terms are sixteen months. On $600,000 of installment receivables outstanding, accounts delinquent forty days on the basis of contract terms were 8% to 9% of the outstandings. The company makes its sales through representatives who operate as independent dealers. Working with these dealers are district managers, and above them are area managers, regional managers, and zone managers. The zone manager is in charge of an entire state, and he is the only one in the sales hierarchy who is an employee of the company. The company delivers its merchandise to the customers through independent carriers and requires a small COD payment to be made by the customer which indicates to the company that the sale is bona fide and the merchandise has been accepted by the customer. Five per cent of every contract is set up as a reserve for bad debts. Even a so-called "hard sell," when properly conducted, may result in a profitable operation and a good finance risk.

THE CONTRACTS AND GOVERNMENT REGULATION

The legal foundations of consumer installment financing can be broken down into two main areas: (1) legal requirements pertaining to the financer and (2) legal requirements pertaining to the retailer. Insofar as the financer is concerned, of primary importance is delivery to him of the retail installment contracts or chattel paper, since at the retail level no filing is necessary on consumer goods. However, Uniform Commercial Code provisions with regard to filing financing statements should be complied with in the same manner as in commercial receivables financing. Similarly, compliance with maximum legal rate statutes is obviously necessary. Proper assignments, including negotiation of notes or retail installment sales contracts, should be provided for.

The Financing Agreement

The underlying agreement between the financer and the retailer is one specially designed for consumer financing (see Fig. 6–5, pp. 147–51). It is addressed to the finance company by the borrower, who makes various representations and warranties and sets the terms and conditions under which he desires to borrow from time to time on the security of collateral assigned to the financer. The agreement's covenants and warranties are basic to the operation of a consumer installment finance account. It usually provides for exclusive financing of all sales, contains a precise definition of prime paper (and thereby, by implication, delinquent paper), and provides for custodianship and sale or lease of records.

Advances and Charges. The agreement contains provisions stipulating the percentage of initial advance and the rate of compensation. There is no set rule as to the percentage of advance, except that generally it should be lower than the advance in commercial receivables financing. This is because the accounts involve individuals and not commercially rated debtors; the collection period is longer because the terms of sale are much longer than those that prevail in commercial transactions; bookkeeping and collection expenses are more costly; and the finance charges are not collected in advance. Normally a 60% to 65% advance on prime paper is made. In certain cases such as with department store receivables, a higher advance can be made. In other situations a lower advance of 50% should be made. Rates of compensation are quoted on a daily rate basis and are usually higher than those that prevail in commercial receivables financing.

Collateral and Ratio. The agreement defines both collateral and prime paper. One criterion of prime paper used in the furniture and appliance fields, used car financing, home improvement financing, and other installment situations is that the purchaser shall have made a payment within sixty days and shall have paid not less than 60% of all matured installments based on original terms. There are variations of this criterion, such as payment within ninety days or payment of at least 66⅔% of matured installments based on original terms. However, the two important elements that must be taken into consideration in setting up criteria for prime paper are *recency* and *frequency*. It is not enough for a purchaser to have made a recent payment. This presents an opportunity for front money (see below, page 135). How frequently he makes a payment, even though it may be a partial payment so that he is meeting at least the aforementioned percentages of original terms, is all important. In the personal or consumer loan business, the recency of payment determines whether or not a customer is current. A customer who has made a payment within the last thirty days, even though it is partial payment and the first one he has made in several months, is considered current. This is a relaxed approach that cannot be allowed in consumer installment financing.

The percentage of advance is expressed in reverse, as it were, as a ratio of prime paper to the unpaid balance of advances— the loan balance. Thus a cash advance of 60% on prime paper would have to be expressed as: ". . . . the ratio of the aggregate unpaid balance of prime paper to the unpaid balance of . . . advances and charges shall be at least 166⅔%."

Custody of Collections. With the introduction of the Uniform Commercial Code, the provision that collections shall be received by the borrower-client in trust for the financer and not mingled with the borrower's own funds is no longer legally important. It was inserted to provide for the so-called dominion and control that the financer was compelled to exercise over receivables on which it had made advances in order to retain a valid lien on the receivables. With regard to the method of indirect collections described earlier (page 122), it is not advisable to use an alternative method that permits the borrower to remit his check to the finance company for the full amount of the day's collections together with a full accounting of all collections. The reasons therefor are set forth in Chapter 3, p. 49.

Reports. The underlying financing agreement further provides that the borrower will furnish the financer monthly with a microfilm of all outstanding accounts assigned as of the close of business on the last day of each month. As a practical matter, the financer does not rely upon the borrower-client to do this Instead, the financer's auditors, using a portable microfilm machine, do the filming in conjunction with their delinquency analysis of the installment receivables. The portable microfilm machine has made it possible for the finance company to take on as new business, operate, and maintain the accounts of retailers and dealers engaged in the business of consumer installment sales with hundreds, even thousands, of customers' accounts. For example, several years ago, a financer undertook to finance the receivables of a well-known department store in Detroit. The receivables consisted of thirty-day charge accounts, ninety-day budget accounts, and twelve-month installment accounts. There were 30,000 active accounts in 103 trays. A microfilm taken every sixty days (or every 30 or 45 days, if the particular circumstances called for it) it enabled the financer to have available on short notice a record of every assigned installment receivable without the expense of clerical help needed to set up and post the hundreds of transactions of sales and payments to a duplicate set of customers' ledger account cards.

Default. The financing agreement contains a section on default. Included among the provisions is a requirement of the amount of net current assets to be maintained by the borrower-client. This is usually based on the most recent financial statement of the borrower.

Miscellaneous Provisions. Among Miscellaneous Provisions, there is a guaranty that every payment falling due on assigned collateral will be duly paid and received by the financer at maturity. This is a means by which the financer is assured that the retailer will replace delinquent receivables with fresh collateral. The financer is also provided with the additional collateral of so-called "add-on sales" to the extent that these sales are not yet specifically assigned. An "add-on sale" is a new sale made to a customer which is added to the existing balance of his installment account. The amount of the "add-on" may determine whether new terms of repayment are set up. Usually the retail installment contract for the "add-on" takes into account the previous balance, recites new payment and contract terms, and generally supersedes the previous contract.

Another provision covers the liquidation of the indebtedness of the retailer-borrower from collections on the installment receivables. The percentage of collection per month is usually set at from 8% to 10% of the outstanding accounts where the term of the installment accounts has been two years so that the indebtedness to the financer may be liquidated within a year.

The underlying financing agreement is usually made effective for one year and is self-renewing unless there is thirty or sixty days' written notice by either party prior to the anniversary date.

Guaranty. Finally, the financing agreement contains the personal guaranty of the principals of the indebtedness of the borrowing company to the finance company. The personal guaranty should be an absolute requirement of the financing agreement. Without it, the financer ought not to consider a consumer installment sales situation.

Licensing Laws and Regulation of Retailers

Besides complying with legal requirements previously mentioned, there is the further problem of determining whether the financer should comply with sales finance company licensing laws in its own jurisdiction or in that of the retailer. New York and New Jersey laws require that finance companies purchasing consumer installment paper or contracts, and collecting them directly, must be licensed. Financers making advances against such paper on a bulk basis (see below) do not have to apply for licensing.

The laws affecting the retailer directly are important considerations, since the retailer's failure to comply with them would make the consumer paper created unacceptable for financing. The consumer's indebtedness may be uncollectible and the financer's collateral therefore worthless. In recent years, state legislatures have expressly fixed,

or have authorized a state agency to fix, finance charges.   It is, therefore, important for the financer to check all applicable state laws
affecting the dealer's operations.

Other legislation has been passed designed to regulate consumer
credit.   Most jurisdictions now require licensing of the dealer and
installment sales forms or other agreements that clearly and
conspicuously show the terms of sale, finance charge, etc. (See
Fig. 6–6, pp. 152–5).   Certain other former abuses are no longer
permitted under the law, and these should be carefully checked
in surveying the retailer's procedures.   In New York State, two
Retail Installment Sales Acts were passed in 1956–1957 which
fixed the finance charge, or credit service charge as it is called, at
10% per year on the first $500.00 of unpaid balance and 8% per year
on the excess above $500.00.   The New York law requires sales
finance companies to be licensed and under the supervision of the
State Banking Department.   The law also stipulates the form of retail
installment contract.   With regard to automobiles, the installment
sales law first passed in 1956 in New York fixed the finance charge
at 7% per year on new cars and from 9% to 13% on used cars, depending
upon the age of the car.   In complying with the law, the retail installment contract, whether used in the sale of an automobile or furniture
and appliances, clearly spells out the terms of sale, including the
cash price, the credit service charge, all other charges, the total time
price, the time balance and the number of monthly payments, and
the amount of each payment in which the time balance is payable.
The law also requires the Notice to the Buyer printed in large type
at the bottom of the contract above the buyer's signature.   The
buyer must be given a copy of the contract.

The reverse side of the original of the retail installment contract
provides for the assignment of the contract by the dealer to the
financer.   If the financer is in turn rediscounting (i.e., refinancing
with a larger company), language covering the reassignment of the
contract is added by a rubber stamp below the dealer's assignment.

OPERATIONAL PROCEDURES

Bulk Assignment

The bulk assignment technique is widely used.   Many commercial
financers have used it in commercial receivable situations that involve

an unusually large number of accounts and/or small invoices. In consumer installment financing, the initial take-over of accounts is accomplished by microfilming the ledger cards of the retailer which may be very numerous. Microfilming, however, follows a card-by-card analysis of the installment receivables in the initial survey. The survey establishes a delinquency analysis and also provides a general "feel" of the calibre or quality of the installment accounts. This detailed analysis establishes the amount of "prime paper" or paper eligible for advance, pursuant to the underlying agreement which states clearly and without ambiguity what is assigned. As indicated previously (page 130), the criteria used in determining delinquency should take into account the factors of recency of payment and frequency of payment.

The initial assignment should be prepared so as to establish the identifiability of the accounts assigned. Prior to the advent of the Uniform Commercial Code there were questions as to the formalities needed for assignment. Even under the Code, despite the granting of a blanket lien on the receivables, the assignment should still use the following language and references:

We herewith assign to you, with the same force and effect as if specifically listed herein below, our installment accounts receivable in the amount of_____, evidenced by original retail installment contracts conveyed to you herewith, further evidenced by a microfilm of the customers' ledger account cards showing the balances due, and further evidenced by adding machine tape of the said balances totalling the amount above, both microfilm and adding machine tape being dated and initialled on behalf of the undersigned, attached hereto and made a part hereof.

It is of primary importance that the financer have possession of the original, executed retail installment contracts. Technically, where the financer has possession, it need not file under the Uniform Commercial Code because the delivery of the contracts constitutes a pledge. If it does not have possession, it must file. A lender, having possession of the contracts, could conceivably defeat the claim of the lender without such possession, even though the latter filed under the Code. The safest course, therefore, is to take possession of the contracts *and* file under the Code.

Wherever possible, sales invoices and delivery receipts should accompany the assignment. Normally, assignments are made about once a week.

The Custodian. An adjunct of the bulk assignment technique is the setting up of a custodian on the premises of the retailer. The custodian, who becomes an employee of the financer, is usually someone employed in the credit or collection department of the retailer, preferably in the collection department. In addition to certifying to the authenticity of assigned accounts, such a person is also charged with the responsibility of accounting for all collections on accounts assigned to the financer. He will see to it that collection reports are prepared and that collections are deposited in the appropriate bank account of the financer. Prior to the Uniform Commercial Code, some lawyers considered this exercise of dominion to be a legal requirement. It is still important as an operational technique.

The custodian is bonded by the financer and is subject to the fidelity protection of such insurance coverage. The ledger trays, ledger cards, and all other matter pertaining to the installment receivables are, as provided in the underlying financing agreement, the property of the financer and should be so marked whenever possible.

Verification of Receivables

In the financer's office, procedures for the operation, policing, and control of a consumer installment receivable account are intensive but not difficult to execute. The verification of every installment account assigned should be arranged on a continuing basis. The importance of this procedure cannot be overemphasized.

Typical Hazards of Financer. The consumer finance field runs the normal risks of fictitious receivables and conversion. The term fictitious receivables is self explanatory. Conversion refers to the appropriation by the dealer for his own use of collections from customers that should have been turned over to the financer. Another practice called "front money" can deceive the financer. This occurs when the retailer reports collections from debtor accounts or actually credits them to the account of the customer in order to make such debtor accounts appear current and in good standing.

Conversion is much less of a risk in consumer financing than it is in regular commercial receivables financing because the collections are diffused among many accounts in amounts smaller than the normal commercial receivables. However, fictitious receivables, "front money," pressure selling, and the assignment of the consumer account before the merchandise has been delivered or when it has been only partially delivered are definite risks.   These and a customer's dissatisfaction that will keep him from paying his account—and conversion, as well—will be discovered, to the extent they exist at all, by proper verification procedures.

Verification Procedures.   Verification of the receivables is the single most important operational technique in commercial financing.   Two forms of verification of consumer accounts have been devised.   One is used to verify an account at its inception (see Fig. 6–1, page 137). The verification clerk writes in the customer's name and address, as well as the date, the customer's account number, and the schedule number on which the account was assigned (for further identification later, if necessary).   The client's name is stamped in.   Then the clerk inserts the contract terms of so many months at so much per month. The total balance due on the contract is not shown, for psychological reasons.   The customer is requested to furnish the date he received the merchandise, the date when he last made a payment—which will elicit information as to any down payment or deposit or the fact that the first payment is due on a certain date—and the amount of the payment.   The customer is provided space at the bottom of the verification for comments.   The verification is then mailed in a window envelope, together with a self-addressed postage-paid envelope in which the verification is to be returned by the customer.   To maintain the element of non-notification, the verification forms are imprinted with the name of an accounting or auditing firm that the financer has adopted for this purpose and has appropriately registered as a business firm name.   The address used may be a special post office box or the financer's own office address.   It is common practice to send a verification request to every single new consumer account assigned by the client, retailer, or dealer-borrower.   Experience has shown that replies will be received from approximately 25% or better of the verifications sent out.   Certain to be heard from are the customers who have some complaint, or who do not agree with the contract terms, or, sometimes, who "don't know anything about the company or the contract."

The second form of verification (see Fig. 6–2, page 138) is used in two ways.   It is used to verify the balances of consumer accounts on an existing portfolio of accounts that is being considered for financing and is to be the basis of the initial advance or loan by the financer It is also used to re-verify the accounts approximately six months after the original verification at the inception of the account.

XYZ COMPANY
ACCOUNTANTS AND AUDITORS

> **THIS IS NOT A
> REQUEST FOR PAYMENT**

TO

_____   Date_____

_____   Account No._____

_____

We are auditing the records of_____

According to their books, you have a contract with them for_____

months, at_____ per month..

      Please furnish the following information:

      a) Date you received the equipment _____

      b) When did you last make a payment _____

      c) Amount of this payment_____

If contract terms are correct, please sign below. If incorrect, please explain the

difference at the bottom of this letter.

Your prompt reply will be appreciated. Please use the enclosed self addressed

envelope which requires no postage.

                  Cordially yours,

                  _____

COMMENTS:

_____

_____

_____

                _____
                    AUTHORIZED SIGNATURE

Fig. 6–1.   Verification Form for New Account

XYZ COMPANY
ACCOUNTANTS AND AUDITORS

**THIS IS NOT A
REQUEST FOR PAYMENT**

TO

Account No. _____

Sched. No. _____

We are auditing the records of _____

According to their books, you owed them on ▷ [   ]

Balance of ▷ [$]

So that you may receive proper credit, please advise whether this balance is correct.

If correct, please sign below. If not correct, explain the difference on the bottom of this letter.

Please return this letter promptly in the enclosed addressed envelope which requires no postage.

Your immediate reply will be greatly appreciated.

Very truly your

☐ *The above is correct*   ☐ *The above is not correct*

*If not correct, explain reason why*_____

MAKE SURE YOU SIGN HERE
BEFORE RETURNING THIS FORM ▷ _____
                              CUSTOMER'S SIGNATURE

Fig. 6–2. Verification Form for Existing Account

						VERIFICATION SUMMARY			

CLIENT'S NAME   DATE OF 1st VERIFICATION   BY (INITIALS)

TOTAL AMT. VERIFIED $ _____ OF GROSS A/R'S OUTSTANDING AS OF _____

OF $ _____

NO.	NAME OF DEBTOR	1st VERIF. A/R'S VERIFIED	REPLIES	PAID	DIFF.	DATE 2nd NOTICE MAILED	REPLIES	PAID	DIFF.

REPLIES: _____
TOTAL PAID: _____   VERIFICATION DEPARTMENT
TOTAL DIFF. _____
NO RESPONSE: _____   BY _____
TOTAL: _____   _____ 19 _____

Fig. 6–3. Verification Summary

The verification forms are made up in triplicate. If there is no reply to the original verification, the duplicate is sent later in the month. The triplicate remains as the office copy to which is attached the reply returned by the customer. The verifications are summarized for statistical purposes on a verification summary form (see Fig. 6-3).

Audits

The auditing procedure should be more frequent than in commercial receivables financing, since the accounts are not ledgered or posted and the financer has no direct experience as to collections. For this reason, a comparison of the current month's cumulative daily collections with the prior month's should be maintained and watched. The chief purposes of the audit are to determine whether collection procedures and experience are satisfactory, to establish collection percentages based on the preceding end-of-month outstanding balances of installment accounts, and to establish delinquency figures. In addition, the auditor should review the retailer's general condition, financial and otherwise, as he would in a commercial receivables situation. Optimum control is provided by an audit program in which microfilming and receivables analysis are leapfrogged with an audit of the books and records in alternate months.

REDISCOUNTING AND FLOOR PLANNING

Rediscounting

In rediscounting, the basic principle is that the larger financer should deal with the smaller company as though the latter were a retail borrower. The financer being rediscounted should be a well-operated company. The rediscounting financer should be certain that the retail operations financed by the smaller financer are sound. Note, however, that rediscounting will normally involve the financing of many retailers (clients of the smaller financer). Also, the larger financer has the protective cushion of the capital of the rediscounting borrower. Most companies have established rule-of-thumb ratios of permissible rediscounting lines to borrower's net worth. Available lines normally do not exceed 2½ or 3 times such net worth.

Floor Planning

Floor planning is an additional service provided by the financer for the retailer. Retailers and dealers require financing not only for installment sales to customers but also for financing their purchases from manufacturers or distributors, i.e. wholesale or inventory financing. This wholesale financing is called floor planning. It enables the dealer to place merchandise on the floor of his sales room and stock his inventory.

Automobile dealers, for example, must pay cash at the factory for their cars. The funds required to stock a dealer's floor adequately with high-priced items such as automobiles is most often too great to be provided by the dealer's own capital.   This is particularly true at peak seasons.   Many appliance dealers and other retailers selling consumer durables of high value also require financing so that they may obtain adequate stocks of goods from manufacturers or distributors.

Sales finance companies who are engaged primarily in buying consumer time sales contracts from automobile dealers and other retailers and are also engaged in the floor planning, provide the factories with payment in full for their goods simultaneously with the shipment of the goods to the dealers.   The dealer displays such merchandise on his floor.   When he sells it at retail, he liquidates the loan with the financer.

Wholesale financing or floor planning is provided to dealers at low rates of interest.   The financer provides this service to the dealer as a means of obtaining the consumer paper generated by him.   The financer thus advances amounts that are very great in proportion to a dealer's own capital.   The financer is also subject to the hazard that the automobiles or other consumer durables serving as security may be sold out of trust.   This means that the dealer, to whom cars (or home appliances such as refrigerators and washing machines or radios and television sets) have been released under a trust receipt, sells and accepts cash for these items of merchandise and then fails to render a prompt accounting for the proceeds to the financer.   The trust receipt is a security instrument and form of lien signed by the dealer, by which he acknowledges that the consumer durable merchandise is the property of the finance company and that it is being held in trust by the dealer, and he promises that it will not be removed or used except upon written authorization from the finance company. The trust receipt remains essentially unchanged under the Uniform Commercial Code (see discussion of trust receipts in Chapter 5, page 109).

In performing the floor-planning or wholesale-financing function, the financer checks the cars, appliances, or other consumer durables on the dealer's floor at least once a month.   These are identifiable by their serial numbers.   The dates and the men used in this checking procedure are alternated so as to obtain effective supervision of the merchandise security under the trust agreement.   When the dealer sells an automobile or other consumer durable, he must immediately deliver either cash payment or the installment contract covering the item to the financer.   If the checker finds that any of the items of merchandise specified in the trust agreement are not on hand, he ascertains when they were sold and then obtains payment from the dealer.

The financer must obtain sufficient consumer (retail) paper from the dealer to justify the floor planning accommodations it extends to him. At least 50 per cent of the dealer's sales of floor planned durables should result in retail paper financed by the financer.

XYZ FACTORS CORPORATION
Retail Accounts
Preliminary Audit Investigation
Date_____19____

Applicant (Exact Corp. Name)_____

Address_____

Audit was made with_____ Title_____

Product_____

Describe Operation_____

_____

Incorporated in_____(State)_____19____

Capitalization_____ Date_____

Net Worth or Capital_____ Date_____

Attach Financial Statement as of _____19____ Certified?_____

Attach D & B Report_____19____ Litigation_____19____

Business History & Moral Risk Aspect_____

_____

_____

Names & Addresses of Banks_____

_____

_____

Seasonal Fluctuations_____

Number of Employees_____ Unionized?_____

Principal Officers (Names & Addresses)   Stock Ownership %

Pres._____

V. P. _____

Secty._____

Treas._____

_____

Name of Controlling Officer_____

Any previous record of Financing or Factoring (Names)_____

_____

Present secured financing other than A/R (Names & Describe)_____

_____

_____

Ageing of Payables as at _____ 19_____
                                                  $_____
_____   _____
_____   _____
_____   _____
      Total $_____

Fig. 6–4. Retail Accounts Preliminary Audit Investigation

Comment on Payables and list several most active creditors and amounts owing:

_____

_____

_____

Consignment sales_____

Consignment purchases_____

Analysis of Accounts Receivable

Month	Balance B.O.M.	Sales	Misc. Debits	Cash Collections	Returns	Misc. Credits
19__ $	$	$	$	$	$	
Totals $	$	$	$	$	$	

Terms of Sale_____ Dilution %_____

Turnover on Cash only_____ Turnover on Cash & Dilution_____

Average Invoice_____ Invoices per Month_____ Number of Debtors_____

Recent Average Monthly Sales $_____ Finance Charge to Customers_____

How do Sales Originate? Canvass_____Door-to-Door_____ Newspaper Adv._____

           Radio Adv._____ Television Adv._____ Leaders_____

Breakdown of Sales (%) Furn._____Appliances_____Telev._____Misc._____

Down Payments:
0-5%_____5-10%_____10-15%_____15-20%_____Over 20%_____

Terms (%):
Up to 12 Mos._____12-15 Mos._____15-18 Mos._____18-24 Mos._____Over 24 Mos._____

Lines Carried: Furniture
             Appliances
             Television
             Soft Goods
             Musical

Fig. 6–4. Retail Accounts Preliminary Audit Investigation—Continued

Delinquency Analysis of A/R:

Month	#O/S	$O/S	Del.#5-30	Del.#31-60	60-90 Del # $ Bal.	Over 90 Del. # $ Bal.	Repossessions

Repossessions (Month-by-month for last 12 mos. and totals for preceding 2 years)

Analysis of Reserve for Bad Debts:

Year	Res. Beg. of Year	Additions	Charge-Offs During Year	Recoveries	Balance End of Year

Financial Information

Per Financial Statement as at_____ 19_____

Current Assets $_____

Current Liabilities   _____

Net Current   _____

Fixed Assets   _____

Other Assets   _____

Long Term Liabilities   _____

Net Worth   _____

Total Debt   _____

Comment on Profit & Loss Status_____

_____

Any liabilities to be subordinated (Names & Amounts) _____

_____

_____

Comment on Fixed Assets_____

_____

Comment on Books & Records_____

Applicants auditor (Names & Address) C.P.A.?_____

Fig. 6–4. Retail Accounts Preliminary Audit Investigation—Continued

Describe Collection System In Detail (Special attention to consistency & frequency of notices, follow-ups, repossession procedures, no-first-payment accounts action, etc.; obtain samples of all forms used; are collections centralized if company operates more than one store?)

Describe Credit Checking Procedures In Detail (Obtain copy of credit application form and attach copy of lien instrument.)

Taxes	Amount Due	Period Covered	When Payable	Last Date	Payment Amount	Amount Delinquent
Fed. Income						
State Income						
Fed. Withholding						
State Withholding						
Social Security						
State Unemployment						
Fed. Unemployment						
Federal Excise						
Others: List						

Comment on Taxes

Your conclusions and recommendations:

Auditor

Executive Comments

Fig. 6–4. Retail Accounts Preliminary Audit Investigation—Continued

Date

To:

XYZ FACTORS CORPORATION
PARK AVENUE
NEW YORK, N.Y.

Gentlemen:

We desire to borrow from you from time to time, upon the following terms and conditions:

Section 1. <u>Advances and Charges</u>

a. You shall advance to us up to   % of the unpaid balance of prime paper (as defined below) assigned to and held by you.

b. Your charges for such advances shall be at the rate of   per day upon the average daily amount of such advances outstanding, allowing five (5) days subsequent to receipt of checks to permit bank clearance and collection of such checks. Charges will be computed monthly and paid by us within five (5) days after receipt of your statement therefor.

c. All your advances and charges, and all our other obligations to you, however, created, shall be secured by all collateral assigned to and held by you.

d. You shall make advances to us weekly, if requested by us. The aggregate amounts of such advances to be made and outstanding from time to time shall not exceed such maximum as you may in your sole discretion determine.

Section 2. <u>Collateral and Ratio</u>

a. "Collateral" means obligations, and any security and guaranty thereon, arising out of our retail sales of merchandise, including additional or supplementary obligations of the same purchasers.

b. "Prime paper" means collateral acceptable to you, payable in installments, and secured by valid title retention or first lien instruments, provided: (1) such prime paper has been duly assigned and pledged to you; (2) delivery of the merchandise has been made to and accepted by the purchaser; (3) no repossession has occurred; and (4) as of the date of determining whether the paper is prime, the purchaser has paid a full contractual payment within   days, and the purchaser has paid   % of all matured installments based on the original schedule of payment. In no event shall our lay-away accounts, firm or officers' accounts, or suspense accounts be deemed prime paper.

c. We shall assign, pledge and deliver to you, in form and manner acceptable to you, all collateral now held by us; and hereafter we shall likewise assign, pledge and deliver to you all additional collateral created by us. Such assignments shall be deemed to include all our right, title and interest in the property described in the collateral and our books, records and files relating thereto. We shall forthwith note on our ledger sheets and other records the fact of assignment to you. We warrant that: all collateral is genuine; all statements therein are and will continue to be true; we have and will convey to you good and unencumbered title; the terms thereof comply with all applicable laws and

Fig. 6–5. Financing Agreement

regulations; and the unpaid amount thereof is as represented at the time of assignment. These warranties shall be deemed automatically repeated with respect to each assignment.

d. Until you otherwise notify us in writing, the ratio of the aggregate unpaid balance of prime paper to the unpaid balance of your advances and charges shall be at least   %. On five (5) days' notice from you that a higher ratio is required, we shall pay you forthwith the amount necessary to establish such ratio. If you shall, for any fixed or indeterminate period, permit a temporary lower ratio to exist, we shall pay you the amount necessary to restore the proper ratio upon the termination of such fixed period or within five (5) days after notice to us, as the case may be.

e. Prior to your first audit of our records relating to collateral, you may in your sole discretion determine what amount is prime paper by applying to each of our controls or subcontrols such percentage as your initial sampling shall have indicated. Between audits, you may· likewise determine the amount of prime paper by applying such percentage as your last preceding audit or sampling shall have indicated.

Section 3.   Custody of Collateral, Records, Collections and
                                    Repossessions

a. All collateral, ledger sheets, files, records and documents relating to assigned collateral shall, until delivered to or removed by you, be kept on our premises in trust for you and without cost to you, in appropriate containers in safe places under your exclusive dominion and control, bearing suitable legends identifying the same as your property. You shall at all reasonable times have full access to and the right to inspect and audit all our books and records. In furtherance of the foregoing, you shall be privileged to employ and maintain in our premises a bookkeeper-custodian selected by you, with full authority to do all acts necessary to protect your interests and to report to you thereon. We shall reimburse you, monthly as billed, for all expenses incurred by you by reason of such employment.

. b. We shall have the privilege, revocable as below set forth, to make collection at our expense of payments from purchasers named in assigned collateral; upon condition, however, that such collections shall be received by us in trust for you and not mingled with our own funds and that we shall, at your option, either (1) forthwith remit all such collections to you in kind, duly endorsed for deposit by you, or (2) remit to you daily our full accounting of all collections effected during the day, together with our check to your order for the full amount thereof, or (3) deposit the same forthwith in a bank account maintained in your name and subject to withdrawal only by you and render you a daily accounting of the items so deposited. Unless the instruments so received by you are dishonored, or unless you shall have re-remitted the amount thereof to us at our request, you shall credit the amount thereof against our indebtedness to you promptly after receipt by you. The above privilege is subject to revocation by you at any time, and shall be deemed automatically revoked upon our default with respect to any undertaking on our part herein or upon the happening of an event of default as defined below.

c. In case any merchandise referred to in assigned collateral shall revert to our possession in any manner, we will forthwith set it apart, mark and designate it as your property, and notify you. In like manner, we shall promptly report to you any allowances granted to purchasers named in assigned collateral. In either event, we shall at your option either deliver repossessed merchandise to you or pay you, in cash or substituted collateral acceptable to you, the full face value of the collateral affected by such repossession or allowance.

Fig. 6–5.   Financing Agreement—Continued

d. You may at any time remove from our premises any documents, files and records relating to assigned collateral, or you may, without cost or expense to you, use such of our personnel, supplies and space at our places of business as may be reasonably necessary for the handling of collections. We will reimburse you for all internal, office and out-of-pocket expenses and costs of collection (including reasonable attorneys' fees) incurred by you in the handling of or effort to enforce collection.

Section 4. Reports

a. We will send to you daily written reports, in such detail as you may request, with respect to all retail sales, repossessions, returns, allowances, collections, and all miscellaneous items affecting the collateral. We will furnish you (1) monthly, a Recordak film of all of our outstanding accounts assigned to you as of the close of business on the last day of each month, a monthly financial and operating statement, and a past due ageing of accounts, all to be certified by our controller or an executive officer; (2) annually, at our own expense, a complete audit report of our operations and condition, made by an independent certified public account satisfactory to you; and (3) upon issuance, copies of all public accountants' audited reports rendered to us while we are indebted to you.

b. We will also send you, from time to time, such other reports, analyses, and operating data as you may reasonably request.

Section 5. Default

a. All our obligations to you shall accelerate and become immediately due upon the happening of any one or more of the following events of default; (1) our failure to make any payment due to you, or our violation of any undertaking on our part herein, remaining uncured for at least five (5) days; (2) our ceasing to do business as a going concern or our commission of any act of bankruptcy or insolvency; (3) the filing by or against us of any petition in bankruptcy, reorganization, arrangement, or receivership; (4) or the failure of our net current assets to equal at least $ (such assets and liabilities being determined by generally accepted accounting principles).

b. Upon the happening of any such event of default, you shall be privileged, in addition to the other rights accruing to you by virtue thereof, to terminate this agreement.

Section 6. Miscellaneous Provisions

a. We guarantee that every payment falling due on assigned collateral will be duly paid and received by you at maturity. We waive presentment, demand, protest, and notice of dishonor as to any instrument. We consent to any extensions, modifications, allowances, compromises, and releases of security which you may grant, none of which shall release us to any extent from our obligations to you. We irrevocably authorize and empower you to endorse our name upon any instrument or document relating to assigned collateral or the merchandise represented thereby, upon any omitted assignments, notifications of assignment, demands, and auditor's verifications relating to assigned collateral, and upon any other instruments and documents required to assert and protect your rights in and to assigned collateral and the merchandise represented thereby.

b. We hereby subordinate, in favor of the payment of all sums due you upon assigned collateral, any and all sums then or thereafter, due to us from the same obligors (whether or not upon obligations thereafter assigned to you), and we hereby assign to you, as additional security, the obligations so subordinated and will remit to you any collections thereon.

Fig. 6—5. Financing Agreement—Continued

c. Upon the termination of this agreement at or prior to the original or any extended expiration date, we will pay to you forthwith all our then outstanding obligations to you. However, if we are not then in default with respect to our undertakings and obligations to you, you may in your sole discretion permit us, in lieu of immediate payment in full, to liquidate our indebtedness to you by continuing to deliver to you all collections upon assigned collateral; provided, however, that the payments so made to you shall not be less than   % per month of the total amount due to you upon termination, and in case of a deficiency in any month, we will pay you such deficiency upon five (5) days notice. If such collections exceed the said required monthly amount, the excess shall be applied to subsequent months, in inverse order of maturity. In the event of such termination, all provisions of this agreement shall continue in full force and effect, except that we shall not assign to you any newly created collateral unless the required prime paper ratio is impaired at any time, in which event we agree to restore it promptly by assignment of additional prime paper or by payment in cash sufficient to restore the required ratio.

d. Your rights and remedies hereunder shall be cumulative, and no waiver by you of any default on our part shall be deemed a continuing waiver. You shall not be responsible for any loss or damage to collateral unless caused by your willful and malicious act.

e. This agreement shall bind and inure to the benefit of the parties and their successors and assigns. It shall continue in effect until   after this date, and thereafter from year to year unless terminated, upon at least   days' written notice by either party, as at the end of said initial term or of any subsequent year. Termination shall not affect our respective rights and obligations as to transactions theretofore had hereunder. This agreement shall not become effective until accepted by you at your office stated below, and all transactions hereunder shall be governed and construed by the laws of the State of

By_____

(Title)

ACCEPTED AT_____   _____
                                 (Date)

XYZ FACTORS CORPORATION

By_____

(Title)

Fig. 6–5.   Financing Agreement—Continued

GUARANTY

In order to induce   XYZ FACTORS CORPORATION   to enter into the foregoing agreement and to make advances thereunder to
                                and in consideration thereof and of other good and valuable considerations, receipt whereof is hereby acknowledged, we jointly and severally guarantee the due payment and performance by said
                       of all moneys to be paid, and all things to be done, pursuant to each and every condition and covenant contained in said agreement or in any supplement thereto, or in any instrument given in pursuance thereof; as well as the due payment of all other obligations which said   may at any time owe to XYZ FACTORS CORPORATION, however created.

The undersigned agree: that this guaranty shall not be impaired by any modification to which the parties to said agreement may hereafter agree, nor by any modification, release or other alteration of any of the obligations hereby guaranteed or of any security therefor, to all of which the undersigned hereby consent; that their liability hereunder is direct and unconditional, and may be enforced without requiring XYZ FACTORS CORPORATION first to resort to any other right, remedy or security; and that this guaranty shall continue in force until XYZ FACTORS CORPORATION shall receive written notice, by registered mail, revoking it as to future transactions.

The undersigned waive: notice of acceptance hereof; the right to a jury trial in any action hereunder; presentment and protest of any instrument, and notice thereof; notice of default; and all other notices to which they might otherwise be entitled. They hereby assign to XYZ FACTORS CORPORATION all claims of any nature which they, or any of them, may now or hereafter have against said

This guaranty, all acts and transactions hereunder, and the rights and obligations of the parties hereto, shall be governed, construed and interpreted according to the laws of the State of

IN WITNESS WHEREOF we have signed and sealed these presents this day of   , 19 .

_____
Witness

_____
Address

_____
Witness

_____
Address

_____
Witness

_____
Address

_____
Witness

_____
Address

Fig. 6–5.   Financing Agreement—Continued

Acc. No. _____

RETAIL INSTALLMENT CONTRACT
XYZ DISCOUNT CORP.

BILLING ADDRESS Name _____
Residence Or
Place of Business Address _____
of Buyer
(PLEASE PRINT) City _____ State _____ Date _____
Telephone _____

Undersigned Seller Sells and undersigned Buyer Individually (If more than one buyer, jointly and severally) purchases, subject to the terms and conditions hereunder the merchandise described below, to be kept at the above address:

ORIGINAL SALE

Description of Merchandise

1. Total Sale _____
2. Sales Tax _____
3. Total Cash Price _____
4. Less Down Payment (Cash) _____
   a. (Trade-in) _____
5. Unpaid Cash Balance _____
6. Credit Life Insurance _____
7. Property Insurance _____
8. Principal Balance _____
9. Credit Service Charge _____
10. Total Time Balance _____
11. Time Sales Price _____

Buyer agrees to pay the Total Time Balance to

XYZ DISCOUNT CORP.

In _____ Monthly Payments beginning on _____

No. of Payments _____ Date _____

in instalments of $ _____ each and a final payment

of $ _____ Describe Trade-In _____

ADD ON SALE

1. Total Sale _____
2. Sales Tax _____
3. Total Cash Price _____
4. Less Down Payment (Cash) _____
5. Principal Add On Balance _____
6. Credit Life Insurance _____
7. Property Insurance _____
8. Principal Balance _____
9. Credit Service Charge _____
10. Add On Time Balance _____
11. Previous Balance _____
12. Total Time Balance _____

NOTICE OF PROPOSED CREDIT LIFE INSURANCE

If an amount is included in item on the face hereof for Credit Life Insurance, such insurance will be provided by an insurance company selected by the seller or sellers assignee on the life of the Buyer whose name first appears as a signer of this contract. Such insurance, subject to acceptance by the insurer, shall take effect as of the date the indebtedness of this contract is acquired by the assignee and shall extend to the scheduled maturity date of this contract. The amount of insurance shall be equal to the unpaid Time Balance from time to time unpaid on this contract but not exceeding $5,000.00. Any proceeds of said insurance shall be applied towards payment of said unpaid Time Balance. If the insurance is declined by the insurer or otherwise does not become effective, notice will be sent to Buyer and any premium or payment for said insurance together with any Credit Service Charge applicable thereto, will be credited to the unpaid Time Balance of this contract.

NOTICE OF PROPOSED GROUP PROPERTY INSURANCE

If, an amount is included in item on the face hereof for Property Insurance, such insurance will be provided under a Master Inland Marine Installment Floater Policy issued to the seller or sellers assignee (hereinafter called "Creditor") by a company accepted and selected by the seller or sellers assignee, covering all merchandise listed on the face of this contract against loss or destruction by one or more of the following hazards: Fire, lightning, collision, marine perils, windstorm and burglary subject to the terms of the policy referred to hereinabove.

It is understood that such insurance is available only if this contract is assigned to Creditor, and that if accepted by the Insurer, will become effective from the date on which finance charges on the indebtedness accrue. The insurance will (in absence of default on installment payments) remain in force subject to the terms of said policy until the discharge of the indebtedness.

In the event that any or all of the covered merchandise is lost, destroyed or damaged by one of the covered hazards, the insurer will tender payment of the loss to Creditor who shall tender further payment, if any, to you as your interest may appear and in such event the Company's liability shall not be more than $5,000.00 or the Time Balance of the original contract, or the actual cash value of the merchandise lost, destroyed or damaged at the time thereof, or the cost of repair, to said merchandise, whichever is the lesser.

If this insurance does not become effective, notice will be sent to Buyer and any payment for said insurance, together with any Credit Service Charge applicable thereto will be credited to the unpaid Time Balance of this Contract, seller or sellers assignee to procure the insurance applied for herein.

This agreement is made and entered into subject to the conditions printed on the reverse side hereof, which conditions are hereby made a part hereof by this reference as though incorporated herein at length.

NOTICE TO THE BUYER: 1. Do not sign this agreement before you read it or if it contains any blank space. 2. You are entitled to a completely filled in copy of this agreement. 3. Under the law, you have the right to pay off in advance the full amount due and under certain conditions to obtain a partial refund of the credit service charge.

Receipt of an executed copy of this RETAIL INSTALLMENT CONTRACT is hereby acknowledged.

≫→
DEALER
SIGN
HERE

Signed _____ (L.S.)
(Seller)

By _____ Date_____
(Individual, Partner, or Officer)

Seller's
Address _____

Signed _____ (L.S.)
(Buyer)

≫→
BUYER
SIGN
HERE

Signed _____ (L.S.)
(Buyer)

Signed _____ (L.S.)
(Buyer)

Signed _____ (L.S.)
(Buyer)

Witness_____ Date_____

Fig. 6–6. Retail Installment Contract

CONDITIONS OF CONTRACT

If merchandise not delivered at signature hereof, serial numbers may be omitted herefrom and inserted in seller's copy after signature by buyer.

In the event of litigation hereunder both parties waive right to trial by jury. For each installment which shall be in default for at least 10 days, Buyer shall also pay, not later than one month after each such default a delinquency charge of five percent (5%) of the amount of each such installment or Five ($5) Dollars, whichever is less. In the event that this contract becomes due and payable, and is referred to an attorney, not a salaried employee of the seller or holder, for collection, Buyer shall pay, in addition thereto, attorney's fees of 20%. As against any assignee who acquires this contract in good faith and for value, Buyer will not assert any claim or defense arising out of the sale, unless within ten days after the assignee mails to the Buyer notice of the assignment the Buyer mails to the assignee written notice of the facts giving rise to said claim or defense.

The merchandise shall remain personal property and title thereto shall not pass to Buyer until the Time balance has been fully paid in cash. Buyer shall be responsible for any loss of or damage to said property. If Buyer fails to pay said Time Balance or any part thereof when due or fails to comply with any other term or condition of this agreement, the entire unpaid balance shall at Seller's election become due immediately and Seller may without notice, demand or legal process, take possession of the merchandise, or so much thereof as Seller may in its sole discretion determine, wherever located and retain all monies paid thereon for the use of said merchandise.

Time is of the essence hereof. This agreement may be assigned without notice to Buyer. The Buyer agrees not to assert against an assignee a claim or defense arising out of the sale under this contract provided that the assignee acquires this contract in good faith and for value and has no notice of the facts giving rise to the claim or defense within ten days after such assignee mails to the Buyer at his address shown above notice of the assignment of this contract.

This constitutes the entire agreement between Buyer and Seller and no oral modification hereof shall be valid.

Buyer certifies that the credit information furnished by him in connection with this sale is true. Buyer certifies that there is to be no extension of credit in connection with the purchase of the above described merchandise other than that evidenced by this agreement.

ASSIGNMENT AND DEALER'S RECOMMENDATION — THIS MUST BE EXECUTED BY THE DEALER

FOR VALUE RECEIVED, the receipt whereof is hereby acknowledged the undersigned does hereby sell assign and transfer unto XYZ DISCOUNT CORP. its successors and assigns, hereinafter referred as "ASSIGNEE", the Retail Instalment Contract above and on the reverse side hereof, and all right, title and interest of the undersigned in and to the Goods described therein and the amounts payable thereunder, hereby granting full power to the ASSIGNEE, either in its own name or in the name of the undersigned, to do every act and thing and to take all such legal or other proceedings which ASSIGNEE may deem necessary or advisable to enforce the terms and provisions thereof.

By executing this assignment, the undersigned agrees to repurchase said Retail Installment Contract on demand for the amount then payable to the ASSIGNEE thereon, including all charges, fees and other expenses incurred in connection therewith, and to pay same forthwith, in the event of breach of any of the following representations, warranties and agreements, which are hereby made to induce the ASSIGNEE to accept the assignment of the said contract:

1. the aforesaid contract is genuine and valid and was duly executed by the Buyer(s) named therein in connection with a bona fide sale to said Buyer(s) of the Goods referred to therein, which Buyer(s) was at the time of such sale competent to contract, and said Buyer(s) was not a minor at the time of said sale;

2. the sale evidenced thereby was effected in accordance with any and all laws and/or regulations affecting the same;

3. the contract correctly sets forth the description of the Goods, which has been duly delivered by the undersigned to, and accepted and retained by the Buyer; that no payment has been made on account of said Contract, except as therein set forth; the down-payment set forth in said Contract was paid by the Buyer and neither all nor any part thereof or of any amount remaining to be paid thereunder has been or will be loaned or otherwise provided directly or indirectly by the undersigned; (any payment which may be made to the undersigned under or relative to said Contract will be received IN TRUST by the undersigned and remitted to the ASSIGNEE promptly in the form received for credit to said Contract);

4. Title to the said Goods was at the time of the sale vested exclusively in the undersigned and said title as hereby conveyed, is free of all liens and encumbrances and is subject to no defenses, offsets or counterclaims on the part of the Buyer; said representation and warranty to survive for fifteen (15) days after the ASSIGNEE mails to the Buyer at his address shown in said Contract notice of this assignment identifying said Contract;

5. If, within thirty (30) days after the ASSIGNEE mails to the Buyer at his address shown in said Contract its standard form of payment book setting forth the payments to be made by the Buyer under the terms of said Contract, the said Payment Book is returned to the ASSIGNEE undelivered to the Buyer for any reason whatsoever, the undersigned expressly agrees to repurchase said Contract on demand for the full amount then unpaid thereon;

6. the sale evidenced by the said Contract was consummated between the Buyer and the undersigned in the regular course of business of the undersigned and at the undersigned's place of business set forth in the Contract (except as the ASSIGNEE and the undersigned may otherwise agree by written exception to the aforesaid warranty and representation);

7. the sale evidenced by the said Contract does not constitute "deal-splitting"; it being intended and agreed that the description of the sale in the said Contract represents the complete purchase by the Buyer; and that no other Contract has been entered into between the Buyer and the undersigned, or is contemplated between them, for the purpose of assigning the same to another person or firm or to be retained by the undersigned (the undersigned knowing full well that the ASSIGNEE is relying upon this warranty in determining the Buyer's credit status).

The undersigned represents that a true executed copy of said Contract was delivered to the Buyer at the time of the execution thereof.

GUARANTEE. Undersigned guarantees prompt and full payment of all sums due according to the tenor of the within contract, to the holder hereof, and, in event of default authorizes any holder hereof to proceed against the undersigned, for the full amount due including attorney's fees, and hereby waves presentment, demand, protest, notice of dishonor and any and all other notices or demand of whatever character to which the undersigned might otherwise be entitled. The undersigned further consents to any extension granted by any holder and waves notice thereof. The undersigned hereby acknowledges receipt of a true copy of this guarantee. WITNESS my (our) hand(s) and seal(s) this.................. day of ....19.........

....

....

.... Guarantor

If more than one guarantor, obligation of each shall be joint and several.

IN WITNESS WHEREOF, the undersigned has hereunto subscribed his, its, or their name, this .... day of .... 19.........

.... (L.S.)

.... (Seller)

By .... Title ....

Fig. 6-6. Retail Installment Contract—Reverse

7

Financing Industrial Time Sales

Robert L. Krause
Vice President, Northern Financial Corporation

SCOPE AND DEVELOPMENT OF INDUSTRIAL TIME SALES FINANCING

Definitions

Industrial time sales financing deals with the acquisition of equipment for commercial purposes (capital goods or income-producing equipment) via the vehicle of installment credit. This credit device is, therefore, also referred to as equipment financing and industrial installment credit. Certain items may be used by consumers and also have an adaptation for commercial use. The basic use of the goods is, then, the chief factor in determining whether they can be considered income producing and so come within the scope of industrial time sales financing. Real estate and anything permanently affixed to real property are excluded. The distinction between the removable and the affixed is not always crystal clear. There are times when one impinges on the other. Such items as air conditioning or sprinkler systems or elevators cannot be removed from a building without impairing or injuring the freehold. This discussion is limited to movable personal property.

The exclusion of consumer goods and real property reduces the financing area and permits homogeneous credit standards and techniques. Consumer financing and real estate financing are very distinct and different fields although they have in common with industrial time sales the fact that the debtor or purchaser pays an acquisition cost in monthly installments over a period of several years. Also excluded from this discussion are financial arrangements other than through the services of a commercial finance company or commercial bank.

Industrial time sales financing is a triangular arrangement between the seller of the merchandise, sometimes referred to as the dealer, the purchaser of the merchandise, and the financer. Their relationship to each other will later be explored more fully. For purposes of definition, however, it is important to note that the absence of any one of the three parties removes the transaction from the area of time sales financing. The basic transaction begins with a credit sale as opposed to a cash sale—the prospective purchaser is either unable or unwilling to pay cash for the item. The seller in his desire to maintain or build up his sales volume is willing to extend credit to the buyer over a period of time. The seller, however, is also financially unable to make the sale on a credit basis and wait for his money. He, therefore, takes the contract of sale to the financer who purchases the buyer's obligation from the seller for an agreed price. This three-way arrangement is not in any sense of the word a loan transaction. The purchaser buys equipment and the financer buys the paper from the seller.

The term "income-producing equipment" may be illustrated by itemizing some of the types that belong to this category: machine tools, hotel and restaurant equipment, store fixtures, vending machines, and manufacturing and printing equipment.

Function of Industrial Time Sales Financing

Dun & Bradstreet reports that most financing of this type of equipment is done in the service industries with retail trade next and manufacturing third. A great proportion of business concerns using industrial time sales financing enjoy a low rather than a high credit rating. It benefits the small business man, primarily. Major corporations and other prime borrowers are usually not involved.

In other words, industrial time sales financing makes possible the acquisition of capital goods by small and medium business through the technique of installment credit. It is a sales finance operation because it permits the seller of goods to expand his volume through the extension of long-term credit to his customers. The expression "long-term credit" is here used to distinguish it from a cash sale or a sale on terms that may be limited to 30 or 60 days. The rationale is based on a belief in the efficacy of permitting a purchaser of income-producing equipment to pay for it as he uses it. Theoretically the equipment produces the income with which the purchaser may meet his obligation. This can result from the creation of an entirely new business enterprise, or a saving on the cost of labor, or simply the improvement of existing services which in itself is calculated to bring in additional income.

Development of Time Sales Financing

Economic Development. Installment credit had its beginnings in the consumer field. The application of this technique to financing of capital goods first occurred at the outbreak of World War I. The war created a need for enormous expansion of manufacturing facilities. Many smaller corporations lacked the cash to increase their plant capacities in proportion to the demands being made upon them. The early pioneers in the field of installment credit such as C.I.T., Commercial Credit Corp., and a few others were quick to adapt the technique to the purchase and acquisition of heavy machinery and other commercial equipment.

The sales finance companies working both in the consumer and industrial field grew and expanded, largely through the support of the commercial banks. It is most interesting to note that while the banks were willing to lend these companies unsecured accommodation, they were nevertheless reticent about entering the field of installment credit themselves. Records indicate that the American Bankers Association made its first study of the field of installment credit in the year 1926. The conclusions that they reached were entirely negative, and they strongly advised their member banks to avoid this area of activity. It was, therefore, left to non-bank agencies who were sufficiently specialized to cope with unique credit problems and to pioneer in new credit areas. In the early years equipment financing grew primarily as a result of the steadily increasing mechanization of manufacturing, mining, and construction industries and the competitive pressures in these industries to modernize production facilities. More recently wider use of mechanical equipment and fixtures in the trade and service operations has developed.

In 1934 an economist named Harry Gerome reporting for the National Bureau of Economic Research said that one of the primary restrictions on the use of machinery in industry was the heavy initial cost of acquisition. Installment selling was a means of overcoming this restriction. It is also the natural development of the pressures on equipment manufacturers to increase sales by offering longer credit terms to buyers in a market chiefly composed of small concerns. The sales finance companies were able to take full advantage of these developments by adapting their own techniques of credit appraisal and collection to this type of financing. These techniques were considered unconventional by established lending agencies. It was, of course, natural that companies experienced in the consumer credit field should have been the first to turn to the financing of income-producing equipment. Of equal importance in this development was the reluctance, mentioned above, of the banking industry either to enter into this specialized and relatively high-cost credit area on a direct basis or to finance equipment manufacturers and dealers. Today this is no longer true, since most commercial banks are heavily engaged in the field of installment credit both in the consumer field and the industrial field.

The needs of the manufacturers and vendors of equipment contributed greatly to the growth of industrial installment credit primarily because they lacked the funds with which to extend long-term installment credit themselves. In addition, the vendors found that by selling their paper to the finance companies they were able to establish a clear separation between manufacturing and selling functions and the function of financing credit. This separation avoids the inevitable domination of the credit department by sales considerations. The finance companies offered additional facilities which made their service attractive. Among these was the fact that they assumed the onus of collections avoiding any possible loss of good will for the seller. Of greatest importance, however, were the legal problems involved in installment selling. The laws varied greatly among the various states and the cost of keeping up with the constant changes was prohibitive. The specialized finance company, however, was able to keep abreast of the laws.

More commercial finance companies began entering the field of industrial time sales by the early 1930's. It became for them an essential part of a plan of diversification set up to protect them from sudden declines in the demand for other types of financing. Today, almost all the finance companies that handle industrial time sales handle other types of loans as well.

Regulatory Legislation. The conditional sales contract, which is the underlying instrument used in time sales financing, dates well back into the nineteenth century. Regulation by law came in the latter half of the nineteenth century. Two considerations entered into such regulation. One was to protect other creditors of the purchaser by preventing his apparent affluence from misleading them into extending unwarranted credit. Hence a filing procedure was adopted to provide notice to the world that a particular item was subject to such a contract. Additionally there was a concern that the conditional vendee should have a right to redeem his interest in the goods in the event of repossession due to a default in payment.

After a miscellany of legislation on the subject by various states, a Uniform Conditional Sales Act was promulgated. This distinguished between a conditional sales contract and a chattel mortgage. The distinction was that in a conditional sales contract title did not pass to the purchaser until fulfillment of its terms.

Although many states adopted this act in the early twenties, minor variations developed regarding certain formalities such as size of print, witnesses to execution, notarization, method of filing, fees, etc. In recent years, this legislation has been replaced by the wide adoption of the Uniform Commercial Code which is discussed in detail in Chapter 9.

DEALER-PURCHASER AGREEMENTS

Conditional Sales Contract

The term "conditional sales contract" implies that the sale that is taking place is subject to certain conditions. The paramount condition is the one stipulating that title to the goods, merchandise, or equipment shall remain vested in the seller until the purchaser has paid the purchase price in full. The following is an example of typical language found in a conditional sales contract form:

Title to said equipment and any replacements and additions shall remain in you and your assigns, irrespective of any retaking and redelivery to us, until said indebtedness is fully paid in money, when ownership shall pass to us.

This is merely one way of expressing this particular stipulation. It is the heart and soul of every conditional sales contract.

Basic Elements. The contract must, of course, recite the names and addresses of the purchaser and the seller. It must also give a complete and detailed description of the equipment that is being sold. The description is extremely important, and model numbers and serial numbers must be given in order to avoid any confusion in identifying the equipment as against other similar equipment that the purchaser may buy from other sources. After reciting the amount of the sales price, down payment, trade-in allowance, finance charge, and total balance due, the contract also spells out the method of payment. The monthly payments to be made, the amount of each, and the date when payment is to commence are set forth. The address where the equipment is to be kept is stated separately if it varies from the purchaser's principal place of business or residence address. The form is signed by the buyer and also by the seller in the form of an acceptance. These are some of the elements that comprise the conditional sales contract. A complete form is given in Fig. 7–1 (pp. 181–6).

Equipment Not Part of Realty. This type of transaction creates problems for the buyer and the seller that the form must attempt to resolve. Previously we discussed the distinction between real and personal property. All well-drawn forms of conditional sales contracts state that the equipment shall remain personal property at all times and shall not become part of the realty where it is to be installed. The mere recitation of this stipulation does not, however, guarantee that a court of law may not at some future date declare the equipment to be part of the real estate nonetheless. This in itself is no catastrophe, for if fixtures are attached to real estate, proper legal precautions can be taken in advance to assure protection to the seller and his assigns. In these circumstances the conditional sales contract must be filed against the real estate itself so that subsequent purchasers of the property will be on notice that the equipment is subject to the lien of a conditional vendor. From a practical standpoint, as opposed to the legal standpoint, it must be remembered that the important drawback to financing equipment or fixtures that become part of the real estate is the simple fact that these items cannot in fact be removed from the property even though appropriate filings have been made.

Obligations of Seller and Buyer. The contract imposes certain obligations on both the seller and the buyer:

1. The buyer is required to keep the equipment insured against loss or damage by fire, wind, theft, and other physical damage. The

amount of insurance must be no less than the unpaid portion of the purchase price. The seller generally has the right to buy the insurance at the expense of the purchaser in the event that the latter does not willingly provide the insurance himself.

2. The purchaser is obligated to pay any taxes that may be due such as sales taxes, personal property taxes, and similar assessments.

3. The purchaser may not sell the equipment or pledge it as collateral for a loan until he has fully paid for it, nor may he move the equipment to another location without first notifying the seller of his intentions.

4. Most well-drawn forms will also contain a provision whereby the purchaser acknowledges the seller's intention to assign or sell the contract to another party. He agrees, therefore, that if he has any claims against the seller, he will settle these with the seller alone and will not attempt to set up any such claim against the seller's assigns. This language is important to the financer who does not wish to inherit any service complaints or problems or assume any responsibility for defective merchandise over which he has no control. In legal terminology this language is known as an estoppel, and it serves to prevent a legal claim of offset by the purchaser against the financer.

Default Provisions. In the event that the buyer does not make his payments as they come due under the terms of the contract or if any provision of the agreement is breached, a series of default provisions goes into effect:

1. The entire unpaid balance of the payments becomes immediately due and payable.

2. The buyer agrees to surrender possession of the equipment on demand.

3. The seller has the right to enter the premises where the equipment may be and take possession of all or part of it. This can usually only be done with the consent of the buyer. The seller is not allowed to breach the peace in removing the equipment nor is he permitted to trespass in the event that the buyer refuses to permit him entry. Despite the language contained in the agreement, it does not necessarily follow that the buyer who has already breached the payment provisions will be more scrupulous with regard to the default provisions.

4. The buyer assumes the cost of retaking, repairing, and reselling the equipment as well as attorney's fees and court costs.

5. After applying the proceeds of reselling the equipment, the buyer is obligated to pay any deficiency that may remain. On the other hand, any surplus must be credited to him.

Purchase Money Security Agreement

At this point let us compare a conditional sales contract with the newer version that under the Uniform Commercial Code is called a purchase money security agreement (see Fig. 7-2, pp. 187-91). There is little essential difference between the two forms. The most important difference lies in the language surrounding the reservation of title. Typical language in the security agreement reads as follows:

A security interest in the equipment sold, and any and all replacements thereof and additions thereto, is hereby reserved by and shall remain in the seller and his assigns until all of the indebtedness hereunder shall have been paid in full.

The work "title" has been eliminated and the term *"security interest"* substituted. This is far closer to the chattel mortgage concept. The seller retains certain lien rights to the equipment rather than retaining "title." The difference, however, is more academic than practical. Under the conditional sales contract the seller did not really retain title in the true sense of the term because he had to comply with a number of legal requirements before actual title was again granted to him. The Code has, therefore, simply called a spade a spade.

Priority over Other Security Interests. Although it is not within the purview of this discussion to become overly involved with legal questions, it is important to point out one significant legal fact about the purchase money security agreement. In security agreements under the Code the secured party, or lender, or its equivalent is granted a security interest in the collateral. A purchase money security interest, however, takes precedence in the event of a conflict of security interests. As an example of the priority of a purchase money interest, take the case of a dealer who has obtained an inventory loan from lender A. A obtains a security interest in all of the equipment on the dealer's premises. The law, very sensibly, permits the dealer, in the ordinary course of his business, to sell any item of this inventory to a customer, free of the security interest of lender A. Consequently, if the dealer sells such an item of inventory to a purchaser under a purchase money security agreement and then sells this paper to lender B, the security interest that lender B has in the equipment takes precedence over the security interest of lender A.

The Time Price Doctrine

The term "time sale" refers to a purchase of goods made subject to an installment contract or time payment plan. The enormous commerce in installment selling, both industrial and consumer, depends very largely on a piece of sophistry known as the time price doctrine. It is based on the following rationale:

A seller is presumed to have two prices. One is a cash price, which requires no further explanation. The time price assumes that the purchaser, who desires credit over a period of time, must pay an added charge to compensate the seller for this additional burden. The difference between the cash price and the time price is referred to as "the time price differential."

This line of reasoning avoids equating the seller of equipment and the money lender, for if the seller is in the same position as a lender, then the time price differential would actually be interest on the loan of money. Interest is regulated in almost every state by very strict statutes which forbid, under varying degrees of penalty, the exaction of an unlawful profit for lending money. These statutes are referred to as usury laws. The laws here again reflect a basic concern on the part of the lawmakers for the weaker, less sophisticated, less informed person who may become the victim of the unscrupulous lender. The usury laws are frequently harsh and were formulated in an era that certainly never conceived of the importance to the economy of the technique of installment selling.

It is generally recognized today that the cost of handling installment credit far exceeds the interest limits that are stipulated by the various usury statutes. No financer can absorb the overhead of handling installment credit if governed by such maximum legal rates of interest. The time price doctrine has, therefore, provided the legal mechanism to remove the time sale from the application of the usury statutes in holding that the transaction is a credit sale and is neither a loan nor a forebearance of money.

There are certain undeniable abuses in the field of retail installment selling. An enlightened view prevailing today differentiates between consumer installment selling and the industrial time sale. Special statutes have been enacted in recent years to regulate consumer credit and thereby reduce the incidence of such abuses. The time price doctrine itself stands quite firmly for the most part and has been upheld by the courts many times.

DEALER-FINANCER AGREEMENTS

When a dealer of equipment and a financer enter into a relationship, it is customary for them to sign an agreement setting forth the ground rules under which they will do business. This document is referred to as the "dealer agreement." Generally this agreement does not compel the dealer to sell his paper to the financer nor does it compel the financer to purchase the paper offered by the dealer. There are exceptions, but by and large the agreement becomes operative only when the dealer offers paper and the financer accepts it. Some financers demand the right of first refusal on all of the dealer's paper, but this requirement has been generally eliminated because of competitive pressures. The financer, of course, only wishes to buy that paper which he finds acceptable from both a credit and legal standpoint, and, therefore, he may refuse paper offered to him. Without exception, financers retain this discretionary right. The most important aspect of the dealer agreement is the one that concerns itself with recourse. Dealer agreements follow three basic formats with regard to recourse which we will call:

1. Full recourse
2. Limited recourse
3. Non-recourse

Full-Recourse Dealer Agreement

The full-recourse agreement is the one most commonly used (See Fig. 7-3, pp. 192-5). It takes the form of a guarantee of payment of the paper that the dealer is selling to the financer, as well as the payment of each and every installment of this paper. There is usually a further stipulation that in the event of default or non-payment, the dealer will immediately pay the entire unpaid balance of such paper. The dealer is also customarily responsible for any costs of collection such as attorney's fees and other expenses that might be incurred in re-taking the equipment and storing it or moving it. In other words, under a full-recourse agreement the dealer retains the full credit risk.

Limited-Recourse Dealer Agreements

Recourse to the dealer can be limited in different ways. The most common variety of limited-recourse agreement is actually nothing more than window dressing. The arrangement stems primarily from a desire on the part of the dealer to limit his over all contingent liability under the terms of the dealer agreement. A dealer who generates a sizable volume of installment sales can find himself guaranteeing payments for a very substantial portfolio of installment paper. The contingent liability figure is usually reported by accountants preparing yearly statements, and such a figure, if it becomes large in proportion to the dealer's net worth, can have an adverse effect on his borrowing capacity for normal business needs. Under such circumstances, the financer may agree to limit the amount of the dealer's contingent liability in any given period to, let us say, one-third of the total unpaid balances of all paper sold to the financer. With such an arrangement, the auditors may safely report a substantially lower contingent liability figure on the balance sheet without in actuality giving the financer any less protection.

This type of limitation generally takes into account the overall performance of the dealer's paper. It also takes into account the fact that the financial responsibility of the dealer could never be sufficient to cover an entire portfolio of paper that went bad. Since the financer is credit-checking each transaction prior to buying the paper and since a normal delinquency ratio is not likely to be higher than 5%, the financer is not actually taking any additional risk in granting this type of limitation. There are undoubtedly limited-recourse agreements that from a practical standpoint pass some of the risk to the financer. Such agreements are rarely used, and we need not devote any time to considering the ways in which such limitations can be provided.

Repurchase Agreement. A far more prevalent form of limited recourse is the repurchase agreement. Such an agreement is not a guarantee of payment on the part of the dealer but rather a commitment to buy back his equipment in the event that the customer defaults in payment. Under this type of arrangement the financer has full responsibility to recover the equipment legally, get possession of it, and be in a position to give good title to the dealer. The agreed-upon purchase price to be paid by the dealer at the time the financer is ready to make delivery to him will vary anywhere from the full unpaid balance due on the equipment at the time of default to a predetermined depreciated value. The prevailing view of accountants with respect to repurchase agreements holds that these do not constitute contingent liability and, therefore, do not have to be reported on the dealer's financial statement.

Non-recourse Dealer Agreements

Non-recourse agreements are quite common. A good deal of paper is purchased under terms whereby the dealer is relieved from all responsibility for the credit risk. The non-recourse arrangement is prevalent in industries where the equipment has a good resale value. Machine tools constitute the best example of a type of equipment that lends itself to non-recourse financing. Actually non-recourse is a misnomer as we are making use of the term. Although the dealer has no responsibility for the credit risk, he is nevertheless selling his paper with certain warranties. These warranties are included in all forms of dealer agreements and in effect constitute a certification on the part of the dealer that the paper is bona fide in all respects.

Dealer's Warranties

The following are aspects of the dealer's paper for which he must remain fully responsible:

1. The dealer had good title to the merchandise at the time of the sale.
2. The purchaser has no counterclaims or offsets or any right of return with respect to the merchandise.
3. The purchaser has received the merchandise and accepted it unconditionally.
4. The paper is genuine and all signatures are valid.
5. The merchandise described in the paper is the identical merchandise delivered by the dealer.
6. The dealer agrees to complete and carry out all agreements and warranties in respect to servicing the merchandise.

If the paper proves to be fraudulent in any respect by virtue of a defect in any of the foregoing, the dealer is fully liable. The non-recourse terminology, therefore, is only applicable to the credit risk; it does not relieve the dealer of his obligation to be honest and to fulfil his warranties.

Computing Financer's Compensation

A very important part of the dealer agreement is the provision that deals with rate. Rate determines the purchase price that the financer will pay to the dealer. It is applied in either of two ways:

Add-on Method. The following example will help illustrate the difference between these two methods of computation:

Cash selling price of equipment	$10,000
Less down payment and/or trade-in allowance	2,000
Unpaid cash balance	$ 8,000
Time price differential (finance charge)	480
Time balance	$ 8,480

The term "add-on" signifies that the cost of paying for the item on time is to be added on. Assuming that the add-on is 6% per annum we also assume that the above transaction is to be repaid in twelve equal, consecutive monthly installments. The add-on is computed on the unpaid cash balance, which in the above transaction is $8,000. It is important to remember that the transaction is between the dealer and the dealer's customer. At this point the financer has not entered the picture.

If the agreement between the dealer and the financer also calls for a 6% add-on rate then the financer will purchase the paper from the dealer for the equivalent of the unpaid cash balance or $8,000.00. The financer will retain the time price differential as its own profit in the transaction.

Discount Method. Under the discount method of computation the financer does not apply his rate to the unpaid cash balance. Rather, his rate is charged against the time balance which includes the dealer's add-on charge. Assuming that the purchase price was based on a 6% discount, the financer would be entitled to deduct $508.80 from the time balance shown above and remit the difference to the dealer as the purchase price for the paper. Thus, the dealer would be absorbing part of the financing cost. The important thing to observe is the fact that a 6% discount results in a higher cost to the dealer than a 6% add-on. Rates vary considerably because of many considerations which need not be gone into here.

Reserves

Another facet of the dealer agreement is that dealing with reserves, also referred to as holdbacks. Typical language in a dealer agreement relating to the question of reserves may be paraphrased as follows: "At the time of purchase the financer will pay to the dealer 90% of the unpaid face amount of such paper after deducting the amount of the financer's discount or rate." In this context the reserve is computed on the face amount or time balance of the paper. It might also be computed on the unpaid cash balance of the transaction. Using the above figures again as an example let us assume that the agreement still calls for a 6% add-on for the financer, which is $480.00. However, in this situation the financer is only required to advance 90% of the unpaid cash balance, or $7,200.00. The financer obtains the same amount of money for advancing $7,200.00 as he would if there were a no hold back arrangement and he advanced the entire $8,000.00. The financer is concerned with what he calls "yield." This term refers to a transposition of the rate into terms of interest on money employed. The reserve obviously does much to enhance the financer's yield assuming that the rate remains the same.

The moneys so withheld, which then constitute a reserve account, serve the additional function of providing protection against losses. The financer is usually permitted to charge any losses he may suffer in connection with the dealer's paper directly against the reserve account at his sole discretion. As specific paper is paid in full, the dealer gets back that part of the reserve account applicable to the matured paper. There may be, however, an understanding between the financer and the dealer whereby periodic adjustments limit the reserves to a specific percentage of the total amount of paper held by the financer. Competition among financers has substantially reduced the utilization of holdbacks. Today the dealer who enjoys a good credit standing is given a 100% advance on his paper as a rule, and holdbacks as such are obtained from dealers who are considered lesser credit risks.

There are two exceptions to this statement. One is the instance where the dealer has sufficient cash on hand and, in the interest of offering his customers a lower rate, permits the financer to retain a reserve, thereby absorbing part of the financing cost. The other instance involves the direct opposite of the foregoing, wherein the dealer charges his customer a rate in excess of the rate charged to him by the financer. Let us assume, for example, that the dealer charges his customer 6% add-on per annum and is in turn charged 5% add-on per annum by the financer. There is a 1% per annum rate differential that the financer will not advance to the dealer but will rather set up on his books as a reserve to be paid to the dealer when the paper has been paid in full.

Miscellaneous Provisions of Agreement

The dealer agreement may contain a great variety of other less-important terms. One of the more controversial of these is the question of the responsibility for correct filing to perfect security interests. Most financers incorporate into their dealer agreements a disclaimer with respect to filing, even though they may assume the burden of transmitting the paper work to the appropriate filing officer. There is also generally a provision in the agreement requiring the dealer to provide the financer with financial information about his operation. Other miscellaneous stipulations may cover the disposition of respossessed equipment, the handling of payments mistakenly made to the dealer, the form that assignments of paper to the financer shall take, and a variety of other minutiae. The agreement attempts to foresee the problems that could arise in the relationship and to provide against misunderstanding and dispute. In this respect it is no different from any other agreement or contract between two or more parties.

FRAUD IN TIME SALES FINANCING

Time sales financing is as vulnerable to fraud as any other type of financing. Although most losses in the finance business are due to poor credit judgment, the financer's greatest fear remains the fraud risk. The knowledgeable and experienced financer knows the pitfalls in handling time sales paper and is consequently able to guard against the more prevalent of the dubious practices.

Fictitious Paper

The most blatant form of fraud is the one involving completely fictitious paper. There are cases on record in which the dishonest dealer has managed to "palm off" on the unsuspecting financer installment transactions that exist only in his fertile imagination. This sort of thing can be done successfully usually only with the assistance of other parties working in collusion to defraud the financer. The most spectacular recent case of this type is the famous Billy Sol Estes scandal. It will be recalled that Mr. Estes generated time paper involving the sale of a type of fertilizer tank to farmers. Many of these farmers cooperated with Mr. Estes in perpetrating the hoax. It later appeared that the ammonia tanks did not exist and that the farmers who cooperated were bribed to do so.

Duplicate Financing

Another type of fraud is the one known as "duplicate financing." In this situation there may be an actual purchaser and even actual equipment. However, there are also more than one set of papers to cover the transaction. The dishonest dealer manages to sell these sets of paper to different financers. To succeed, this scheme would also seem to require the cooperation of the purchaser. The financer who holds the paper may check both purchaser and equipment and be satisfied that they exist. What he does not know, of course, is that one or more other financers hold the identical collateral.

Prebilling

The foregoing are the two most spectacular kinds of fraud perpetrated in this type of financing. However, there are a number of other less elaborate but equally devious practices that cause losses to the unwary lender. A very prevalent practice, and one indulged in by dealers who would readily deny that they had perpetrated fraud, involves failure to deliver the equipment described in the contract. This is sometimes known as "prebilling." In this instance the dealer has an order for an item of equipment that is not in stock and must be ordered from the factory. He may be short of cash, and the factory may insist on sending him the equipment under sight draft. He finds it expedient, therefore, to have his customer sign the installment credit forms, and he discounts these before the equipment has passed through his hands. With the money given him by the financer he then pays for the equipment and subsequently makes delivery.

The dealer will insist that his intentions were entirely honorable, and yet this practice is fraudulent. He has accepted money from the financer at the time that the paper is discounted under a flagrant misrepresentation. The paper he has sold has no validity at the time he sells it because it does not represent a completed transaction. The unsuspecting lender has given up his funds against delivery of a worthless piece of paper. Since the purchaser has not received the equipment, he is not obligated to pay for it. The financer, therefore, has neither access to the equipment nor does he have a valid obligation of the purchaser. The dealer who engages in this sort of scheme does so because he lacks money. Very likely, his business is going rapidly down hill. If in the course of his maneuvers he is forced into a bankruptcy he may never complete the transaction, or transactions, that he has already discounted with the financer. The money he has received may be dissipated. At such a time the financer is holding worthless paper upon which he cannot recover.

Misrepresentation of Terms of Sale

Another unfortunately common practice involves the misrepresentation of the terms of a specific time sale transaction. In these situations the figures are manipulated, usually by inflating the amount of down payment and trade-in allowance far beyond the true figures. This kind of thing has a number of variations. The most common is the concealment of a complete lack of down payment. In this instance it is a simple matter to inflate the selling price and to assert a down payment equal to the amount by which the true selling price was adjusted upward. The result is that the financer takes in the transaction believing that the purchaser has a certain equity in the equipment which in fact he does not. There are times when an unscrupulous dealer in his anxiety to sell his merchandise may agree to add several thousand dollars to the selling price of a piece of equipment, thereby in effect obtaining a loan for his customer over and above the value of the equipment without the financer ever being aware of the fact. A rather common practice of this variety involves what we may call "hidden costs." Take, as an example, the dealer selling restaurant equipment. His customer is planning to open a very elaborate establishment, and the equipment dealer agrees to provide many of the construction items as well as equipment. Electrical wiring, ceiling, wall paneling, flooring—these are all things not readily financeable since they cannot be removed from the premises and still retain any value. The unsuspecting financer is easily deceived into advancing more money than he wishes to by the simple expedient of showing only a lump sum price covering the equipment that is being sold. Failing to analyze these costs, the financer does not realize that he is in effect providing the financing for items of negligible resale value.

"One-Name" Paper

One of the great safeguards in time sales financing is the fact that the buyer in a given transaction is a wholly independent person who has no relationship to the seller beyond the transaction itself. The contract of sale is "two-name paper," as opposed to a very hazardous variety known as "one-name paper." In the latter category, the buyer and the seller are either one and the same or so closely inter-related as to be in fact the same. In such a situation, where the seller has complete control over the buyer, the opportunities for fraud are ripe indeed. The vending industry produced a lot of "one-name paper" in years past which at the time seemed innocent enough. Manufacturers and distributors of vending equipment, jealous of the profits that their customers were making, decided to operate equipment themselves. Separate corporations were set up for the purpose of running these vending machine routes, and paper was created by virtue of the sale of equipment from the manufacturing corporation to the operating corporation. On the face of things, this appeared to be "two-name paper." However, with only a modest amount of scrutiny we see that this is truly "one-name paper" since the operating company and the manufacturing company are owned by the same people. The mere fact that a commonly owned manufacturing concern and operating firm buys and sells equipment in this manner is not in itself fraudulent. However, for the financer this situation is very difficult to police. There is no independent buyer who, benefitting from competition in the industry, pays the price of the market place, nor is the buyer likely to complain of any failure of consideration. In every other respect as well the seller is able to manipulate the customer in any way that he sees fit.

There are many ways in which an unscrupulous dealer can deceive the financer. The varieties are endless, and new wrinkles are added every year. The techniques of handling industrial installment paper help to protect against these deceptions. The most important element is the development of a healthy skepticism on the part of the financer.

OPERATIONAL PROCEDURES

Credit Investigation

The process of handling time sales paper begins with the credit functions of investigation and analysis.

Dealer. First, the dealer from whom the paper is accepted must pass this scrutiny. It is standard procedure to obtain the dealer's financial statement and to check out his references. The credit standards of the various financers in the field tend to vary. However, the basic concern of this initial credit investigation is to establish the integrity and reliability of the dealer. This holds true whether the paper is to be purchased with or without recourse. This truth becomes clearly evident when we reflect upon those incidents which each of us has at one time or other experienced in making a purchase from an unscrupulous seller. The normal reaction is to seek retaliation. However, the victimized purchaser in a cash sale usually has no recourse. In a credit sale, on the other hand, he obviously can retaliate and frequently does by the simple expedient of not paying.

In investigating the credit of the dealer one must be very much concerned with antecedent information. The owners of a dealership must be experienced in the business. They must enjoy a reputation for fair and honest dealings. They must have the physical facilities necessary to service their customers properly. It is important that they have working capital adequate to the volume of business that they transact, and they must, above all else, sell a reliable product.

Purchasers. Having decided to accept paper from a specific dealer the credit man must turn his attention to the credit worthiness of each customer of the dealer. The investigation of these credits must, of necessity, be speedily accomplished because the dealer, anxious to make a sale, is relying very heavily on the financer for a prompt decision. The amount of the effort that goes into the investigation is geared to the size of the transaction. If larger dollar amounts are involved, the dealer will have to obtain financial statements from his customers. He will invariably need to obtain bank and trade references to give the credit man sufficient information.

Credit judgment at this juncture is based largely on experience, on the ability of the credit man to interpret and evaluate the underlying facts, and on his ability to discriminate between significant and insignificant factors. Since the general objective in installment credit is to make credit available to those who need it, risk selection is more inclined toward liberal than restrictive standards. This does not imply that there need be haphazard selections, because there are reliable time-tested guides at the credit man's disposal.

In deciding whether or not to accept a certain paper from the dealer the credit man must ascertain the following about the purchaser:

1. His financial status and ability to pay
2. His capability and competence
3. Personal characteristics such as age, reputation and habits, type and location of residence

Consideration must also be given to the equipment being purchased, its durability and resale value. The size of the down payment is an important factor. The buyer must have enough of a stake in the equipment to maintain his desire to retain it. The amount of down payment also has a strong influence on the ability to resell the equipment for the amount owing in the event of the buyer's default. In a transaction in which the dealer is on recourse, the efficacy of that recourse will also influence the credit decision.

Purchase of Paper

Having approved the credit, the financer awaits the completion of the transactions. When delivery is complete and the merchandise is accepted fully by the purchaser, the dealer submits the properly executed papers to the financer and receives his money in accordance with the terms of their dealer agreement. The dealer must individually assign the paper to the financer. When promissory notes are used, these must be endorsed by the dealer. It is important to remember that the installment sale is between the dealer and his customer. The financer is not involved in the transaction until the time that the dealer offers the paper for discount. The obligation of the purchaser and the security interest in the equipment both run to the dealer; consequently the dealer must assign these interests to the financer.

The documents, at time of purchase, must be carefully scrutinized. All names and addresses must be correct and must correspond to information in the credit file. The amounts must coincide with those previously stated. The description of the equipment must be complete. All dates and signatures must be properly affixed. Corporate titles must be accurately set forth, and acknowledgements, if required by the laws of the state where the transactions occurred, must be accomplished. Special requirements must have been met such as landlord's and/or mortgagee's waivers, guarantees, and subordinations.

Notice of Assignment and Inspection of Equipment

After purchasing the paper from the dealer, the financer notifies the purchaser of the assignment. In most instances the purchaser receives a payment book with the notice of assignment. He is thus informed that payments are to be made to the financer, and the payment book is provided to facilitate the forwarding and proper crediting of his remittances.

The credit investigation has previously established the existence of the purchaser and his credit worthiness. The mailing of the notice of assignment and payment book directly to the purchaser confirms that this same individual or corporation is, in fact, the actual purchaser. The prudent financer will also make a physical inspection of the equipment on the purchaser's premises to make certain that there has been no collusion between the buyer and the seller. This type of inspection can be inexpensively accomplished by certain credit agencies who operate on a national scale and who send inspectors from their local branch offices to check on the equipment. Economic considerations generally dictate that these inspections be done in connection with transactions over a certain dollar amount. However, when handling low-balance paper an occasional spot check can be useful. The inspection should include scrutiny of the serial numbers on the equipment if it is so numbered. The discovery of a disparity in serial numbers may spell trouble for the financer.

Verification and Maintenance of Insurance Coverage

Under the terms of a properly drawn conditional sales contract or similar instrument, the purchaser of the equipment is required to maintain adequate insurance protection against loss by fire and other physical hazards. The financer must obtain a copy of the purchaser's insurance policy which must contain a loss-payable endorsement in favor of the financer. The purchase money instrument should permit the seller or his assigns to obtain the insurance coverage at the buyer's expense if the latter fails to provide it of his own accord. Policy expiration dates must be flagged and general diligence maintained by the financer to assure protection against insurable losses.

Collection

The next function in the procedure is the one on which the success of the operation ultimately depends, namely the function of collection. Having put the account on the books, it must now be "lived with" for as long as five years and in some instances even longer. To the dealer on recourse the collection effort of the financer is the most important service being provided.

Handling Delinquent Accounts. The first step requires setting up a system for flagging accounts that do not meet their payments on the due date. A grace period of from five to ten days is allowed

from the due date for the payment to be received and credited to
the account. Those that do not pay must be culled out and set
into the collection follow-up. Systems for accomplishing this vary;
the latest methods, of course, employ electronic data processing
equipment.

The delinquent account will initially receive printed forms of
notice. If these fail to bring response, the account will be assigned
to a collection man who then regularly follows up with the debtor
by letters, telegrams, and phone calls until he has gotten him to
bring his account up to date. Where the dealer is on recourse it
is advisable as well as effective to keep him apprised of the status
of his accounts. He receives copies of all past-due notices going
to his customers, and at the end of every month he is sent a listing
of all past-due accounts which shows the extent of their delinquency
and the balances owing from each.

Examination of Payments. As payments come in they should be
carefully scrutinized and not be permitted to receive automatic handling. If a dealer sends in payments for one or more of his accounts
this must be questioned. Dealer payments are regarded as a "red
flag" which could signify any one of a number of situations injurious
to the financer's interests. It could mean that the dealer has taken
back the equipment without notifying the financer, or that the transaction is actually fraudulent. It may mean that the purchaser is unable
to pay, and the dealer, who is on recourse, is attempting to keep
the account current to avoid having to repurchase it in full. Payments from third parties, persons not originally involved in the account, must also receive special attention. Such a remittance may
result from many different circumstances, but the financer must determine whether or not they are innocent.

Transfer of Possession and Assumption Agreements

Most frequently a third-party payment signifies that the original
buyer has transferred possession of the equipment to someone else.
According to the sale agreement, he is not allowed to do this without
obtaining the consent of the seller or the seller's assigns. The restriction is important in order to control the whereabouts of the equipment
and retain the prerogative of extending credit to risks of the financer's
own selection. The original buyer, however, does not relieve himself
of liability by the simple act of transferring possession to someone
else. A change of the location of the equipment and a change in

the name of the party possessing it also require amended filings, and a failure on the part of the financer to be alert to these changes could cause him to lose his security interest.

Changes of this nature are not infrequent, although most purchasers will notify the financer of their intention to sell the equipment to some one else, subject to the underlying purchase money instruments. The new buyer intends to assume the obligation, and an "assumption agreement" is entered into with the original buyer to which the financer lends his formal consent. Normally, under the terms of such an agreement the original buyer remains fully liable. When notified in advance that an assumption is contemplated, the financer will investigate the credit of the new buyer. Even though the original buyer remains fully liable, the financer will want to be satisfied that the equipment, his collateral, will not be in the hands of disreputable people and that he can reasonably expect the new buyer to make the payments as they come due. The new buyer becomes the primary obligor, and the original buyer becomes the guarantor with whom the financer will lose direct contact. In Code states an amendment to the original filing must be made, and in non-Code states a duplicate original of the assumption agreement itself is filed in the office where the original filing was made.

Forebearances

It is not uncommon for a collection man to be confronted with a request for an extension of the original terms of the purchase money instrument. Assuming that the request is reasonable and warranted it may be granted. An interest charge is made to cover the additional time granted to the buyer in which to complete his payments. The granting of this extension is legally known as a forbearance.

Even though the transaction originated as a time sale and the original finance charge was governed by the time price doctrine, the forbearance has the same legal status as a loan, and the charge made in connection therewith is governed by the usury statutes. This can pose a serious dilemma to the financer who finds that the legal limit of the interest he can charge for the forbearance is substantially lower than the rate that governed the original transaction. It can be, in fact, so much lower as to compel him to refuse to grant the forebearance. The penalty for usury can be quite onerous in some states, as has been mentioned. The financer is, therefore, cautious in granting extensions and deplores the frequent practice of many dealers in many industries who attempt to meet the situation by writing a new installment sales contract. This is, of course, mere subterfuge and can also serve to lose the security interest protection afforded by the original filing if that filing is supplanted by the filing of the newly written contract. Under the Code, filings are valid for five years. Hence, extensions, depending on the amount of additional time involved, may also require amendment filings and may involve re-filing of the contract which the original terms may not have required. These are all pitfalls to which the financer of this type of paper must be alert.

Prepayment and the Rule of 12/78ths

There is more popular misunderstanding in connection with prepayment of installment sales contracts than any other phase of this subject. Although practices may vary and prepayment penalties do exist, for the most part it is the practice of financers to accept prepayment and to allow rebates of the unearned portion of the finance charge on the basis of a formula known as the Rule of 12/78ths. A misconception exists with respect to this formula, and it is thought by many that the Rule of 12/78ths in and of itself contains a prepayment penalty, or at least is so calculated as to cause a serious disadvantage to the person wishing to prepay.

This is a calumny born out of ignorance which the explanation that follows will seek to dispel. The Rule of 12/78ths is a sum-of-the-digits method of calculation. It gets its name from the sum of the series 12, 11, 10, 9, 8, 7, 6, 5, 4, 3, 2, 1, which equals 78. The twelve numbers represent the twelve months of a one-year installment sales contract. In the first month of this contract $12/78$ths of the finance charge is earned and $66/78$ths is unearned. After the second month, 12, and 11 or $23/78$ths of the finance charge is earned and $55/78$ths is unearned, and so forth. The misconceptions mentioned above arise from the fact that the uninformed expect the finance charge to be applied equally over the twelve months so that only $1/12$th is earned each month. This completely overlooks the fact that the earning of the finance charge is based on the amount of money that remains unpaid. In an installment transaction the early months involve the largest portion of money outstanding, and, therefore, the financer must be compensated accordingly. The Rule of 12/78ths, which is extended to cover transactions of any length, seeks merely to preserve whatever rate, or yield as the financer prefers to call it, was written into the transaction at its inception. In other words, if the installment contract was written at a rate that yielded 10% per annum in terms of interest on money employed, then by using the Rule of 12/78ths at the time of prepayment, the financer will have earned 10% per annum up to the prepayment date.

Satisfaction and Statement of Termination

The last occurrence in the handling of a time sales account is the receipt of the final payment. The purchaser is now entitled to unencumbered ownership of his equipment. The only thing that remains to be done is the issuance of a satisfaction. In Code states, a statement of termination is signed and sent to the filing office or offices to clear the security interest from the record.

ORIGINAL FOR XYZ

CONDITIONAL SALES CONTRACT

This form is subject to State legal requirements.

Purchaser's Name ....

Address ....
(If corporation, give location of principal place of business in State; if individual or partnership, give residences)

City .... County .... State ....

To ....
(Name of Seller)

....
(Address of Seller's Place of Business)

Date ...., 19.......

We, the purchaser whose name and address are given above, hereby purchase from you the equipment or property (hereinafter referred to as "equipment") described below or on the attached schedule:

for which we agree to pay you or your assigns a Total Time Sales Price of [#2 plus #8 below] $........
(1) BONA FIDE CASH SELLING PRICE .... $........
(2) DOWN PAYMENT { BY ALLOWANCE $........
                   BY CASH $........ } (*Describe Briefly Goods Accepted in Trade*)
(3) Difference between (1) and (2) (Base Time Price) .... $........
(4) Amount included for insurance and other benefits .... $........
    (Specify type of coverage and benefits and cost of each type)
(5) Official fees ....
(6) Principal balance (sum of 3, 4 and 5) .... $........
(7) Finance charge or Time Price Differential .... $........
(8) We agree to pay the TOTAL TIME BALANCE OF .... $........
in .... successive monthly payments, each of $........, commencing the .... day of ...., 19.......

Fig. 7-1. Conditional Sales Contract

and on the same date of each month thereafter until paid, the final payment to be the balance then unpaid hereon, together with interest from maturity at the highest lawful rate (not over 1½% per month) as evidenced by negotiable promissory note.

Title to said equipment and any replacements and additions shall remain in you and your assigns, irrespective of any retaking and redelivery to us, until said indebtedness is fully paid in money, when ownership shall pass to us. Said equipment shall remain chattels and personal property at all times and will be installed in the following premises:

_____ , City _____ , County _____ , State _____
(Street Address)

but shall not become part of the realty or freehold. We agree to keep said equipment insured against loss or damage by fire, wind, theft and accident, in an insurance company or companies satisfactory to you, in an amount not less than the unpaid portion of the purchase price, such insurance to be payable to you as your interest may appear, and the policies therefor to be delivered to and retained by you until the purchase price is paid in full. If we fail at any time to provide said insurance, you may have the equipment insured and the cost of such insurance shall be paid for by us. We further agree to pay promptly when due all taxes, assessments, license fees and other public charges levied or assessed and to satisfy all liens against said equipment. If we breach any provision of this agreement or remove, dispose of or encumber said equipment or attempt so to do, the entire unpaid balance of the aforesaid payments shall become immediately due and payable without notice or demand and we agree to surrender possession of said equipment on demand; you and your assigns may without notice or legal process enter any premises where said equipment may be and take possession of all or any part thereof, (and at your option abandon or transfer to us any portion of the equipment you choose) retaining all payments made as partial compensation for our use of said repossessed equipment, which may be sold with or without notice at private sale or at public sale at which sale you or your assigns may purchase; there shall be credited upon the amount unpaid the proceeds of such sale less the expenses of retaking, repairing, holding and reselling the equipment and reasonable attorney's fees (20% if permitted by law), and we agree to pay the balance as liquidated damages for the breach of this contract, any surplus, however, to be paid to us. Waiver or condonation of any breach or default shall not constitute a waiver of any other or subsequent breach or default. We will settle all claims against you, the seller, directly with you, you hereby agreeing to remain responsible therefor, and we will not set up any such claim against your assigns.

Any provision of this agreement prohibited by laws of any state shall, as to said state, be ineffective to the extent of such prohibition without invalidating the remaining provision of this contract.

No oral or implied agreement, guaranty, representation, or warranty shall bind you or your assigns.

If an installment is not paid within ten days after it is due we agree to pay a delinquency charge of $5.00 or 5% of the installment, whichever is less.

For the sole purpose of resolving any problem of conflict of laws with respect to filing or recording hereof, it is hereby declared and agreed that this instrument shall be deemed to be executed, completed and effective for such purpose when the property is received at the address at which it is to be located, and that questions of filing or recording shall accordingly be determined by the law of such place.

NOTICE TO THE BUYER:

(1) Do not sign this contract before you read it or if it contains any blank spaces.
(2) You are entitled to an exact copy of the contract you sign.
(3) Under the law you have the right to pay off in advance the full amount due and to obtain a partial refund of the finance charge.

We waive all exemptions and acknowledge receipt of a true copy of this agreement.

Witness _____

Witness _____

(Signatures of two witnesses)

By _____ (Seal)

_____ (Seal)

} Signature of Purchaser

(Owner, Partner or Officer and Title)

Accepted:

By _____

} Signature of Seller

(Owner, Partner or Officer and Title)

Witness _____

(Signature of witness)

(Please sign all copies in ink.)

(Type or print names under signatures.)

*This instrument was prepared by _____

*(Use in Arkansas, Indiana and Ohio)

Fig. 7-1. Conditional Sales Contract—Continued

THIS FORM IS FOR USE IN THE
FOLLOWING STATES:

ALASKA

ARKANSAS

CONNECTICUT

FLORIDA [acknowledgements 1 or 2 and 3 or 4]

GEORGIA

IDAHO.............[acknowledgements 1 or 2]

ILLINOIS

INDIANA

KANSAS

KENTUCKY

MASSACHUSETTS

MICHIGAN ....[after 1/1/64]

MONTANA

☞1 ACKNOWLEDGMENT BY INDIVIDUAL PURCHASER

STATE OF .... COUNTY OF .... SS.:

I .... do hereby certify that on this........day of

of.............County of..............19...., before me personally appeared...................., a Notary Public, in and for the State

to me known to be the individual described in and who executed the within instrument and acknowledged

that he signed, sealed and delivered the same as his free and voluntary act and deed for the uses and pur-

poses therein mentioned.

IN WITNESS WHEREOF, I have hereunto set my hand and affixed my official seal the day and year

of this certificate above written.

....
(AFFIX   Notary Public   My Commission Expires ....
NOTARIAL SEAL)

☞2 ACKNOWLEDGMENT BY CORPORATION PURCHASER

STATE OF .... COUNTY OF .... SS.:

On this......day of........., 19...... before me, a Notary

Public in and for the State of.................., County of..............

personally appeared.......................to me personally known and known to me

to be the.................of the corporation which executed the within instrument,

who being by me duly sworn, did say that he is the.................of

................., the within named buyer, that he knows the seal of said

corporation, that the seal affixed to said instrument is the seal of said corporation, and that said instrument

was signed, sealed and delivered in behalf of said corporation by authority of its Board of Directors and the

said.................acknowledged the execution of said instrument to be his free, true

and lawful act and deed and the free, true and lawful act and deed of said corporation by him in his said

capacity and by it voluntarily executed for the uses, purposes and consideration therein mentioned.

Witness my hand and official seal the day and year in this certificate first above written.

....
(AFFIX   Notary Public   My Commission Expires ....
NOTARIAL SEAL)

☞3 ACKNOWLEDGMENT BY INDIVIDUAL SELLER

STATE OF .... COUNTY OF .... SS.:

I .... a Notary Public, in and for the State

of.............County of..............do hereby certify that on this........day of

NEW HAMPSHIRE
NEW JERSEY
NEW MEXICO
[acknowledgements 1 or 2 and 3 or 4]

NEW YORK
OHIO
OKLAHOMA
OREGON.......... [after 9/1/63]
PENNSYLVANIA
RHODE ISLAND
TENNESSEE
UTAH
WYOMING

(AFFIX
NOTARIAL SEAL) .... Notary Public .... My Commission Expires ....

ACKNOWLEDGMENT BY CORPORATION SELLER

STATE OF ...., COUNTY OF .... SS.:

On this.......... day of.........., 19......, before me, a Notary Public in and for the State of.........., County of.......... to me personally known to be the identical person who signed the attached instrument and known to me to be the.......... of the corporation which executed the same as Seller, who being by me duly sworn, did say that he is named Seller, that he know the seal of said corporation, that the seal affixed to said instrument is the within the seal of said corporation and that said instrument was signed, sealed and delivered in behalf of said corporation by authority of its Board of Directors, and said.......... acknowledged the execution of said instrument to be his free, true and lawful act and deed and the free, true and lawful act and deed of said corporation by him in his said capacity and by it voluntarily executed for the uses, purposes and consideration therein mentioned.

Witness my hand and official seal the day and year in this certificate first above written.

(AFFIX
NOTARIAL SEAL) .... Notary Public .... My Commission Expires ....

to me known to be the individual described in and who executed the within instrument and acknowledged that he signed and sealed the same as his free and voluntary act and deed for the uses and purposes therein mentioned.

IN WITNESS WHEREOF, I have hereunto set my hand and affixed my official seal the day and year of this certificate above written.

ASSIGNMENT

For value received, the undersigned hereby sells, assigns, and transfers to XYZ Financial Corporation, its successors or assigns, all right, title and interest in and to the within contract, the amounts payable thereunder, the property therein described, and the rights therefrom ensuing. The undersigned hereby guarantees: the full performance of said contract and prompt payment of all sums provided therein, together with all collection expenses; that the merchandise described in the contract was actually delivered and/or installed and accepted by the purchaser named therein; that nothing has been done or exists to limit or affect the validity of said contract. The undersigned agrees that any extension, compromise or settlement that may be granted or made by the holder hereof to or with the parties to said contract shall not in any manner release the undersigned.

Date ....

.... (Seller)

By ....

Title ....

Fig. 7-1. Conditional Sales Contract—Continued

CONDITIONAL SALE CONTRACT

....
Conditional Seller

....
Conditional Buyer

Contract Balance ....$................................

Equipment located at:

....
Address

....
County

....
City and State

When the equipment is to be affixed to real estate in Indiana, New Hampshire or New Jersey the following statement should be filled in and filed for record **before installation.**

Lot No. ....

Block No. ....

Addition ....

County ....

Other Description ....

Record Owner ....

The equipment is to be affixed to the above premises but shall not become part of the freehold.

....
Name of Conditional Seller

By ....
            Signature   Title

Fig. 7–1. Conditional Sales Contract—Continued

ORIGINAL FOR XYZ

PURCHASE MONEY

SECURITY AGREEMENT
(Industrial Equipment)

SELLER
(Secured Party).. | Date ....

Address ....

City .... State ....

BUYER
(Debtor) ....

Address ....

City .... County .... State ....

Equipment Sold (include manufacturer's name, type of unit, identifying numbers and other pertinent information): *(If more space is needed, attach schedule.)*

....

Equipment shall at all times be located at ....

but shall not become part of the realty. (If Equipment is a fixture: The Equipment is affixed or to be affixed to realty at said address, the

record owner of which is ....).

Buyer (meaning all buyers, jointly and severally) has purchased from Seller, on a time price basis, received delivery of and accepted the foregoing Equipment on the terms appearing on the face and back hereof:

Fig. 7–2. Purchase Money Security Agreement

1. Cash Price .... $
2. Down Payment:
   Cash ....
   Trade-In .... Total ....
3. Unpaid Cash Balance (1 minus 2) ....
4. Official Fees ....
5. Insurance (specify) ....
6. Unpaid Principal Balance (3 plus 4 plus 5) ....
7. Time Price Differential (Finance Charge) ....

APPLICABLE IN MASSACHUSETTS: "The Finance charges provided herein are not regulated by law. They are a matter for agreement between the parties."

8. Net Balance Due .... $
9. Time Price (2 plus 8) .... $

Buyer agrees to pay the net Balance Due to Seller or its assigns in .... consecutive monthly installments (................ @ $................ and .... @ $................) commencing .... 19........; and after maturity to bear interest or legal charges at the lightest lawful rate.

A security interest in the Equipment sold and any and all replacements thereof and additions thereto (all hereinafter referred to as "chattels") is hereby reserved by, and shall remain in Holder. meaning Seller and assigns, until all of the indebtedness hereunder, meaning the "full amount of the purchase price and all other sums for which Buyer is liable hereunder or under any accompanying promissory note or notes, shall have been fully paid in cash. Proceeds of collateral are also covered. Buyer agrees that Holder may grant extensions or accept renewals or assign this contract or negotiate any notes executed herewith without relieving Buyer of any obligations hereunder or waiving its security interest. This contract, if assigned, shall be free from any defense, counter-claim or cross-complaint by Buyer, it being understood that all claims or demands on the part of Buyer against Seller shall be independent of any action or claim by any assignee against Buyer. Buyer agrees to procure forthwith and maintain fire insurance with extended or combined additional coverage on the chattels for the full insurable value thereof for the life of this contract plus other insurance thereon in amounts and against such risks as Holder may specify, and promptly deliver each policy to Holder with a standard long form endorsement attached thereto showing loss payable to Holder as respective interest may appear; acceptance of policies in lesser amounts or risks shall not be a waiver of the foregoing obligations. If Buyer defaults in payment of any part of the purchase price when due, or fails to comply with or defaults in any of the provisions of this contract or defaults deem itself insecure, the full amount of the indebtedness then unpaid shall, at Holder's option, become immediately due and payable, and Buyer agrees to assemble the collateral and make it available to Holder at a place to be designated by holder which is reasonably convenient to both parties. Holder also may without notice or demand and without legal process enter into any premises where said chattels may be and take immediate possession thereof. Upon default, Holder shall be entitled to legal attorney's fees (not to exceed 15 per cent) and shall have all of the rights of a secured party under the Uniform Commercial Code, including the right to claim a deficiency from Buyer upon disposition of the chattels. It shall also account to Buyer for any surplus. Buyer agrees that five days notice of disposition of the chattels is reasonable and that sale to a dealer is a reasonable method of disposition.

Buyer agrees to keep the chattels free of taxes, liens and encumbrances, agrees to take good care of said chattels and be responsible for their loss or damage by reason of fire or for any reason, and shall have no right to sell or assign the chattels or its rights under this contract without the consent in writing of Holder. Buyer will reimburse Holder for any amounts expended by Holder in any action to protect its security interest in the chattels, including Holder's election to remedy a default, but any action so taken will not be a waiver of such default nor will any waiver of any default constitute a waiver of any other prior or subsequent default. Buyer waives any and all right to trial by jury in any action or proceeding arising herefrom or based hereon.

This contract contains the entire agreement between the parties hereto and is not subject to cancellation. Unless specifically contained herein, there are no agreements, guaranties or warranties, express or implied, in connection with the sale of the chattels. If any installment is not paid within ten days after it is due Buyer agrees to pay a delinquency charge of $5.00 or 5% of the installment, whichever is less. All provisions of this contract prohibited by the law of any State shall as to said State be ineffective to the extent of such prohibition without invalidating any other provision or condition. The undersigned expressly waives all exemption and homestead laws and acknowledges receipt of a true copy of this agreement.

ACCEPTED: ....
Date

Seller .... Buyer ....

By .... By ....

Title .... Title ....

Witnesses to Buyer's signature ....

(For Arkansas and Ohio) This instrument was prepared by ....

.... Address ....

Fig. 7–2. Purchase Money Security Agreement—Continued

GUARANTY

In consideration of Seller making the sale set forth on the reverse hereof, each of us as a primary guarantor guarantees jointly and severally, to Holder, meaning Seller and assigns, the payment of the indebtedness and performance of all other conditions and covenants set forth on the reverse side hereof, when due, as well as payment of all other obligations owing to Holder by Buyer, however arising. Holder need not proceed against Buyer or liquidate any security. Each of us will be bound by any deficiency established by sale of the obligation or security, and shall pay such deficiency or demand. Notice to us of such sale shall not be required. Each of us waives notice of acceptance hereof; any and all right to a trial by jury in any action or proceeding based hereon or arising hereunder, and presentment, demand for payment, protest and notice of protest as to the obligations or any notes executed therewith. Holder may compromise its rights against Buyer or others, grant extensions of time, or release by operation of law or by agreement Buyer or others without affecting the liability of each of us. Death of any of us shall not discharge this guaranty. This guaranty binds our respective heirs, administrators, representatives, successors or assigns.

(Sign individually without corporate titles)

Name   Address

.... (L.S.) ....

.... (L.S.) ....

.... (L.S.) ....

FOR USE
IN THE
FOLLOWING STATES

ALABAMA (after 1/1/67)
ALASKA
ARKANSAS
CALIFORNIA
COLORADO
CONNECTICUT
DELAWARE
    (after 7/1/67)
DIST. OF COLUMBIA
FLORIDA (after 1/1/67)
GEORGIA
HAWAII (after 1/1/67)
ILLINOIS
INDIANA
IOWA
KANSAS
KENTUCKY
MAINE
MARYLAND
MASSACHUSETTS
MICHIGAN
MINNESOTA
MISSISSIPPI
    (after 3/31/68)
MISSOURI
MONTANA

NEW HAMPSHIRE
NEW JERSEY
NEW MEXICO
NEW YORK
NORTH CAROLINA
(after 7/1/67)
NORTH DAKOTA
OHIO
OKLAHOMA
OREGON
PENNSYLVANIA
RHODE ISLAND
SOUTH CAROLINA
(after 1/1/68)
SOUTH DAKOTA
(after 7/1/67)
TENNESSEE
TEXAS
UTAH
VERMONT (after 1/1/67)
VIRGINIA
WASHINGTON
(after 6/30/67)
WEST VIRGINIA
WISCONSIN
WYOMING

For valuable consideration, the receipt whereof is hereby acknowledged, the undersigned hereby sells, assigns, transfers and sets over to XYZ FINANCIAL CORPORATION, 70 Pine Street, New York, New York 10005, its successors and assigns, all of its rights, title and interests (a) in and to the within instrument and any accompanying promissory note or notes, and all rights and remedies thereunder, including the right to collect installments due thereon, and the right either in assignee's own name or in undersigned's name to take such legal proceedings or otherwise as undersigned might have taken save for this assignment, (b) against all other parties, other than the Buyer named in said instrument, obligated for the indebtedness set forth thereon, whether so obligated by said instrument, said note or notes or otherwise, and (c) in and to the property described in said instrument. Undersigned guarantees payment in accordance with the terms of the foregoing Guaranty.

The undersigned warrants that the within instrument is genuine and in all respects what it purports to be; that all statements therein contained are true; that the said instrument and the accompanying note or notes are genuine, collectible, enforceable, and the only instrument and notes executed for the property described herein; that at the time of the execution of this assignment the undersigned had good title to the property covered thereby and the right to transfer title thereto; that said property has been delivered and accepted in accordance with the terms of said instrument; that all parties to the said instrument have capacity to contract and that the undersigned has no knowledge of any facts which impair the validity of said instrument or render it less valuable; and warrants compliance with all filing and recording requirements; that title to the said property originated with the undersigned and not with the buyer, and that prior to the execution of the said instrument, the Buyer did not either directly or indirectly have any interest in the property described therein, that the down payment was made by the buyer in cash or as otherwise specifically stated in the instrument and that no part thereof was advanced by the undersigned to the Buyer and that undersigned will not advance any part of the unpaid purchase price, and that the Buyer has not and will not either directly or indirectly receive from or through the undersigned any part of the consideration for this assignment. The undersigned shall have no authority to accept collections, repossess the equipment or modify the terms of the note or instrument. Notice of acceptance hereof is hereby waived.

Dated: ....

....
Seller-Dealer

By ....

Its ....

Fig. 7-2. Purchase Money Security Agreement—Continued

MASTER DEALER AGREEMENT

To: XYZ FINANCIAL CORPORATION
PARK AVENUE
NEW YORK, N.Y.

...............................19....

1. From time to time we desire to sell you certain notes, chattel mortgages, conditional sale agreements, lease agreements and other obligations (all herein called 'paper') endorsed or assigned by us all of which we hereby warrant will be valid and enforcible deferred payment obligations, in accordance with the terms thereof, of the respective debtors to whom we have leased or sold merchandise, and which we further warrant are not subject to any disputes, set-offs, counter-claims, or right of return. You are not obligated hereunder to buy any paper which is not acceptable to you, but when any such paper is sold to you, the terms and conditions of this Master Dealer Agreement shall apply to each such sale.

2. (a) We represent and warrant that any paper sold to you will have resulted from the sale or lease of our own property. We further represent and warrant that any merchandise covered by said paper shall have been unconditionally accepted by the debtors and that at the time of the assignment of any paper by us to you the merchandise will be in the possession of the debtor and will be the identical merchandise described in the paper. We agree to complete and fully carry out the terms of any and all agreements and warranties in respect to servicing the merchandise, the sale of which is represented by paper sold to you.

(b) Your rights and remedies hereunder shall be cumulative and you may exercise any right or remedy, whether against the debtors under the paper, against the security therefor, against the sums withheld or retained by you hereunder, against us or against any combination of the foregoing, in such order as you see fit without thereby releasing any other right you may have.

(c) You do not assume any obligation or liability of ours in respect to any paper or otherwise and we will hold you harmless from and against any expense or liability incurred by you as the result of any obligation, liability or action of ours.

(d) In the event that any paper sold to you be rejected or returned by the debtor named therein, or come into our possession for any reason whatsoever, we agree to hold the same separate and apart from merchandise and property of our own, in trust for you, and we agree to notify you immediately of such fact, and to continue to hold the said merchandise in trust for you pending your instructions as to its disposition.

3. You shall have the sole right to make collections on all paper and to notify each debtor of our assignment to you. We agree not to solicit or make any collections with respect to any paper sold to you except pursuant to your written instructions, and to forward to you promptly all communications, inquiries and the identical remittances which we may receive with reference to said paper, and you may endorse our name upon any checks, notes, money orders or other commercial paper received in payment upon said paper.

4. The purchase price of each paper accepted by you will be the unpaid face amount thereof (in the case of a lease, the aggregate of the unpaid monthly rental payments) less the appropriate discount specified in Paragraph 9 hereof. At the time of purchase you will pay to us ......% of the unpaid face amount of each paper from which there will be deducted the amount of your discount. The balance of the purchase price is to be retained by you as a reserve and held in a general Reserve Fund.

5. The Reserve Fund may be used by you to pay any defaults and losses which may occur upon any and all paper purchased by you from us. You may, but are not required, to charge against such Reserve Funds at any time in your discretion any sum or sums which may at any time become due and be payable to you through transactions with us, whether under the terms of this agreement or not.

(a) Unless we specifically request in writing the reassignment of any paper held by you which is charged against the Reserve Fund, said paper shall be held by you as part of the Reserve Fund and any collections upon such paper shall be added to and treated as part of said Reserve Fund.

(b) The Reserve Fund may also be used by you to pay or satisfy any loss, cost, damage or expense which you may suffer or incur by reason of any breach by us of any provision of this agreement or of any provision of any assignment of paper as contemplated hereunder.

(c) So long as we are not in default under any of the terms and conditions of this agreement, you agree to pay us from the Reserve Fund the original sum withheld from the purchase price of each paper when said paper has been paid in full.

(d) In the event we stop selling paper to you or you stop buying paper from us for a period exceeding ninety (90) days, you may hold and apply the Reserve Fund until all paper purchased from us and all debts and obligations owed to you by us have been paid in full.

6. We guarantee that all paper which we sell to you, and each installment thereof, will be paid on or before its maturity. In case of default or non-payment of any such paper or any installment thereof we will immediately pay you the entire unpaid balance of such paper, without first requiring you to exhaust the security or to proceed against the debtor or other obligor. In the event we should fail to pay such amount promptly on demand, or should otherwise fail to perform any obligation to you, we agree, upon your demand, to pay you the entire unpaid balance of all paper which we may have sold to you, whether or not such paper is in default. We further agree to pay all attorney fees,

Fig. 7-3. Full-Recourse Dealer Agreement

late charges and other collection expenses you may may incur to enforce this guarantee or any paper we may sell you. We waive notice of acceptance hereof, non-payment, presentment, demand, protest and notice of protest and all other notices otherwise required to be given to us or to any other person, and agree that our liability shall not be affected, or impaired by any extension, settlement, compromise, or release of any contract debtor or other obligor in connection with any paper, you may make, grant, or effect to or with any debtor or obligor on such paper, nor by any release or failure to enforce any security. The waiver of any default hereunder shall not operate as a waiver of successive defaults, but all rights hereunder shall continue notwithstanding one or more waivers. This agreement shall inure to and bind our respective legal representatives, successors and assigns, and any company affiliated with you which may transact business hereunder. All paper shall be assigned or endorsed by us in such form as you may require, but should any such assignment be omitted or incomplete, you or an officer or employee of your company may place or complete the necessary or appropriate assignment or endorsement thereon.

7. You or your representatives shall have the right to audit our books and records at any time. We will give you, in such detail as you may request, written reports on all sales, and collections, if any, on all paper sold to you hereunder. We will also furnish any other accounting which you may request from time to time. Every .... months after the date hereof or oftener if you so request, we will furnish you financial and operating statements and reports on our current operations and conditions, and will furnish you when issued copies of all audited statements of our financial condition and operations.

8. We understand that for our convenience, and without any liability on your part, you will furnish us from time to time on request such forms of conditional sales contracts, chattel mortgages, notes, or other forms as you may have approved for use in states in which we sell our products. It is understood that you do not warrant or represent that such forms comply with statutory requirements. You are under no obligation to file, record, re-file, or re-record any security instruments or notices; and if you should do so it is understood that such act is for your own benefit and that we will not assert any claim against you for any loss which may result from improper, inadequate or untimely filing or recording (including re-filing and re-recording).

9. With respect to all paper purchased hereunder, you shall deduct discounts from the unpaid face amount thereof as follows:

By ....% minimum discount per month per paper is $3.00.

10. The term of this agreement shall be for one year from the date hereof. Thereafter, this agreement shall continue from year to year under the same terms and conditions as herein set forth unless 30 days prior to the termination of the original terms of this agreement or 30 days prior to the termination of any of said renewal terms thereof, we shall have given you 30 days notice in writing that we do not intend to renew this agreement. You shall have the right to terminate this agreement at any time upon 30 days' notice in writing, but in the event we do not comply with any of the provisions of this agreement, this agreement may be terminated by you at once without notice.

11. (a) Neither this agreement nor any portion or provision hereof can be changed, modified, amended, waived, supplemented, discharged, cancelled or terminated orally or in any manner other than by an agreement in writing signed by the party to be charged.

(b) Each of the parties hereto does hereby waive trial by jury in any action or proceeding, of any kind or nature, in any Court, to which they may both be parties, whether arising out of, under or by reason of this agreement, or any assignment, account, or other transaction hereunder, or by reason of any other cause or dispute whatever between them, of any kind or nature.

(c) This agreement is made in the State of New York, and this agreement and all acts, agreements, assignments of accounts, transfers and transactions hereunder, and all rights of the parties hereto, shall be governed, as to all matters, by the laws of the State of New York.

....
      Corporate, Individual or Firm Name

By ....

Accepted at New York, N.Y.

This ....Day of ....19....

XYZ FINANCIAL CORPORATION

By ....

Fig. 7-3. Full-Recourse Dealer Agreement—Continued

8

Perfecting Liens Under Pre-Code Law

Monroe R. Lazere

In recent years, forty-nine of the fifty states of the United States (and the District of Columbia) have adopted the Uniform Commercial Code.[1] The advent and impact of the Code are discussed in Chapter 9. The purpose of this chapter is to describe briefly the various laws that governed commercial transactions in different states before the wide adoption of the Code. It will serve as historical background for the types of questions covered by the Code and illustrate the former complexity of the problems. Further, measured in terms of the history of law, the Code is new. Institutionally, there probably will remain in common parlance for several years an overlap or overtone of pre-Code vocabulary and reference. Thereafter, of course, this particular discussion may well be rendered obsolete. At present, it seems worthwhile as a means of adjusting the text to the normal social lag, as well as to provide some background understanding of the matrix from which the Code was developed. Perhaps Shakespeare summarized this notion best: "What is past is prologue."

PROBLEMS IN ASSURING FINANCER'S ACCESS TO SECURITY

Financers, as previously defined, are secured lenders. Whether they are banking or non-banking institutions is here immaterial. To assure himself that he could in fact avail himself of the security or

---

[1] At this writing, only Louisiana has not.

collateral supporting his loan, the financer had to be certain that he had perfected his lien on the particular collateral.

Need for Perfected Liens

The question of perfection arose when the borrower attempted to place another lien on the same collateral. Such an attempt would sometimes give rise to two claimants to a lien on the same collateral. Double hypothecation aside, the assignment was valid between the parties, without reference to technical perfection.

The question of technical perfection of the lien also became vital under the Federal Bankruptcy Law. Indeed the question of perfection usually arose in a bankruptcy context. The borrower had become insolvent, the secured lender (then a secured creditor) asserted his claim to the collateral and might be challenged by the unsecured creditors (or their representative, a trustee in bankruptcy or a receiver). The most frequent basis of the challenge was a claimed failure by the secured lender-creditor to perfect his lien. In essence, the question was whether the secured lender had performed all of the steps required by law. These legal steps were set forth in the state law by which the transaction was governed.

Law Governing Transactions

Which law governed the transaction sometimes presented a question in itself. The perfection of real estate mortgages was and is invariably governed by the law of the state in which the real estate is located. Inventory and equipment loans were usually perfected as prescribed by the law of the state in which such tangible collateral was located. Accounts receivable, however, are a form of intangible, conceptual property whose "location" was variously held to be in the place (1) where the account-creditor was, or (2) where the account-debtor was, or (3) where the tangible evidence thereof—i.e., the accounts receivable ledger—was maintained. (The Code adopts criterion number 3). In some cases, the parties were permitted to agree contractually to apply still another law, usually the law of the state in which the lender had his office.

Thus the procedure of perfecting liens on his collateral was rather complex and hazardous for the financer prior to the Code. First, he had to select the particular state whose law was applicable. Then, he was required to ascertain the requirements of that state's law with respect to perfecting his lien on the particular collateral involved. The three major types of collateral utilized by financers were and are accounts receivable, inventory, and equipment. All of these were and are personal property. Real estate loans are omitted from this discussion.

ACCOUNTS RECEIVABLE

Rules for Perfecting Liens

With respect to the perfection of liens upon accounts receivable, there were three significant views. Some states had adopted, by judicial decision, the old common-law rule known as the English Rule. It required notification to the account debtor (the borrower's customer) to perfect the lien. In the event, therefore, of two assignments of the same receivable, the first assignee to notify prevailed. Other states had adopted another view known as the American Rule. Under this rule, the written assignment for consideration was itself sufficient without further steps being required. This made possible what was known as the non-notification form of accounts receivable financing. While several states adopted the rule by judicial decision, many adopted it by statutory enactments referred to as validation statutes. New York and New Jersey were among the states adopting the American Rule by judicial decision. Massachusetts and Connecticut were among those adopting it by statute. The effect of the American Rule was to enable the first assignee to prevail, regardless of which of several assignees first notified the account debtor. Some twenty-two states formerly followed this rule.

The third significant rule for the perfection of liens on accounts receivable took the form of a recordation statute, which required the lender to file, in a specified government office, notice of intention to finance receivables of a particular borrower. Such a filing thus became a prerequisite to perfection. This requirement at one time obtained in some twenty-one states.

One state—North Dakota—required the assignor's books of account to be marked to set forth the details of the assignment. This idiosyncratic rule was patently an extremely difficult method of perfection for the lender to undertake.

The American Rule with its ease and simplicity encouraged the development of non-notification financing. Certain objections were, nevertheless, voiced against it by some credit men. The charge was made that it constituted a "hidden lien" which was abhorrent to American jurisprudence and prejudicial to general (unsecured) creditors.

Such discounting of receivables, it was urged, would enable the borrower to dissipate his funds, to the detriment of suppliers. Close analysis, however, readily reveals the fallacy of this line of reasoning.

Receivables financing merely accelerates the flow of cash from the receivables. In theory, the borrower could achieve the same acceleration by offering attractive discounts to his customers for much more rapid payment. It is the borrower's use of the money thereafter that determines the effect on the position of the general creditors. The mere acceleration of the borrower's receipt of the proceeds of his receivables via the financer does not *ipso facto* prejudice his general creditors.

Dominion and Control

One other pre-Code requirement relating to the financing of accounts receivable should here be mentioned. This had to do with the question of dominion and control over the receivables. The question arose in the case of *Benedict* vs. *Ratner*.[2] It was decided by the United States Supreme Court in 1925 and held that an assignee of receivables lost his lien thereon if he permitted the assignor to deal with the receivables as though they were his own, i.e., to utilize for his own purposes the proceeds of the receivables without any arrangement for applying the proceeds to repay the loan or any obligation to account for the collections. The Court held that the assignor's complete exercise of dominion and control over the receivables was inconsistent with the assignee's claim of a lien thereon. The Court's conclusion was that to accept and claim an assignment of receivables while permitting the assignor to deal with the receivables as though they were his own constituted a fraud on creditors and voided the assignment.

The *Benedict* vs. *Ratner* case give rise to much discussion as to whether it required the financer to obtain, in kind, the checks of its borrower's account debtors. The consensus was that the doctrine only required a transfer of proceeds from borrower to lender. That is, if the borrower had deposited the checks of its account debtors into its own account and then promptly transferred the same amount by its own check to the financer, sufficient dominion and control would have been exercised. Nevertheless most financers required their borrowers to remit the account debtors' checks in kind. This was done, however, not for legal reasons but for administrative reasons.

[2] 268 U.S. 353.

It provides closer supervision for the financer. Hence even currently, although the Code eliminates the dominion-and-control doctrine, financers usually require delivery to them of the account debtors' checks. This subject is discussed more fully in Chapter 3 (see page 49).

Purchaser's Prohibition of Assignment

Prior to the Code, another possible restriction sometimes prevented the perfection of the assignment of accounts. This arose where the purchaser included in his purchase order a prohibition against the assignment of the receivable created by delivery of the order. The purchaser may have wished to avoid possible confusion in the event that he would wish to claim an off-set against his supplier. Or a large organization may have feared that a notice of the assignment might be overlooked and payment improperly made to the assignor, resulting in the account debtor's also being liable to the assignee. For whatever reason the purchaser inserted such a provision, the New York courts upheld its validity,[3] and several other states followed this view. Not surprisingly, the exact language of particular prohibitions then became important. If the language stated that such an assignment was void, then a trustee in bankruptcy could claim the proceeds, for the attempted assignment was ineffectual. If the language of the purchase order merely prohibited the seller from assigning the receivable, then such assignment would be considered a violation of seller's promise but it would not be void. The purchaser then would have to resort to action for damages against the seller, who at that point would probably be bankrupt. Known as the *Caristo* doctrine, the legal power of the account debtor to restrict the assignability of accounts receivable has been expressly eliminated by the Uniform Commercial Code.

Factoring

As has been indicated in prior chapters, the factoring arrangement entails the purchase of receivables by the factor from the client. Since no pledge or lien was involved, the question of perfection of a lien on the collateral arose. But merchandise returned by the account debtors belonged to the factor until the client (shipper) repurchased it. To maintain a legal hold on such merchandise during that period, factors frequently considered that perfection

---

[3] *Allhusen* v. *Caristo Construction Corp.*, 303 N.Y. 446 (1952).

of the assignment gave them title to the receivables and the merchandise. Under the American rule no problem arose. Under the English rule, no problem arose since factors normally notified the account debtors, as more fully described elsewhere (page 82). In states operating under recordation statutes, however, the more cautious factors complied with the requirements thereof.

INVENTORY

In connection with inventory loans, the pre-Code law again presented a melange of requirements. Various states had different requirements on the subject, as well as different terminology. In some states, for example, a "chattel mortgage" could be obtained on inventory, while in other states such a device was available only as a lien on equipment. This discussion uses the pre-Code law of New York State as the chief prototype. This is justifiable on the ground that a large volume of transactions were conducted under that law, since New York was and is the home office of many finance companies and factors. Further, many new refinements of law and technique have been developed there.

Common Law Pledge

The simplest type of inventory loan involved no filing or complicated legal requirements. This was the common law pledge, and it still exists in the pawnshop type of loan. Here the lender took physical possession of the article and advanced the agreed amount. In order to redeem the article, the borrower had to repay the agreed amount. Inventory lending in commercial enterprises was and is patently somewhat more complex. Nevertheless, the legal theory could be similarly satisfied. The merchandise inventory could be delivered to a public warehouse and held there for the account of the lender, to be released only with his written consent. In legal contemplation, the common law pledge was thereby effected commercially.

A variation of this arrangement—and much more practical commercially—was the development of the field warehouse. Under this arrangement, a warehouse company leased a portion of the borrower's premises, which was physically separated from the remainder of such premises, and there set up a warehouse. Receipts were issued in the normal way. A fundamental legal requirement was that the field warehouse area be designated by signs indicating the existence of a field-warehouse arrangement. The theory was that any creditor of the borrower who visited the borrower's premises and saw an impressive amount of inventory would thus be put on notice that the portion in a specified area was not unqualifiedly the property of the borrower. Again, a fear of hidden liens was behind this requirement.

Factor's Lien

This fear of hidden liens led to some confusion in connection with the requirements for a factor's lien. Such a lien was defined in Section 45 of the Personal Property Law of New York and permitted a lien on borrower's inventory, present and future, and wherever located. The factor's lien (which could also be held by a non-factor) also attached to the accounts receivable generated by the sale of the merchandise. Written agreements were required, and notices had to be filed in any county or town or city in which the liened merchandise was located. In addition, a notice had to be filed in the county, city, or town in which the lender had his office. The reason for the last requirement was obscure, since the purpose of the filing was to put creditors of the borrower on notice.

And in many states—including New York—an additional step was necessary. A sign was required to be posted on the borrower's premises setting forth the name of the factor or lender (lienor). This requirement quickly led to some mischief. Periodic inspections could be made by the lender to assure the presence of the sign. But shortly after such a visit, the wind or the borrower could bring the sign down. Some lenders developed the practice of taking pictures of the sign, but this obviously was useful only as of a given moment. However, since the filing of notice had already given notice to the world of the existence of a lien on the borrower's inventory, the sign posting was a truly superfluous source of technical attack upon perfection of the lien. New York therefore soon repealed this provision.

Trust Receipt

The security device known as the trust receipt was generally utilized by lenders to create or maintain a lien, during short transitory stages, on inventory or documents of title representing inventory. The usual transition was to effectuate a change of location or physical character of the merchandise or the changing of the documents representing the merchandise into the actual merchandise. The Uniform Trust Receipts Act was adopted by a majority of the states, including New York. It also provided for the protection of a lender secured by negotiable instruments when they had to be transported, deposited, registered, or the like. This discussion focuses on trust receipts involving merchandise or documents of title representing merchandise.

For a valid lien on merchandise, new value had to be given at the time the borrower obtained possession of the merchandise from either the lender or a third party. If the borrower already had possession of the merchandise, a valid trust receipt could not be created. Likewise in the case of documents, a trust receipt could be created when the lender advanced new value at the time the borrower obtained possession of the documents from the lender or third party. With respect to documents only, a valid trust receipt could also be created if the documents initially were in possession of the borrower but were exhibited to the lender at his office at the time that new value was advanced.

Nature and Filing of Instrument. The trust receipt itself was a written instrument describing the entruster (lender), the trustee (borrower), and the merchandise or documents that were the subject matter of the trust relationship. Notice to the world was given by filing a Statement of Trust Receipt Financing identifying the parties and subject matter. In New York State, filing was made with the Secretary of State of New York and could be effected thirty days after execution of the transaction. Within that period, the lien was valid as against other creditors. It could, however, be defeated by the borrower's executing another trust receipt on the same subject matter to a lender with no actual knowledge of the first trust receipt. Hence, prudence dictated prompt filing despite the liberal statutory time provision.

Sale of Inventory. The lien of the trust receipt followed into the receivables generated by the sale of the merchandise. The lender, however, was required to demand an accounting of the proceeds of the sale within ten days of his learning of such sale or his lien was extinguished. (Note the similarity here to the doctrine of *Benedict vs. Ratner* discussed above, page 199.) And finally, as with the factor's lien, the lien did not affect the rights of a purchaser of the merchandise, provided he was a bona fide purchaser for value in the normal course of business.

EQUIPMENT

Place of Filing to Perfect Lien

The state laws governing the perfection of chattel mortgage loans were varied as to signatories, notarization, witnesses, and place of filing. Almost uniformly, however, the state laws required a filing to perfect a lien on fixed assets. This again stemmed from the concept of notice to the borrower's creditors that a visible physical asset was encumbered and therefore not unqualifiedly the property of the borrower. In New York State the filing was required in the county where the chattels were located—a reasonable requirement. Less logical and a frequent source of claim of failure of perfection was the requirement that a filing be made in the county of the borrower's residence. For corporations, this meant the county of incorporation. Frequently the county of incorporation might be the county in which the original incorporating lawyer had his office, but with which the operating corporation had no further contact or had long since lost contact. Nevertheless, a failure to file in such county could result in a lender's loss of his collateral.

Holder of Title to Collateral

For filing purposes, there was no distinction between a chattel mortgage and a conditional sales contract. The conditional sales contract—usually arising out of the purchase of additional (usually new) equipment—left title in the seller until payments were completed. Default in payment would enable the seller (or financer) to repossess the equipment. In a chattel mortgage, title was initially in the borrower. The lender took the mortgage on the equipment to secure a loan, leaving title (in most states) in the borrower, subject to the lender's right to take possession thereof upon default in the borrower's scheduled payments. In both types, the written agreement was enforceable as between the parties. But failure to properly perfect the lender's security interest on the equipment left the door open to an attack upon such interest on the part of the creditors.

Time of Filing

The time of filing also involved some legal niceties. At one time New York provided for a filing within a reasonable time after the consummation of the transaction. What constituted a reasonable time could become a subject productive of litigation. This statute was later amended to provide that a filing within ten days after execution would be effective as of the date of execution. Filing thereafter would be effective as of the actual date of filing.

How these variations on the theme of perfection of liens for various types of collateral were fused into a major harmony is described in the discussion of the Uniform Commercial Code in Chapter 9.

9

Secured Transactions Under the Uniform Commercial Code

Eli S. Silberfeld
Partner, Kupfer, Silberfeld, Nathan and Danziger

HISTORICAL BACKGROUND

According to the dictionary, a "code" is a systematic collection of the laws, rules, and regulations applicable to or governing one or more topics or activities. The Uniform Commercial Code is a code, as its name indicates, and it is applicable to a very broad range of topics and activities that make up the daily life of the modern business and financial community. Known familiarly by its initials as the U.C.C., it is a monumental piece of work, and it has had a significant impact on commercial financing.

The Advent of Civil Codes

Uniform laws are no novelty in human history. The archeologists tell us that as soon as men began to organize themselves into families, clans, tribes, nations, and empires, codes appeared. The early codes were apparently concerned principally with religious and moral affairs, and with the penalties imposed for violation of the rules. As trade and commerce began to develop, and governmental units grew larger, civil topics began to appear in the codes. When the Kingdom of Babylonia acquired political, intellectual, and commercial control over most of western Asia, it promulgated a set of uniform laws known as The Code of Hammurabi which contained nearly 300 laws. They covered crimes and taxes, of course; but they also touched on family law, sales, property rights, civil rights, loans, interest rates, pledges of security, and even guaranties. Those last items sound rather "modern" indeed.

So far as is known, there never was a code devoted exclusively to *civil* matters until Napoleon promulgated the *Code Civil des Francais* in 1804. The Code Napoléon is therefore the direct ancestor of all subsequent uniform civil laws, including the U.C.C. It had a vast effect on the civil codes thereafter adopted, such as the German Civil Code of 1895. Substantive traces of the Code Napoléon can still be found in the laws of Louisiana—which, of course, was a French possession in Napoleon's time.

Uniform Laws in the United States

In the United States, the basic legal climate was not favorable to the development of civil codes or uniform laws. We inherited the English common-law system, under which commercial law was a gradual accumulation of court decisions rendered over a period of centuries, resembling the growth of a living organism. By contrast, a code is created as a complete, systematized entity when it is enacted by a legislature. The transition from a common-law to a code point of view has been difficult, because it requires a complete change of approach.

In addition, our Federal union is a group of sovereign states, each of which jealously reserves control over its own local matters.

As a result there was increasing diversity in commercial law as among the various states, which in the early days was not too serious. However, when interstate trade and commerce mushroomed during the nineteenth century, merchants and bankers found themselves facing a chaotic situation. Finally, the lawyers stepped in about seventy-five years ago and started the uniform laws movement. A semiofficial group called the National Conference of Commissioners on Uniform State Laws was organized, and began the difficult process of drafting uniform laws. Among the earliest were the Negotiable Instruments Law (which dates back to 1896) and the Uniform Sales Act. New York State adopted them in 1909 and 1911 respectively, and within a few years they were enacted by practically all the rest of the states. Other uniform laws followed, including some of particular interest to the commercial finance industry, such as the Uniform Conditional Sales Act, the Uniform Trust Receipts Law, and a Factor's Lien Act which emanated from New York State in 1911.

Everything seemed to be going well; but some scholars have noted that one of the salient characteristics of uniform laws, at least in this country, is that they are not necessarily uniform, even though they hopefully start out that way. Many of those mentioned were enacted with local variations, with the result that, after a few years, the commercial finance and factoring industry, along with businessmen generally, came to realize that the ideal of uniformity in the civil laws governing commercial and financial transactions was proving to be a frustrating illusion.

Recognizing the situation, about twenty-five years ago the American Law Institute started the U.C.C. project in conjunction with the National Conference of Commissioners on Uniform State Laws. It took ten years for a talented and dedicated group of lawyers to draft the U.C.C. The first state to adopt it was Pennsylvania, in 1954, and practically every state has followed suit. The U.C.C. went into effect in New York in 1964. References to the U.C.C. hereafter will be to the version in effect in New York State, which is substantially representative of the code elsewhere.

REGULATION OF SECURED TRANSACTIONS

Scope of the Code

The U.C.C. is only a single-volume work, but it touches just about every legal question that a businessman, manufacturer, banker, or commercial financer is likely to encounter in the ordinary course of his operations. It is a compilation of statutory law, divided into nine Articles. Briefly, these Articles cover and codify the following topics, as to each of which the U.C.C. in general supersedes all prior statutory or common law:

Article 1 states the purpose and policy of the U.C.C. and contains definitions of a number of words and phrases, some of them previously in general use and some quite novel.

Article 2 covers *Sales* of goods. It does not cover transactions involving land.

Article 3, which is entitled *Commercial Paper,* deals with checks, drafts, notes, trade acceptances, and other instruments that evidence obligations to pay money or are the means by which money is transferred from one party to another.

Article 4 covers *Bank Deposits and Collections.* It sets out the rules of law that come into play when the holder of a check or other instrument deposits it with his bank to be collected for him.

Article 5, entitled *Letters of Credit,* covers the rules applicable to the majority of import and export transactions in which the buyer of goods supplies the shipper with a letter of credit—that is, an undertaking by a bank to pay the shipper for the goods shipped to the buyer.

Article 6, *Bulk Transfers,* is the set of rules covering the situation in which a businessman sells his business without notifying or taking care of his creditors. It specifies how and to what extent the buyer may become liable to the creditors if the transaction is not properly handled.

Article 7 is entitled *Warehouse Receipts, Bills of Lading, and Other Documents of Title.* When goods are put into a warehouse, the warehouse company issues a warehouse receipt acknowledging that it has received the goods and is holding them. When goods are delivered to a railroad, or a trucking company, or a steamship line, or an air-freight carrier, a similar receipt is given, which is called a bill of lading. Article 7 spells out the rights and obligations of the issuers, holders, and transferees of such documents representing goods.

Article 8 deals with *Investment Securities.* These are stocks, bonds, or debentures issued by corporations. Article 8 defines them and the rights and interests they represent, and tells how they are issued and transferred.

Article 9 is entitled *Secured Transactions; Sales of Accounts, Contract Rights and Chattel Paper.* This is the Article with which we are primarily concerned, because it is the modern-day Bible of the commercial finance and factoring industry.

We will now consider the theory and approach of Article 9 and its impact on commercial financing—which has been considerable indeed. To simplify the discussion of that impact, only *business* financing, such as is extended to manufacturers, jobbers, and other wholesale businesses, will be discussed. Consumer finance is a distinct topic in itself and subject to somewhat different rules and techniques.

Provisions of Article 9

The philosophy of the U.C.C. as a whole, and of Article 9 in particular, is expressed at the outset:

The underlying purposes and policies of this Act are to simplify, clarify, and modernize the law governing commercial transactions . . . [and] to make uniform the law among the various jurisdictions.[1]

To accomplish these purposes in the commercial financing field, the draftsmen of Article 9 took four significant steps. These involved the removal of procedural differences, unification of nomenclature, and the establishment of the concepts of perfecting security interests and universal notice filing.

Abolition of Legal Distinctions. Article 9 abolishes the welter of fine legal and procedural distinctions that existed among the various types of financing. Until Article 9 arrived on the scene, there was a different common-law or statutory formula for the creation and consummation of practically every type of financing device, and scarcely any two States had even the same set of formulas.

For example, in pre-Code days accounts receivable financing was done in some places merely by taking written assignments; in others, filing in a public office was required; in still others, notification had to be sent to the people whose accounts were being assigned; and in one or two states notations of the assignments had to be entered in the assignor's accounts receivable ledgers. Considering that accounts receivable are now being financed or factored at the rate of many billions of dollars each year, and that the financing agency, the borrower, and the account-debtors are often located in different states, it is obvious that the parties would have to hack their way through a legal jungle in order to handle the business and that the risk—and the cost—would be enormously increased if the former diversity of law still existed.

Another example is the wholesale financing of automobiles—a very large and important item in our economy. Prior to the U.C.C., it was handled in some places under trust receipts; in states that did not recognize trust receipts, conditional sales were used; but where the state law did not recognize conditional sale agreements, the parties had to resort to the questionable chattel mortgage route. Each of those security devices required different documentation; some re-

---

[1] Sec. 1–102. All section references in this chapter are to the Uniform Commercial Code.

quired public filing, and others did not; and even the place of filing varied.

Article 9 recognizes that, in our complex and fast-moving economy, financing methods have to be tailor-made to fit the needs and practices of the particular industry being financed and that new models are introduced from time to time as the economy grows and changes. Article 9 also recognizes that, regardless of their widely varying details, all financing devices are fundamentally alike and have the same fundamental objective. So, says Article 9, let them all be treated alike in the law, and let them all be labeled alike so that the old artificial distinctions will be eliminated.

Accordingly, Article 9 recites that it applies

. . . to any transaction (regardless of its form) which is intended to create a security interest. . . . [2]

What this declaration means, as a practical matter, is that people engaged in the business of commercial financing can concentrate on being businessmen and no longer need concern themselves with such abstruse legal problems as conflicts of laws or the nice distinctions between chattel mortgages and conditional sales contracts. Article 9 states that all security devices have equal legal stature and that under the U.C.C. the laws of all the states are uniform. In such a context, the operating and executive personnel of commercial finance companies and factors can focus all their attention on operating problems and business risks; they no longer have to be part-time lawyers or amateur metaphysicians.

UNIFORM NOMENCLATURE. Pursuing this underlying philosophy, Article 9 brushes aside the complicated terminology that has developed over the years. When a transaction is set up, it is no longer necessary to make a meticulous, and sometimes hazardous, selection of appropriate words and phrases to identify the parties or to spell out the legal intent of the documentation. Article 9, in effect, eliminates from the working vocabulary such items as factor, lender, lienor, mortgagee, entruster, conditional vendor, borrower, customer, mortgagor, trustee, conditional vendee, pledge, assignment, sale, hypothecation, discount, security, chattel mortgage, conditional sale agreement, financing agreement, factoring agreement, and many others. Instead, the U.C.C. supplies a basic vocabulary for *all* financing and factoring transactions. The principal ones are these:

[2] Sec. 9–102(1)

1. *Security interest*—"an interest in personal property or fixtures which secures payment or performance of an obligation."
2. *Secured party*—"a lender, seller or other person in whose favor there is a security interest, including a person to whom accounts, contract rights or chattel paper have been sold."
3. *Debtor*—"the person who owes payment or other performance of the obligation secured, whether or not he owns or has rights in the collateral . . . includes the seller of accounts, contract rights or chattel paper."
4. *Security agreement*—"an agreement which creates or provides for a security interest."
5. *Collateral*—"the property subject to a security interest . . . includes accounts, contract rights and chattel paper which have been sold."

The Concept of Perfection. Article 9 covers *secured* transactions. This means transactions in which the secured party intends to obtain collateral that is not only of adequate value but also legally valid. The law books are full of cases in which the legal right of secured parties to keep and realize upon their collateral has been lost on absurdly technical and flimsy grounds; and in many instances, secured parties have found, to their chagrin, that their collateral position was destroyed because they had inadvertently failed to take the right legal steps. These unfavorable results should not be too surprising in view of the confusion and diversity in the statutory law and the court decisions.

To correct this frustrating situation, Article 9 propounds the concept of "perfection." It does so by spelling out in precise terms the steps necessary to obtain a perfected security interest in the collateral. It says that a security interest becomes perfected—that is, legally effective and immune to attack—when all those specified steps have been taken.[3] In the typical commercial financing case there are four such steps, which can be taken in any order:

1. The secured party and the debtor sign a security agreement which spells out the terms of their arrangement and describes the collateral.
2. The collateral comes into existence.
3. The secured party makes an advance to the debtor.
4. The secured party files a financing statement.

Article 9 thus tells secured parties what they must do to perfect their collateral and protect it against attack. Of the four steps speci-

---

[3] Sec. 9–303(1).

fied, the filing of a financing statement is really the only procedural novelty.

Notice Filing. The concept of notice filing rounds out the new image of commercial financing under Article 9. It means that, in order to perfect his security interest in collateral left in the debtor's possession (as it usually is in most types of financing or factoring), the secured party must put a financing statement on file in a specified public office where it is available for public inspection.

The financing statement is a simple printed form. It shows the names and addresses of the secured party and the debtor and describes the type or types of the collateral involved. It gives official notice to all the world that the secured transactions are going on, and thus it protects all parties concerned against fraud and other perils that might be encountered if the transactions were kept secret. Most important, it assures the secured party that his collateral has been perfected and is safe from attack.

The Financing Statement and Related Forms

The financing statement form and two other related printed forms in use in New York are prescribed by the Secretary of State of New York, and are available at stationers and printers. The following example will serve to demonstrate actual financing statement procedures that would be employed in a typical case.

John Jones is an officer of Jones Finance Corp., which is a commercial financer and factor. Jones Finance Corp. is about to enter into a security agreement with Smith Manufacturing Corp., a producer of widgets. The collateral will be the inventory of Smith Manufacturing Corp. (that is, the metals and other components used in the manufacture of widgets, the partially finished widgets, and the finished widgets packed and ready for shipment) and the accounts receivable created when Smith Manufacturing Corp. ships widgets to its customers.

At the outset, Jones' first concern is to find out whether there are any financing statements already on file against Smith Manufacturing Corp. This inquiry is important, because if someone else is already on file with respect to Smith's inventory or accounts, Jones will not be able to perfect his proposed security interest in those types of collateral unless he or Smith can persuade the previous secured party to terminate his financing statement.

Inquiry is made by using Form UCC-11 (see Fig. 9–1). Once the field has been cleared, Jones is ready to proceed with his financing statement.   This is Form UCC-1 (Fig. 9–2).

With the financing statement duly filed and the security agreement with Smith Manufacturing Corp. duly signed, Jones can go ahead with the transactions, knowing that he has and will continue to have a perfected security interest in the collateral under Article 9.   Surely, this simple and uniform procedure represents a spectacular improvement over the former crazy quilt of rules which required one to file different types of documents depending upon what kind of financing he was extending and what type of collateral he was receiving, which even varied the place of filing from one transaction to the next, and which in some cases (such as accounts receivable financing) did not provide for any filing at all.   Certainty has indeed been substituted for uncertainty.

Finally, after a long and satisfactory relationship, Jones' arrangements are terminated, Smith Manufacturing Corp. pays Jones what they owe him, and Jones releases his security interest on the record. This is accomplished by using Form UCC-3 (Fig. 9–3).

THE IMPACT OF ARTICLE 9

Practical Benefits

From the practical point of view, Article 9 has exerted a beneficial influence upon commercial financing in a number of respects.   The notice-filing concept, implemented by the filing of financing statements, has removed the mass of problems formerly existing as to the proper method of perfecting security interests.   Precision has been substituted for confusion.

Article 9 has abolished the legal distinctions that formerly existed among the many types of financing agreements, but a commercial financer or factor is still free to use any of the forms of agreements that he developed in pre-Code days, with scarcely any changes being required.   In this way, he retains the ability to mold each transaction in such form as will best serve the practical needs of the situation, and he no longer has to worry about whether he has selected the proper label for it: Under Article 9, every type of security agreement creates a security interest and thus affords the secured party the legal protection that he wants.

In earlier times, the legal path of commercial financing was lib-

REQUEST FOR COPIES OR INFORMATION. Present in DUPLICATE to Filing Officer.

1. Debtor (Last Name First) and Address	Party requesting information or copies: (Name and Address)	For Filing Officer, Date, Time, No.-Filing Office
Smith Manufacturing Corp. 1 South Street Southville, New York	John Jones 2 North Street Northville, N. Y.	

☒ INFORMATION REQUEST: ☒ COPY REQUEST:

Filing officer please furnish certificate showing if there is on file under the code as of ___April 13,___ , 19 X6 at ___9:00___ A. M., any presently effective financing statement filed pursuant to the UCC naming the above named debtor and any statement of assignment thereof, and if there is, giving the date and hour of filing of each such statement and the name(s) and address(es) of each secured party(ies) therein. Enclosed is uniform fee of $3.00.

Filing officer please furnish exact copies of each page of financing statements and statements of assignment listed below, at the rate of $1.00 each, which are on file with your office. Enclosed is $ _1.00_ fee for copies requested. In case any of said statements contain more than one page the undersigned agrees to pay the sum of $1.00 for each additional page payable in advance.

Date ___April 12, 19X6___   _John Jones_ (Signature of Requesting Party)

File No.	Date and Hour of Filing	Name(s) and Address(es) of Secured Party(ies) and Assignee(s), if any
12345	Feb. 2, 19X6 10: A.M.	XYZ Truck Co., Main St., Southville, N.Y.
12467	Feb. 3, 19X6 9:30 AM	XYZ Adding Mach. Co., POB 12, Albany, N.Y.
12774	Feb. 7, 19X6 9:30 AM	XYZ Trading Co., Broadway, New York, N.Y.

CERTIFICATE: The undersigned filing officer hereby certifies that:

☒ the above listing is a record of all presently effective financing statements and statements of assignment which name the above debtor and which are on file in my office as of ___April 13,___ , 19 X6 at _9:00_ ___A.___ M.

☒ the attached _3_ pages are true and exact copies of all available financing statements or statements of assignment listed in above request;

___April 15, 19X6___   _A. B., Deputy Secy of State_
Date   By (Deputy) Filing Officer
                                   Signature of Filing Officer

COPY 1

(9/65) NY STANDARD FORM - FORM UCC-11 — Approved by John P. Lomenzo, Secretary of State of New York

Fig. 9-1. Request for Copies or Information: Form UCC-11

This FINANCING STATEMENT is presented to a Filing Officer for filing pursuant to the Uniform Commercial Code.

No. of Additional Sheets Presented:		3. Maturity Date (optional):

1. Debtor(s) (Last Name First) and Address(es):

Smith Manufacturing Corp.,
1 South Street
Southville, New York

2. Secured Party(ies): Name(s) and Address(es):

Jones Finance Corp.,
2 North Street,
Northville, New York

4. For Filing Officer: Date, Time, No. Filing Office

April 18, 19X6 9:30 AM
Number 12345
Department of State of
New York

5. This Financing Statement covers the following types (or items) of property:

-- All inventory, present and hereafter acquired.

-- All accounts and contract rights, present and hereafter created.

☒ Proceeds are also covered.   ☒ Products of the Collateral are also covered.

8. Describe Real Estate Here:

6. Assignee(s) of Secured Party and Address(es)

7. ☐ The described crops are growing or to be grown on.*
    ☐ The described goods are or are to be affixed to:.*
    *(Describe Real Estate Below):

9. Name(s) of Record Owner(s):

No. & Street	Town or City	County	Section	Block	Lot

10. This statement is filed without the debtor's signature to perfect a security interest in collateral (check appropriate box)

☐ under a security agreement signed by debtor authorizing secured party to file this statement.
☐ already subject to a security interest in another jurisdiction when it was brought into this state.
☐ which is proceeds of the original collateral described above in which a security interest was perfected:

Smith Manufacturing Corp.   Jones Finance Corp.

By *Bill Smith*   By *John Jewell*
Bill Smith (Signature(s) of Debtor(s) President   John Jones Signature(s) of Secured Party(ies) Treasurer

(1) Filing Officer Copy — Numerical

(9/65) NY STANDARD FORM - FORM UCC-1 — Approved by John P. Lomenzo, Secretary of State of New York

Fig. 9–2. Financing Statement: Form UCC–1

This STATEMENT is presented to a filing officer for filing pursuant to the Uniform Commercial Code.

1. Debtor(s) (Last Name First) and Address(es)	2. Secured Party(ies): Name(s) and Address(es):	No. of Additional Sheets Presented:	3. (optional) Maturity Date	4. For Filing Officer: Date, Time, No.-Filing Office
Smith Manufacturing Corp. 1 South Street Southville, New York	Jones Finance Corp. 2 North Street Northville, New York			Dec. 20, 19X8 9:30 A.M. Dept. of State of N.Y.

5. This statement refers to original Financing Statement No. 12345   filed (date) Apr. 18, 19X6 with Dept. of State

6.   [ ] A. Continuation   The original Financing Statement bearing the above file number is still effective.

    [X] B. Termination   The Secured Party of record no longer claims a security interest under the Financing Statement bearing the above file number.

    [ ] C. Release   From the Collateral described in the Financing Statement bearing the above file number, the Secured Party of record releases the following:

    [ ] D. Assignment   The Secured Party of record has assigned the Secured Party's rights in the property described below under the Financing Statement bearing the above file number to the Assignee whose name and address are shown below:

    [ ] E. Amendment   The Financing Statement bearing the above file number is amended as set forth below: (Signature of Debtor is required if Collateral is added.)

Section _____ Block _____ Lot _____

(fee $2.00 or $3.00 if any item is continued on an additional sheet)

Termination fee $1.00

Jones Finance Corp.

By _____ *Tom Jones*   Vice-Pres.
Tom Jones
Signature(s) of Secured Party(ies)

By _____
Signature(s) of Debtor(s) (only an amendment)

(1) Filing Officer Copy — Numerical
STANDARD FORM - FORM UCC-3 — Approved by John P. Lomenzo, Secretary of State of New York

Fig. 9–3.   Financing Statement Change: Form UCC-3

erally strewn with technical booby-traps and legal pitfalls. The draftsmen of the U.C.C. were aware of it: They noted that the finance industry had long been plagued by a sort of "fanatical and impossibly refined reading" and interpretation of statutory requirements.[4] That situation no longer prevails.[5] As one court has put it: After the Uniform Commercial Code is adopted, litigations "will not turn upon minor technicalities."[6] As an illustration of this new attitude, there was a case in that same court in which a secured party had filed a financing statement giving the name of the debtor as "Excel Department Stores." The correct name should have been "Excel Stores, Inc." In former days, such a variance might well have been fatal. Article 9, however, says that a financing statement "is effective even though it contains minor errors which are not seriously misleading,"[7] and the court accordingly held in favor of the secured party.[8] In effect, this liberal attitude means that, although persons engaged in commercial financing can never afford to be careless, they no longer have to devote a substantial portion of their time and energy to proofreading or technical legal matters.

One interesting by-product of the financing-statement system is that the financial and other details of the arrangements between secured parties and debtors can be kept strictly confidential in all cases. The financing statement (Form UCC-1, see page 216) discloses only the names of the parties and the type of collateral. It does not disclose the amount of the loans, the interest rate, or any other financial details. By contrast, in pre-Code days there were certain transactions that could not be perfected except by putting the entire agreement on public file. That was the case, for example, in chattel mortgage financing, conditional sale agreements, and lease financing.

One of the most useful innovations of Article 9 is the so-called "blanket lien." It is now possible for a security agreement to provide that the secured party shall have a continuing security interest in all the present and future collateral of the type or types specified in the agreement and in the financing statement. In the example above, Smith Manufacturing Corp. gave Jones Finance Corp., as collateral, all existing and future inventory and accounts receivable. The agreement could also have included other types of collateral,

---

[4] Sec. 9–402(5), official comment.
[5] See 50 *Cornell Law Quarterly* 128, 130, n. 29 (1964).
[6] *In re Waterbury Packing Co.*, 309 F.2d 743.
[7] Sec. 9–402(5).
[8] *In re Excel Stores, Inc.*, 341 F.2d 961.

such as existing and future machinery and equipment. Under such a blanket lien arrangement, all those types of collateral are automatically subject to the security interest as soon as they come into existence, without paper work or other formalities. No such facile device was possible prior to Article 9.

The uniformity of Article 9 tends to promote interstate finance and factoring business. As long as the parties are situated in U.C.C. states, they know what the law applicable to their transactions will be. Article 9 spells it out in precise terms,[9] and it is not necessary to puzzle over that legal mystery known as "conflicts of laws," which is surely one of the most difficult subjects in all jurisprudence. For example, Section 9-103(1) says that if a debtor maintains his accounts receivable records in New York State, then the creation of perfected security interests in his accounts receivable is governed by New York law and the financing statement must be filed in New York, even though the parties may have offices or legal or business connections in other states—as is frequently the case nowadays. Thus, a tremendous advantage is gained by the elimination of conflicts of laws questions. From the standpoint of the financing industry, it is certainly one of the most significant practical benefits of Article 9.

Psychological Impact

Article 9 has brought about a subtle and favorable change in the attitude of businessmen and courts toward commercial financing. Previously, laymen tended to regard non-notification receivables financing with suspicion as being somehow surreptitious, and to regard businessmen who were receiving such financing or factoring accommodation as being on the brink of insolvency. This attitude was unfortunately reflected in the view, occasionally expressed by unsophisticated judges, that a security interest in receivables was a "secret lien" because there was no public filing, and that it therefore was reprehensible and deserved to be struck down on some legal or equitable theory or other. Article 9 was intended to put a stop to all this. The filing of financing statements certainly disposes of the secret lien straw-man. Article 9 constitutes a forthright legitimization—if, indeed, any were needed—of the industry, and an official recognition of its vital function in our economy.

In financing circles, some people expressed the fear that the filing of financing statements under Article 9 would result in unduly fierce

[9] Sec. 9–103.

competition. Competitors, they thought, might find it very easy to check the filing records, ascertain the names and addresses of businessmen obtaining commercial financing accommodation, and then approach them to solicit their business. Whether this type of piracy has actually come about is doubtful. Indeed, it is not at all certain that it ought to be called "piracy." Competition certainly existed in the industry before Article 9 came along, and we are forever being reminded that competition is a basic ingredient of the capitalist system. Article 9 has not changed that.

The blanket lien device, just because it is so simple under Article 9, could conceivably be over-exploited. If a secured party takes far more collateral than is reasonably proportionate to his advances or if, when he is already adequately secured by one type of collateral, he nevertheless takes other types as additional—and unnecessary—coverage but makes no additional corresponding advances, he might be inflicting an unintended strangle-hold upon the debtor, choking off credit that the debtor would otherwise have available from other sources. For instance, when a debtor seeks to obtain inventory on normal credit terms, his suppliers might hesitate to ship the merchandise when their credit departments learn that practically all of his assets are subject to a security interest.

Finally, the very facility of the Article 9 procedure may expose secured parties to an unexpected peril—namely, a deterioration in the alertness and attention to detail that is vital to the success of every commercial finance or factoring organization. A secured party holding a blanket lien can very easily tend to become careless in his control procedures. He may feel that, since he has a security interest in everything, he *must* be amply collateralized. This attitude could be dangerous. A blanket lien may be relied upon only if the secured party continually watches his collateral, so as to be sure that he does not extend financing beyond what is justified by the *actual* collateral position. Just as eternal vigilance is the price of liberty, so eternal policing of collateral is the price of success in commercial financing. This was a truism in pre-Code days, and it so remains.

10

Import and Export Financing

Monroe R. Lazere

The world has become so small that international trade and finance are becoming a regular part of many business enterprises. Unfortunately, many people tend to look upon a foreign transaction as an ogre. This is a pity because the international field is one of the most challenging and rewarding in the world of business.

Like domestic sales, both import and export transactions have three major elements. They are: an agreed sales price, a time and method of delivery, and, most important, the method of payment for the goods. There are, of course, many refinements and variations of these three fundamentals, but they are always present. Since this book deals with commercial financing, the present discussion is primarily concerned with the last-mentioned item, method of payment.

In foreign transactions, for both exports and imports, four basic types of credit are extended: letter of credit, documents against payment on a collection basis through a bank, term draft, and open account. The first two types represent secured credit and the latter two unsecured credit. As will be seen, the key to the secured transactions is retention of control over the merchandise or documents of title until payment is effected.

OPEN ACCOUNT

The type of credit whose workings are most immediately obvious is open account. The seller sends the shipping documents directly

221

to the buyer who, of course, takes title to the merchandise. The buyer will pay the seller directly in accordance with the terms of the sale. This is by far the most hazardous type of credit that can be granted. It should of course be granted only to very well rated concerns. If the buyer gets into financial difficulties and cannot pay, suing him on an open account is complicated, drawn out, costly, and very cumbersome. Furthermore, whenever a foreign country gets into difficulties because of dollar shortages or related problems of exchange, this type of credit is usually the last to be honored. Decisions on this type of credit are usually based on accepted sources of credit information. Obviously, past experience is important and can within reasonable limits be relied upon. In recent years a protective device has been developed to reduce the hazards of this double exposure. It is known as F.C.I.A. insurance and is discussed below (see page 231).

LETTER OF CREDIT

Suppose the available information is insufficient or it is desirable to have more protection to assure collection. Then the safest device is the letter of credit.

Definition

There are many definitions offered for a letter of credit. The most satisfactory is that a letter of credit is a written instrument issued by the buyer's bank constituting that bank's promise to make payment to the seller or accept seller's drafts upon it, provided the seller complies with the terms and conditions of the letter. In effect, it constitutes a contract between the bank and the seller.

LETTER OF CREDIT VS. CONTRACT OF SALE. This contract is separate from the sales contract between seller and purchaser, for the letter of credit deals with documents, not merchandise. The distinction is fundamental. The purchaser cannot and must not rely upon his bank, which issues a letter at his request, to protect him against defective merchandise shipped thereunder or the possibility of a dishonest supplier shipping cartons of sawdust. If the documents are in order, the issuing bank must pay under the terms of the letter or breach its own contract with the seller (i.e., the letter of credit itself). The purchaser must satisfy himself as to the responsibility of the seller and then rely on the specifications in his purchase contract to call forth the desired merchandise.

The confusion between the two contracts constitutes the chief source of difficulty that businessmen experience with letters of credit. In sum, banks that issue letters of credit are not equipped to administer the contract of sale. For that reason letters of credit usually indicate the amount of the sale price, the period of time allowed for making shipment, and the shipping and other documents that the buyer or his bank wishes to receive. One cannot read into the terms of a letter of credit any condition that does not appear therein, even though the contract of sale may specifically cover that condition. Banks merely handle shipping and other documents and are not responsible for the quality, quantity, or delivery of the merchandise. The banks merely examine the documents. If the documents conform to the terms of the letter, this constitutes a necessary, as well as a sufficient, condition for payment. The bank must thereupon honor its engagement to the seller.

Irrevocable and Revocable Letters of Credit

The buyer's bank may issue the letter of credit commitment in an irrevocable or revocable form. In the former case it is a binding and continuing commitment (see Fig. 10–1), whereas in the latter case the commitment may be revoked at any time prior to actual payment without notice to the beneficiary.

The revocable letter is therefore of limited value and offers extremely limited protection. Indeed, such an instrument is not a letter of credit at all since it lacks the fundamental element of a letter of credit, to wit, the support of the credit standing of the issuing bank. Rather than a letter of credit, such a document is more appropriately designated a revocable advice. It is an instrument seldom used and is recognizable by language indicating that it is revocable at any time without notice and "conveys no engagement or obligation on our (the advising bank's) part or on the part of our above-mentioned correspondent (the issuing foreign bank)." (See Fig. 10–2.)

Uses of Revocable Advice. But such an instrument is not completely valueless. As above stated, it is not and cannot serve as a true letter of credit. Yet, as between forwarding documents through a bank on a collection basis (see below) and such an advice, there is some advantage in the advice.

First, as the advice usually states, it is for the guidance of the shipper in the preparation of his documents. Secondly and more important, it indicates that the purchaser has probably arranged for the financing of the shipment. In a documents-on-collection arrangement, the shipper must finance the shipment until delivery and his receipt of payment. Hence, the revocable advice has some value to the shipper. But care must be exercised to avoid treating it with the same reliance as a letter of credit.

Confirmation

An irrevocable letter of credit may be confirmed or unconfirmed by the local advising bank. In this context, the term "confirmation" means an engagement to be responsible for payment of the letter of credit. This is particularly important for American exporters shipping to foreign customers who cause their foreign banks to open letters of credit. A particular foreign bank may be completely unknown to the American exporter, and the American bank advising the exporter of the creation of the credit may not be undertaking any responsibility for payment. The American exporter may therefore unknowingly find himself in a precarious position. A confirmation of the letter of credit, on the other hand, assures the American exporter that the American advising bank is responsible for payment. This is, of course, the best commitment that the seller can obtain. In American import transactions, since the purchaser is opening his letter of credit through an American bank, the American bank is directly responsible for payment. It is therefore rarely confirmed by the foreign bank, unless local law or custom requires it.

Advantages of Confirmation. If the letter of credit is payable at sight, payment can be obtained from the advising bank (if it is confirmed) at the time of presentation of the shipping documents in accordance with the terms of the credit. If it is unconfirmed by the advising bank, payment may also be obtained at the time of presentation of documents if the advising bank chooses to do so. If the advising bank does not so choose, however, the exporter will have to wait until the issuing bank examines the documents and then instructs its correspondent (the advising) bank to pay the beneficiary of the letter of credit. For, in this arrangement, the American bank is merely an agent for its principal, the foreign bank. Hence if the foreign bank does not have sufficient funds on deposit with the American bank, the latter may refuse payment of the draft. Similarly, if any possibility of a discrepancy arises between the terms of the letter and the documents presented, the advising bank may prefer to await instructions from the issuing bank. If the shipper insists that the documents are in order he has no claim against the local bank. His claim can be asserted only against the distant foreign bank. These possibilities clearly illustrate the advantages of a confirmed letter of credit as opposed to an unconfirmed letter of credit.

Language of Confirmation. A confirmed letter of credit may be distinguished from an unconfirmed letter of credit by an examination of its face. If the letter from the American bank is designated an "advice" and contains language to the effect that "this advice contains no engagement or obligation on our part," then the American bank is not responsible for payment (see Fig. 10–3). The American bank is responsible for payment only if the credit contains express language to the effect that "we (the American bank) confirm their (the foreign bank's) irrevocable credit and engage with you that all drafts drawn under and in compliance with the terms of this credit will be duly honored." In this or equivalent language lies the engagement of the advising bank; the credit may also bear a legend at the top indicating that it is a confirmed irrevocable credit (see Fig. 10–4; the term "straight" in the heading indicates that any drafts thereunder are not negotiable). The language of engagement again illustrates the principle that the letter of credit is a contract between the bank and the seller, distinct from the sales contract between seller and purchaser. The intermediary or correspondent bank can merely advise the seller or undertake an engagement with him.

A revocable letter of credit is never confirmed by the advising bank.

Payment on Acceptance or Deferred Basis

A letter of credit can also be payable on either an acceptance or a deferred basis. On an acceptance basis, the exporter draws a draft on the advising bank (if the letter of credit is confirmed) that may be payable in 90 days, 120 days, 180 days, or any agreed period. Once the advising bank accepts the draft drawn upon it, the exporter can request the acceptance to be discounted by the advising bank or any other bank after paying the prevailing discount charges. Occasionally, the negotiations between buyer and seller can result in the buyer's paying the discount charges. Sometimes this can result in modification of the price. Sometimes, however, the buyer may already have his optimum price and still prefer to defer payment for a time after sight (presentation of documents). This may be because the buyer wishes to have merchandise or equipment actually on hand before making payment. In such event, the letter of credit would indicate that discount charges are to be charged to buyer's account, the confirming bank would charge the issuing bank therefor, and the latter would charge the buyer's account. If the letter of credit is issued on an acceptance arrangement, such drafts when accepted are known as bankers' acceptances.

On a deferred-payment basis, a draft may not be drawn. The exporter has to wait until the maturity date of the agreed period of time before payment is effected; he does not have the opportunity of discounting the obligation and receiving his funds immediately. But this may be by his own choice. The exporter may be reluctant to draw a draft on the theory that if the drawee does not pay on maturity he, the drawer, will be liable. Since the drawees on such drafts are almost uniformly prime banks this danger is rather remote, and such deferred non-draft arrangements are rare.

Pitfalls in Use of Letters of Credit

While a letter of credit may theoretically be unsecured as between the bank and the purchaser, that possibility will be omitted from this discussion. The secured letter of credit is created when the terms thereof require that the documents of title be payable to the bank or its order. This enables the bank to claim the merchandise on arrival or endorse the documents to its customer's order under a trust receipt which preserves its security interest in the merchandise in the possession of the buyer as well as the receivables generated by the sale of the merchandise. The forms and technicalities involved in trust-receipt financing are discussed in Chapter 5.

The device of the letter of credit, however, may prove to be of illusory value. The possible pitfalls are many; two true tragedies may illustrate the point that extreme caution must be exercised in these transactions.

Specification of Partial Shipment. A letter of credit was issued in a very simple form calling for ten different types of merchandise to be shipped. The credit on its face appeared to be perfectly normal and did not contain any unusual conditions. In order to make the shipment the beneficiary had to make purchases from ten different suppliers. Nine of the suppliers delivered their merchandise, but the tenth could not. When the shipper presented his documents covering nine tenths of the shipment he could not obtain payment because he had overlooked the fact that the credit did not allow for partial shipments. The buyer could not use these goods because the missing item was required to make the other items usable. In the meantime, the market price dropped substantially on most of the items, with the result that the buyer bought the merchandise elsewhere at a lower price. The shipper was left with the merchandise.

Specified Transport. Another unhappy incident occurred when one of the terms of the credit was that the shipment had to be made on the XYZ steamship line to a remote seaport. The shipper bought the goods and made arrangements to ship them. To his very great surprise, he found that there was no vessel on that line that would arrive in the port of embarkation in time to pick up the merchandise. The merchandise was highly specialized in nature, and when it could not be shipped in time the seller suffered a serious loss. Both stories bear a common moral. The shipper must read the letter of credit carefully to ascertain whether he can fully comply with its terms.

Inspection Requirements. For the importer, an inspection of the merchandise before on-board loading may be useful. The letter of credit can be drawn to require a certificate of inspection of a responsible third party such as the Superintendence Company, a world-wide company performing such services on a fee basis. For the exporter such a requirement would be legitimate, but the provision of the letter of credit must be carefully read. Seemingly innocuous clauses are frequent sources of trouble. If an inspection report is required, the person or company who is to make the inspection report should be independent. The person or company must have somebody available and capable of making the inspection report required. Very suspect is the provision that "our President, Mr. John Smith" must sign his approval on the commercial invoice or on the inspection report. Mr. John Smith may not exist or may not be available to sign the reports. Even worse, he may not be willing to do so.

Insuring Merchandise in Transit

Insurance coverage for merchandise in transit is an essential consideration in all import or export transactions. Marine and war risk coverage are usually provided. Who arranges for such coverage and who pays therefor should be part of the terms of the contract of sale. American exporters and importers obviously prefer that all-risk coverage be obtained from a United States insurer and payable in dollars. Such a policy (or a certificate thereof) may properly be required as a necessary document to be presented under a letter of credit established by an American importer.

DOCUMENTS AGAINST PAYMENT ON A COLLECTION BASIS THROUGH A BANK

With this type of credit the buyer can arrange to purchase goods and make a commitment directly to the seller to the effect that he will pay for the merchandise when the shipping documents are presented to him by a bank. The seller will then send the shipping documents first through his own bank which will forward them to a correspondent bank in the city of the buyer. The correspondent bank will release the shipping documents to the seller only against payment. Thus the seller maintains control of the merchandise by not permitting the shipping documents to leave his control, or the control of the bank, until payment has been made.

Pitfalls

The primary risk here is that the buyer may refuse to pay for the goods because of a decline in the market price or because he is financially unable to do so. Since in such cases the seller will have to arrange to dispose of the goods with a very great likelihood of loss, the buyer should be investigated so that it is reasonably certain that he will be able to pay upon presentation of the documents.

The exporter must be certain that an import license has been granted on the other side, if one is required. Advance consideration should be given to the problems of disposing of the merchandise to third parties. The economic and political structure of the buyer's country should be considered as it affects the shipper's ability to maintain control of the merchandise and resell it. The shipper must also be concerned with fines and demurrage charges if the merchandise is not cleared through customs within a certain time after arrival. Exchange problems in the country of the buyer must be examined. The usual procedure is for the buyer to pay the value of the shipment in local currency which is converted into United States dollars. However, if the country lacks sufficient dollar exchange, payment may be withheld for many months. In some instances, delays have been as long as one year or more. Obviously, if the shipper does not receive dollar reimbursement within a reasonable period of time, the interest charges on the loan received from the bank or other financer against this item could wipe out the profit on the transaction. Further, by the time dollar exchange becomes available, the rate of exchange may have deteriorated and the shipper may not get the full dollar reimbursement until the buyer makes good on the deficiency. Export financing, therefore, involves not only credit risks but also exchange and legal problems.

TERM DRAFT

In this arrangement, the procedure followed is usually the same as in the case of documents against payment through a bank. The only difference is that instead of paying for the goods upon presentation of the documents, the buyer will accept the seller's draft drawn on him payable at thirty days, sixty days, or whatever period has been agreed upon between the buyer and the seller. Once the draft has been accepted, the buyer receives the shipping documents and, of course, title to the merchandise. The trade acceptance is, therefore, an unsecured obligation and the moral and financial standing of the buyer are vital. All the pitfalls described above relative to documents against payment are also fully applicable here.

FINANCING TECHNIQUES

The function of the finance company or other secured financer in the field of international trade is similar to its function in domestic trade. Because it is equipped and staffed to test, control, and administer the collateral, it can provide greater accommodation than can a more traditional lender in the same situation. Thus an importer may sometimes obtain a more generous letter of credit line from such a financer than from a more traditional lender. The financer guarantees payment to the bank, but it is the bank that opens the letter of credit. The credit is opened as though the financer's client were the direct customer of the bank. This is arranged by underlying agreements executed at the time of application to the bank for the opening of letters of credit. The financer retains his security interest by receiving the documents endorsed to its order, releasing them on trust receipt to the borrower and preserving its lien through the inventory, receivable, and collection phases of the transaction.

"Back-to-Back" Letter of Credit Financing

In export financing, the financer may provide the accommodation that enables the borrower to purchase the merchandise and convert it into foreign receivables, which may also be financed by the finance company. Two common protective devices utilized by such financers are worthy of mention. The first is termed "back-to-back" letter of credit financing. Here the borrower's customer opens a letter of credit.

Domestic Letters. If the borrower is an importer, this letter of credit may be opened by a domestic customer and called a domestic letter of credit. Buttressed by this letter of credit, the financer would then cause its bank to open a foreign letter of credit setting forth the same documentary requirements. Care must be exercised to insure that the foreign letter provides for shipping and termination dates well within the corresponding dates of the domestic letter. Otherwise the financer may receive documents and shipment after expiration of the domestic letter and be faced with a problem of reselling the merchandise. When the documents are presented under the foreign letter, the financer takes possession thereof. He thereupon presents them to the bank issuing the domestic letter and obtains payment thereunder. Many letters of credit are in terms non-assignable. In such event, the financer retains possession of the domestic letter of credit and obtains a letter requesting and authorizing the paying bank to remit the proceeds to the financer.

Foreign Letters. In export transactions, the theory is similar but the elements are reversed. Here the borrower has a foreign letter emanating from the bank of a foreign customer, and the financer causes its bank to open a domestic letter in favor of the borrower's supplier. Again termination and shipping dates must be carefully arranged. The financer therefore provides the necessary financial bridge to enable the borrower to complete the transaction.

F.C.I.A. Insurance

Another protective technique available to American exporters is F.C.I.A. insurance. Announced in October, 1961, and operative in February, 1962, the Foreign Credit Insurance Association constitutes a joint venture of the American insurance industry and the United States government-owned Export-Import Bank of Washington (Exim-bank). It was developed in response to the then pressing gold balance-of-payment problem and was designed to enable American exporters to compete favorably as to credit terms with exporters of many other countries. Some of these countries had already developed similar insurance programs.

Originally the insurance companies and the Eximbank jointly shared the commercial risk. However, effective August 1, 1964, the credit insurance was assumed by the insurance industry, with the Eximbank providing re-insurance over certain limits of liability. Credit insurance covers losses arising from non-payment by the foreign buyer due to financial inability. Political risk insurance is assumed solely by Eximbank. Political risks include blockages or delays in dollar exchange; cancellation or non-renewal of export licenses; prohibition of import authority; war, rebellion, or revolution confiscation of buyer's business; changes in local currency regulations; transport of insurance charges incurred as a result of such political disturbances—all of which are not due to the fault of the buyer.

The coverage is normally for short-term credit (up to 180 days), unless involving capital goods or similar merchandise which are normally shipped under medium terms (181 days to five years). Depending on the term of credit and the rating of the country of destination, political risk coverage may vary from 70% to 95% of loss. Commercial credit insurance may be up to 85% of loss.

If a commercial financer is financing the exports, the policy may be endorsed for the benefit of the financer. Such an arrangement permits the financer to provide more favorable and liberal terms to its client, the American exporter. The policy premium is usually a small percentage of the volume of exports covered. The policy will of course not be used as a substitute for the normal credit investigations and credit judgment of the exporter and his financer. Indeed the co-insurance provisions stipulate that the exporter retains at least 15% investment in any loss and hence should exercise normal and reasonable prudence.

The Financing Contract

The relationship between financer and client is formalized by a written contract between them. The contract provides that the financer, in the event of default, can dispose of the merchandise. The financer also retains the discretionary right to accept or reject a particular application for guarantee of a specific letter of credit. This enables the financer to determine in advance whether sufficient firm purchase orders are available to dispose of the merchanise, and/or the buttressing letters of credit are in order, etc. The contract also provides for the financer's compensation and the method of payment.

A very basic stipulation of the contract is the amount of deposit which the merchant must keep with the financer. This is usually stated as a percentage (e.g., 15% or 20%) of the face amount of the letter of credit that the financer causes to be opened. This requirement stems from the fundamental recognition that letter of credit financing is essentially inventory financing. Although the transaction technically deals with documents, in reality it deals with the goods represented by the documents. Hence the cash deposit enables the financer to establish a protective margin between the estimated value of the goods and the amount it may be called upon to advance. The problems of shrinkage, deterioration, and marketability of the goods are much the same as described in the discussion of inventory financing (Chapter 5). In import financing, the deposit is also designed to provide a cash reserve to pay the import duties and freight charges, in the event the client is unable to do so. Such charges, if not paid by the client, constitute an additional advance that may have to be made by the financer to obtain possession of the goods in order to liquidate his loan. These amounts are therefore pre-calculated and covered by the amount of the deposit.

Paying American Exporter on Shipment

Another foreign trade arrangement is available in which the American exporter can be relieved of all credit risk and receive cash upon shipment. This service has been developed by some American finance companies and factors. In effect they are granting credit to the foreign buyer and pay the American exporter in full upon shipment. The foreign buyer can afford a finance company's charges because such rates are probably the same or less than the foreign buyer's cost of local bank credit, if it is available. Furthermore, the American exporter is willing to allow a cash discount or otherwise participate in the cost of financing because his export sales are immediately transformed into cash sales. Such transformation into cash sales is in fact the objective of the plan. The result is similar to, but the technical arrangement is different from the confirming-house arrangement. The confirming house in effect serves as the buying agent for its foreign principals. It confirms the order to the supplier, thereby agreeing to pay on the supplier's terms. It thereafter becomes the exporter of record. Under the newer plan, the finance companies do not act in a trading capacity. Rather they act as fiscal disbursing agent for the foreign buyer who chooses his own supplier and arranges his own terms of purchase.

As can be concluded from the above discussion, the function of the financer in import-export financing is quite similar to his function in domestic financing. Equipped to administer collateral and thereby provide greater accommodation than unsecured or more traditional lenders, the financer accelerates the cash flow of the importer or exporter.

FIRST NATIONAL CITY BANK

CABLE ADDRESS "CITIBANK"

399 PARK AVENUE, NEW YORK, N. Y. 10022

IRREVOCABLE CREDIT
X Overseas Supplier, Inc.
Rio de Janeiro
Brazil

DATE January 15, 19____

| ALL DRAFTS DRAWN MUST BE MARKED: DRAWN UNDER CREDIT NO. | 12345 |

DEAR SIRS:

WE HEREBY AUTHORIZE YOU TO VALUE ON First National City Bank, New York, New York

FOR ACCOUNT OF Y Importers, Park Avenue, New York, New York
UP TO THE AGGREGATE AMOUNT OF Ten thousand ($10,000.00) and 00/100 dollars------------------
AVAILABLE BY YOUR DRAFT(S) AT Sight   **FOR** 100% **INVOICE COST TO BE ACCOMPANIED BY**

1. Customs invoice in duplicate.

2. Commercial invoice stating that it covers shipment of two hundred (200) bags of coffee.

3. Full set on board steamer bills of lading made out to the order of First National City Bank, New York (LC 12345) marked "Notify" Y Importers, Park Avenue, New York, New York.

4. Partial shipments permitted.

   Insurance to be effected by buyers.

BILLS OF LADING MUST BE DATED NOT LATER THAN March 1, 19__
BILLS OF EXCHANGE MUST BE NEGOTIATED NOT LATER THAN March 10, 19__
THIS CREDIT IS SUBJECT TO THE UNIFORM CUSTOMS AND PRACTICE FOR DOCUMENTARY CREDITS (1962 REVISION), INTERNATIONAL CHAMBER OF COMMERCE BROCHURE NO. 222.
WE HEREBY AGREE WITH THE DRAWERS, ENDORSERS AND BONA FIDE HOLDERS OF DRAFTS DRAWN UNDER AND IN COMPLIANCE WITH THE TERMS OF THIS CREDIT THAT SUCH DRAFTS WILL BE DULY HONORED ON DUE PRESENTATION TO THE DRAWEE.

YOURS VERY TRULY,

COM 627 (L) REV. 8-85

ART 904 REV. 12-84

AUTHORIZED SIGNATURE

Fig. 10—1. Letter of Credit
234

FIRST NATIONAL CITY BANK

CABLE ADDRESS "CITIBANK"

399 PARK AVENUE, NEW YORK, N. Y. 10022

ADVICE OF AUTHORITY TO PAY

NEW YORK

X   Exporter & Co.
500 Fifth Avenue
New York, New York

Date February 10, 19___

| ALL DRAFTS DRAWN MUST BE MARKED:
DRAWN AS PER ADVICE | 54321 |

DEAR SIRS:

WE ADVISE YOU THAT   Y' Bank, Colombo, Ceylon

HAVE AUTHORIZED US TO HONOR YOUR DRAFTS UNDER THEIR CREDIT NO. 678910

FOR ACCOUNT OF   Z General Merchandise Co., Colombo, Ceylon

FOR A SUM OR SUMS NOT EXCEEDING A TOTAL OF   Ten thousand ($10,000.00) and 00/100 dollars

TO BE DRAWN AT   sight   ON US TO BE ACCOMPANIED BY

1.   Commercial invoice in triplicate stating that it covers thirty thousand
     (30,000) yards of cotton piece goods.

2.   Insurance certificate/policy in full set in negotiable form covering
     marine and war risks.

3.   Full set on board ocean bills of lading issued to order of shipper, endorsed
     in blank and marked "Notify Z General Merchandise Co." and "Freight
     Prepaid."

4.   Partial shipments are not permitted.

      DRAFTS SO DRAWN, WITH DOCUMENTS AS SPECIFIED, MUST BE PRESENTED AT THIS OFFICE
NOT LATER THAN March 15, 19___.

      THIS ADVICE IS SUBJECT TO THE UNIFORM CUSTOMS AND PRACTICE FOR DOCUMENTARY CREDITS
(1962 REVISION), INTERNATIONAL CHAMBER OF COMMERCE BROCHURE NO. 222.

      THIS ADVICE, WHICH IS SUBJECT TO REVOCATION OR MODIFICATION AT ANY TIME WITHOUT NOTICE
TO YOU, CONVEYS NO ENGAGEMENT ON OUR PART OR ON THE PART OF THE ABOVE MENTIONED CORRE-
SPONDENT AND IS SIMPLY FOR YOUR GUIDANCE IN PREPARING AND PRESENTING DRAFTS AND DOCUMENTS.

                         YOURS VERY TRULY,

COM 512B* (L) REV. 7-68

ART 904 REV. 12-64

AUTHORIZED SIGNATURE

Fig. 10—2.   Revocable Advice
235

FIRST NATIONAL CITY BANK

CABLE ADDRESS "CITIBANK"

399 PARK AVENUE, NEW YORK, N. Y. 10022

CORRESPONDENT'S IRREVOCABLE STRAIGHT CREDIT

DATE February 10, 19___

X   Exporter & Co.
500 Fifth Avenue
New York, New York

ALL DRAFTS DRAWN MUST BE MARKED: DRAWN AS PER ADVICE	54322

DEAR SIRS:

WE ARE INSTRUCTED BY   Y Bank, Colombo, Ceylon

TO ADVISE YOU THAT THEY HAVE OPENED THEIR IRREVOCABLE CREDIT NO. 678910   **IN YOUR FAVOR**

FOR ACCOUNT OF   Z General Merchandise Co., Colombo, Ceylon

FOR A SUM OR SUMS NOT EXCEEDING A TOTAL OF Ten thousand ($10,000 $\frac{00}{100}$) and 00/100 dollars

AVAILABLE BY YOUR DRAFTS AT   sight   **ON US TO BE ACCOMPANIED BY**

1.   Commercial invoice in triplicate stating that it covers thirty thousand
     (30,000) yards of cotton piece goods.

2.   Insurance certificate/policy in full set in negotiable form covering marine
     and war risks.

3.   Full set on board ocean bills of lading issued to order of shipper, endorsed
     in blank and marked "Notify Z General Merchandise Co." and "Freight
Prepaid."

4.   Partial shipments are not permitted.

     THIS ADVICE IS SUBJECT TO THE UNIFORM CUSTOMS AND PRACTICE FOR DOCUMENTARY CREDITS
(1962 REVISION), INTERNATIONAL CHAMBER OF COMMERCE BROCHURE NO. 222.

     **THE ABOVE-NAMED OPENER OF THE CREDIT ENGAGES THAT EACH DRAFT DRAWN UNDER AND IN COM-
PLIANCE WITH THE TERMS OF THE CREDIT WILL BE DULY HONORED, IF PRESENTED AT THIS OFFICE (TOGETHER
WITH THE DOCUMENTS AS ABOVE SPECIFIED) ON OR BEFORE** MARCH 15, 19___ .

     **THIS LETTER IS SOLELY AN ADVICE OF THE OPENING OF THE AFORESAID CREDIT AND CONVEYS
NO ENGAGEMENT BY US.**

                              YOURS VERY TRULY,

COM 810A (L) REV. 8-83

AUTHORIZED SIGNATURE

ART 904 REV. 12-64

Fig. 10—3. Advice of Irrevocable Letter of Credit

FIRST NATIONAL CITY BANK

CABLE ADDRESS "CITIBANK"   399 PARK AVENUE; NEW YORK, N. Y. 10022

CONFIRMED IRREVOCABLE STRAIGHT CREDIT   DATE February 10, 19____

X   Exporter & Co.
500 Fifth Avenue
New York, N.Y.

| ALL DRAFTS DRAWN MUST BE MARKED: |
| DRAWN AS PER ADVICE 54323 |

DEAR SIRS:
   WE ARE INSTRUCTED BY   Y Bank, Colombo, Ceylon

TO ADVISE YOU THAT IT HAS OPENED ITS IRREVOCABLE CREDIT No. 678910   IN YOUR FAVOR

FOR ACCOUNT OF   Z General Merchandise Co., Colombo, Ceylon

FOR A SUM OR SUMS NOT EXCEEDING A TOTAL OF Ten thousand ($10,000$\frac{00}{100}$) and 00/100 dollars

AVAILABLE BY YOUR DRAFT(S) AT   sight   ON US TO BE ACCOMPANIED BY

1. Commercial invoice in triplicate stating that it covers thirty thousand
    (30,000) yards of cotton piece goods.

2. Insurance certificate/policy in full set in negotiable form covering marine
    and war risks.

3. Full set on board ocean bills of lading issued to order of shipper, endorsed
    in blank and marked "Notify   Z General Merchandise Co." and "Freight
    Prepaid."

4. Partial shipments are not permitted.

THIS ADVICE IS SUBJECT TO THE UNIFORM CUSTOMS AND PRACTICE FOR DOCUMENTARY CREDITS
(1962 REVISION), INTERNATIONAL CHAMBER OF COMMERCE BROCHURE NO. 222.

   THE ABOVE-NAMED OPENER OF THE CREDIT ENGAGES WITH YOU THAT EACH DRAFT DRAWN UNDER AND
IN COMPLIANCE WITH THE TERMS OF THE CREDIT WILL BE DULY HONORED ON DELIVERY OF DOCUMENTS AS
SPECIFIED IF PRESENTED AT THIS OFFICE ON OR BEFORE March 15, 19__.
WE CONFIRM THE CREDIT AND THEREBY UNDERTAKE TO HONOR EACH DRAFT DRAWN AND PRESENTED AS
ABOVE SPECIFIED.

                        YOURS VERY TRULY,

COM 811A (L) REV. 12-64   PRINTING OF 3-66   AUTHORIZED SIGNATURE
ART 904 REV. 12-64

Fig. 10—4. Confirmed Irrevocable Letter of Credit

11

Equipment Leasing

Monroe R. Lazere

NATURE OF EQUIPMENT LEASING

Leasing is one of the oldest of legal relationships. Historically, it involved an arrangement in which an owner permitted another the right to use his property for a period of time pursuant to stipulated conditions. Familiarly, in real estate transactions it involves the granting of a right to use the realty for a period of months or years. Obviously such leases are for a substantially shorter term than the usable life of reality. However, in the case of ninety-nine year leases (or substantially equivalent terms) the realty becomes an integral part of the enterprise's operation. This discussion is limited to personal property and, even more specifically, to income-producing equipment for a business enterprise. Patently, such income-producing equipment has a usable life considerably less than that of realty. Obsolescence, depreciation, and ordinary wear and tear combine to reduce the usable life of the average piece of equipment to a limited number of years.

Indeed, this very fundamental fact gives rise to many of the unresolved problems concerning equipment leasing. The relationship between the usable life of the equipment, the dollar cost thereof, and the terms of the lease has been the major source of the debate on the legal and accounting treatment of leasing transactions.

The equipment leasing device really blossomed after World War II. In the 1950's it was in its infancy. In the 1960's the estimated annual volume of transactions was $600 million, and for the 1970's an annual volume of $7 billion appears to be a reasonable expectation

Terminology

The newness of the concept of equipment leasing has also contributed a multiplicity of overlapping terms. At the extreme ends of the leasing spectrum the terminology is clear. A business enterprise may lease trucks for the movement of its merchandise over a period of several weeks. This short-term use of relatively long-lived equipment is clearly a "pure" lease, or "true" lease, or "operating" lease. In common parlance it is frequently called a "rental." At the other end of the spectrum is the situation in which a piece of equipment with a usable life of perhaps ten years is leased by a business enterprise for five years at a rental that enables the lessor to recover the cost of the equipment plus his compensation for the use of the funds over that period. At the end of the lease period, the lessee has the option of purchasing the equipment for one dollar. Under such an arrangement, the lessee has effectively acquired the use and title to the equipment over a period of time. Such a lease appears to differ only in form and not in substance from a purchase under a purchase money security agreement (or, before the advent of the Uniform Commercial Code, a conditional sales contract). Such a lease has been described as a "finance" or "financial" lease. Between the extremes of the spectrum, of course, lies a large twilight area of transactions with many variables.

LEASES VS. INSTALLMENT PURCHASES

Understandably, the novelty of the device of equipment leasing has resulted in differences of opinion among financers regarding its proper function. To analyze leasing effectively one must recognize what it can and cannot do. Purchase money security agreements (in non-Code states, conditional sales contracts) are another means of acquiring equipment (as well as the use of the equipment) without an immediate full outlay of cash.

Several arguments favoring leasing over installment purchases appear in the literature. Since many of them almost fall of their own weight, their enumeration need not long detain us. Examples are: the formalities of leasing are less cumbersome, and leasing companies make decisions more rapidly than other lenders. The argument was also made that lessors know the equipment better than other lenders. While this last proposition may be accurate with respect to lessors specializing in particular equipment (e.g., automobiles or computers), it surely does not apply to a leasing company handling a fuller range of equipment. Surely such a lessor would be no more familiar with the equipment than would a similarly broad-gauged installment sales financer.

Obsolete Arguments for Leasing

Other arguments favoring leasing over installment sales financing were originally valid. The validity was lost, however, as the device became more familiar. In this category of arguments was one urging that in government cost-plus contracts the entire rental would be taken as "costs" even though the equipment would be retained by the contractor by exercising a nominal option at the end of the term. Government contracting officers have now eliminated this possibility. Also, it was urged that leasing could be utilized to avoid restrictions in departmental capital budgeting. Now such budgeting usually includes restrictions on finance leases as well. And finally, leasing was urged as a method of avoiding restrictions regarding capital expenditures found in long-term debt agreements. Such agreements are now usually broadened to apply the restrictions to finance leases.

Thus some early supporting arguments have been seriously diluted, even eliminated. Newer and perhaps more persuasive justifications have developed. It may therefore be appropriate to discuss some of the more serious theoretical arguments in close relationship to their chronological development. In such a chronology, 1962 represents a key year, for then the investment tax credit provisions became law. Thenceforth the theoretical and practical justifications for leasing underwent a profound change.

Size of Down Payment

In the 1950's, however, leasing salesmen offered leasing as virtually a panacea for the company short of operating cash. They urged that the required down payment was less than in installment purchasing. Initially, this was true. The usual lessor required prepayment of one month's rental for each year of the lease term or $8\frac{1}{2}\%$ of the total dollars involved. Under the pressure of such competition, however, the financers of equipment installment sales generally reduced their requirements from 25% to 10% of the purchase price. Hence the differential on this score became less dramatic.

Size of Monthly Payments

Further, the lower monthly payments promised by the leasing sales-men seemed illusory. Where, as was usually the case, the lessor acquired the equipment for a particular lessee, he would obviously anticipate the full recovery of the cost of the equipment plus compen-sation for the use of funds during the lease period. Hence the lessee's option to purchase the equipment at the end of the lease period was usually nominal because the investment then remaining in the equipment was insubstantial. After 1962, as will later appear, it became economically feasible for the lessor to schedule monthly payments that would leave a more substantial investment in the residual portion at the end of the lease term.

Tax Deductions

Another argument pressed by proponents of leasing was that the lease payments were deductible as an operating expense, thereby effecting a considerable tax savings for the lessee. It must be noted, however, that a purchaser of equipment may take depreciation and interest as tax deductible expense. Studies of comparative tables of parallel transactions (utilizing the same depreciation formula, cost of equipment, and interest charge) have been made. The conclusions thus reached clearly indicate that leasing does not increase or decrease the total tax savings. Leasing, however, does enable the lessee to distribute his tax savings more evenly over the term of the lease. The installment purchaser has higher tax savings earlier in the purchase period and lower in the later period. Further, as the lease term or purchase period increases, the annual differential on tax savings seems to become less.

Creditworthiness of Lessee

A fourth argument utilized by the advocates of leasing was that leasing obligations were not required to be reflected on the lessee's balance sheet as debt. Hence leasing equipment (as opposed to purchasing it) would not affect existing credit lines with lenders and suppliers. Such lines are, of course, predicated in part upon the amount of debt incurred by the debtor. To the prospective user or lessee, this argument had great appeal. This is explored further on page 244. While the no-debt argument was advanced by the sales department, the credit department of the financer was usually more circumspect. In practice, no financer considered advancing the cost of a specified piece of equipment for the lessee without being reasonably certain of the capacity of that lessee to repay the advance. Or, in the alternative, the financer had to feel that the equipment itself had sufficient liquidation value so that in the event of lessee's default, the lessor could recapture his investment through a sale of the equipment.

Since the lessor expects to be repaid—as does the financer under an installment sales contract—the credit standards should be the same for both devices. This obviously contradicts the popular notion that an applicant who is too weak financially to qualify for installment sales financing can solve the problem by seeking a lease. Patently, if a prospect does not qualify for purchase money security interest financing with, for example, a 10% down payment, there is nothing in a lease that improves his credit. Conversely, if the credit factors warrant approval for lease financing, they would also qualify for installment sales contract financing. In short, in this context, leasing must be deemed just another form of equipment financing and the same credit standards should be applied. All facts about a company's financial condition should be examined—its operations and its ability to meet its obligations, including its lease obligations.

"TRUE" LEASE VS. DEBT

Effect of Filing

It has also been argued that additional recognition of a lease as debt is found in the filing by lessors of financing statements under the Uniform Commercial Code or the recording of the lease with the proper agency in non-Code states. The method of perfecting security interests in equipment is described in Chapter 7. That discussion is equally applicable to leases. Such filings make leasing transactions matters of public knowledge. By this action the lessor, it has been urged, puts future creditors on notice that such leases are debts. Hence the argument that a lease is not fixed debt became considerably weaker. Certainly this conclusion would be valid in a "finance" lease, and the filing would therefore be a vital protection to the lessor.

It should be stated, however, that some lessors argue that such filing merely constitutes an inexpensive safety play, for actually it does provide a simple notice of the lessor's interest. Indeed it is a safer method than relying upon an identification plaque that can be removed from the equipment. It can therefore reduce some potential identification disputes with trustees in bankruptcy, receivers, etc. Conceivably, therefore, the lessor of a "true" lease with limited non-cancelable payments and large reversionary interest might also wish to file a financing statement. Such filing would also protect his security interest in the event that a referee in bankruptcy subsequently were to hold his agreement to constitute an installment sales contract. A filing without prejudice (i.e., with appropriate language describing the transaction as a "true" lease) would then constitute an insurance policy with nominal premium. Hence the filing per se of a financing statement does not resolve the problems of whether the lease obligations are debt and to what extent.

Legal Criteria

The legal criteria for classifying a lease run as follows: A true lease exists if the lessor's reversionary interest has a substantial economic value. On the other hand, if the exercise of a nominal monetary option enables the lessee to take title at the end of the lease term, then the lease may be considered a finance lease or quasi-purchase. Here the lessee would find it economically unsound to forego his option. In such case, the lessee has, during the lease term, virtually paid for the equipment plus the use of the funds employed in financing it.

The standards paraphrased above were set forth in many pre-Code statutes. In essence, they also represent the intent of Section 1-201(37) of the Uniform Commercial Code defining a "lease intended for security."

Obviously the determination of the facts and the development of conclusions making such standards operative will vary in each case. The relative novelty of the leasing format sometimes makes prediction of a court decision in a particular case uncertain. Because of a dearth of established authority, the decision may frequently turn on the predilections of the particular judge or referee and/or the matrix of circumstances from which the case arises. For example, if a large piece of leased equipment (with no financing statement filed therefor) lends an aura of affluence to the bankrupt, a persuasive creditor's attorney may convince the referee that the transaction is a purchase. Then the absence of a financing statement might throw the equipment into the general creditors' pot. This problem points up the advisability of filing a properly worded financing statement (without prejudice) covering a true lease.   Lessee resistance to such a filing may develop because the possible balance sheet advantage (no debt) may then be lost.

Accounting Treatment

The problem of whether leasing obligations should be treated on the balance sheet of the lessee as fixed debt has been examined by the accounting profession.

A.I.C.P.A. Criteria.   In 1964 an opinion of the Accounting Principles Board of the American Institute of Certified Public Accountants set forth guidelines for the reporting of leases in the financial statements of lessees.   In doing so it made no "distinctions between leases of real property and leases of personal property."   It is not clear why such distinctions were not made.   It is submitted that such distinctions can be made and probably would be very useful.   In any event, Opinion No. 5 recommends that where a lease arrangement is in effect a purchase, then the accounting treatment should indicate the asset and liability involved.   The Opinion is expressly applicable only to non-cancelable leases (or leases cancelable upon a remote contingency) and sets forth some criteria to determine whether the lease is actually a purchase.   Any one of the following criteria would indicate that a lease is a purchase:

1. The property was especially acquired by the lessor for the lessee and is probably usable only by the lessee.
2. The lease term corresponds to the probable usable life of the property; and the lessee is obligated to pay costs such as taxes, insurance, and maintenance.
3. The lessee has guaranteed the lessor's obligations with respect to the property.
4. The lessee has treated the lease as a purchase for tax purposes.

The Opinion attempts to standardize the accounting treatment and apparently seeks to set more stringent standards than formerly prevailing.   It is submitted, however, that many routine leasing transactions would fall outside the criteria established.   For example, a lessor purchases a lathe having a ten-year life for a particular lessee and leases it to him for five years with a nominal purchase option at the end of the lease term.   Although the property was purchased for the lessee it is usable by not only the lessee but others as well. The lease term does not correspond to the usable life of the property. The lessee has not guaranteed the lessor's obligations, nor has the lessee treated the lease as a purchase for tax purposes. Nevertheless, here the initial term is "materially" less than the useful life of the equipment. Hence, under paragraph 10 of the Opinion it should be reported as a purchase. However, if the useful life were six years and the initial term five years, a grey area obviously would develop. Further, if the total lease payments are small in relation to the lessee's net worth, accountants reasonably might differ on the proper treatment. Some accountants would feel justified in not reflecting such lease obligations on the liability side of the balance sheet.

Adequate Disclosure. To the layman some distortion of the lessee's financial position seems to result. Indeed, such a possible buildup of equipment leases, unreflected on the balance sheet, presently constitutes a major attraction for leasing deals. Where, however, the lease obligations appear to the lessee's accountant to be material (in relation to net worth, for example) he may feel compelled to footnote them. Assume now that the lessee's accountant feels compelled to report in the footnotes of the balance sheet the type of lease above described. It seems highly unlikely that the average reader of the statement would be able to absorb the full import of such information. It has seriously been questioned, therefore, whether footnoted information of this nature is properly presented, for such presentation resembles the raw materials of a financial statement, rather than a finished product. It is in this twilight area that a very real and significant, albeit intangible, advantage exists for leasing deals.

"Hell-or-High-Water" Clauses. It should be noted that most leasing agreements contain what have become popularly known as "hell-or-high-water" clauses. As indicated by the colorful description, these clauses require the lessees to make the agreed payments to the lessor notwithstanding operational difficulties encountered in the equipment. It therefore frees the lessor of any warranties relating to the equipment, for the lessee must make payments come "hell or high water." Such a lease seems to resemble very closely the installment sale contract in which the lender's security interest is free of the manufacturer's warranties. Nevertheless, as above indicated, the lease obligations may not necessarily appear as balance-sheet debt.

Lessee's Equity in Equipment. Another difficulty arises in the accounting treatment which revolves around the condition that lease obligations may be reflected as a liability, provided the lessee is developing an "equity" of some kind. Apparently this need not necessarily be an ownership equity. Presumably it can be a "use" equity. Understandably, accountants are reluctant to assign a value to this "equity" because such evaluation falls into the realm of economics rather than accounting. It may be asked why the total amount of the firm commitments for lease payments could not be capitalized as a "use equity." Here, the use of the cost figure appears reasonable. Whatever the merits of this issue may be, the net result of the present treatment is an absence of a reportable asset and corresponding liability. Consider the case of a ten-year, non-cancelable lease on equipment having a ten-year life. There are no options at the end of the lease term. Assume that it otherwise falls within the conditions of Opinion 5 described above. No equity seems to be accruing to the lessee, and therefore an accountant would feel justified in omitting the reporting of the lease liabilities. On the other hand, the same equipment on a ten-year installment sales contract would result in balance-sheet debt for the purchaser. The reason for the difference in treatment seems tenuous, but the lessee apparently gains an advantage over the purchaser. This advantage, however, could mislead the lessee's creditors. It could also encourage the lessee to over-extend himself.

BANK LESSORS AND THE INVESTMENT TAX CREDIT

The year 1962 was pivotal for equipment leasing. In that year a ruling of the Comptroller of the Currency authorized national banks to purchase and lease capital assets. This, of course, encouraged national banks to enter the field and will probably also exert pressure on state banking authorities to grant similar powers to state banks. (This became an actuality for New York State in 1966.) The year 1962 brought another fundamental change to the leasing field. This was the amendment of the Internal Revenue Code to provide for the 7% investment tax credit. The tax credit could be taken by the lessor or passed on to the lessee. The accelerated depreciation (set forth in the Internal Revenue Code of 1954) could not be passed through to the lessee. The maximum of 7% (which constitutes an abatement of final tax otherwise computed) is available where the equipment has a usable life of eight years or more. It drops to 4.66% for an asset with a usable life of at least six but less than eight years and to 2.33% for an asset with a usable life of at least four but less than six years. These provisions were designed to encourage capital investment and thus stimulate the economy which was felt to be growing insufficiently at the time. The administration's desired result was soon realized, and the impact of the provisions was dramatic. Commitments for the acquisition of capital equipment burgeoned substantially. Leasing and other devices for financing these orders all blossomed.

Low-Profit, High-Investment Industries

For the equipment leasing field, two major new concepts resulted. The first centered around industries that were not particularly profitable and therefore could not take direct tax advantage of the investment tax credit and accelerated depreciation features. Among such industries were railroads, trucking operations, and some airlines. Lessors could utilize the new tax credit and the accelerated depreciation features of the old law and then pass on the saving to the lessees in the form of interest rates, reflected in very low downpayment requirements and low leasing payments. In this area leasing held a unique advantage as compared with other financing techniques. Since the equipment involved jet aircraft, railroad cars, trucks, etc., with large dollar value per unit, the total dollar volume of such transactions mounted rapidly and substantially. Since the leasing company effects substantial tax savings by these two tax devices, it can ease the burden on the lessee and still profit handsomely on its investment.

Non-payout Lease

Another leasing development fostered by the dual tax advantages was the non-payout lease. This form of lease provides for a firm commitment by the lessee for a total amount which will not recover for the lessor the full cost of the equipment. Options to renew the lease or purchase at the then fair market value may then be available to the lessee. This method of leasing covers very select types of equipment such as jet aircraft and computers where manufacturer support is available to the lessor. This support may consist of the manufacturer's guarantee to cover any loss on the final disposition of the equipment up to an agreed percentage of original cost. The lessor's ability to utilize the accelerated depreciation for its tax purposes is here clearly established by the very non-payout structure of the arrangement. In setting up its deal, the lessor relies upon expert opinion regarding the future value of the equipment at key points of time.

Large leasing companies engaged in this activity are optimistic regarding the future outcome of their arrangements. Predictably, the non-payout lease will flourish in the fields dealing with equipment that has developed or can very probably develop markets for second- and third-hand units. Such equipment would have some determinable market value for many years. The automobile is such an item of equipment, and the non-payout lease (including maintenance) developed early in that field, even before the advent of the investment tax credit. (It also flourished in the consumer area.) It seems quite likely that a parallel development is in the offing with respect to jet aircraft and computers. The anticipated wide demand for such equipment apparently has and will continue to create subsidiary markets for second- and third-hand units, thus assuring the lessor of their saleability. These markets eliminate the lessor's need for the above described manufacturers' support.

Effect of Government Regulation of Economy

Current economic thought includes the regulation of the economy by monetary, fiscal, and tax policies of the Federal government. As indicated above, this theory gave rise to the legislation regarding the investment tax credit and the earlier accelerated depreciation provisions in order to stimulate an economy then considered sluggish. Conversely, when a rapidly expanding economy exhibits inflationary tendencies, these regulators may be reversed. The economic valves that were opened may then in effect be closed. Such a possibility could readily result in a repeal or suspension of the favorable tax provisions, and in such event, some of the above described competitive advantages may be lost permanently or temporarily. The temporary suspension of the investment tax credit during the latter months of 1966 and early 1967 is a case in point.

The survival of one by-product of the investment tax credit seems assured. By and large, as discussed above, the non-payout lease technique probably will continue to be a viable device.

THE EQUIPMENT LEASE TRANSACTION

Let us follow through the practical application of a financial leasing transaction. XYZ Corporation is interested in a certain piece of equipment, perhaps a large piece of plastics machinery. The prospective lessee contacts a financer, giving it the specifications of the equipment, the vendor, the cost, and the length of time for which he wishes to lease it initially (see Fig. 11–1). The initial term is

TO: XYZ LEASING CORPORATION

LEASE REQUEST

COMPANY

Name of Company __XYZ Corporation__

Address __23 South Street   Newark, New Jersey__

Type of Business __Manufactures Plastic Toys__   Telephone Number_____

Person to Contact __John Smith__   Title __President__

Form of Organization: Corporation ☒   Partnership ☐   Proprietorship ☐

State of Incorporation __New Jersey__

EQUIPMENT

Seller's Name: __XYZ Plastics Company__   Address: __First and Main__

__Wheeling, West Virginia__

Manufacturer's Name: __XYZ Automatic Tool Company__   Address: __Richmond, Indiana__

Equipment Description (Attach Descriptive Literature, Sales Brochures, Specifications and terms if any)

Model #: __123AB 456__   Equipment: __Plastics Molding Machine__

(Continue on Separate Sheet)

Equipment is: ☒ New   ☐ Used   If used, how old is the equipment: _____Yrs.

The Equipment will be used for: __Production of Plastic Toys__

What Phase of Process: __Molding of Raw Material__

The Equipment is specially designed or built for intended use: ☒ Yes   ☐ No

The Equipment is to be modified for particular use: ☐ Yes   ☒ No

Cost of modification, if any: $_____ Number of Shifts to be run: __Three__

Has your own purchase order been issued: ☐ Yes   ☒ No   (If Yes, Please Attach Copy)

Has an invoice been received: ☐ Yes   ☒ No   (If Yes, Please Attach Copy)

Has the Equipment been shipped to or received by you: ☐ Yes   ☒ No

Cost: $ __85,000.00__   Sales Tax: $ __None__

Terms of Lease __Sixty__ Months   Desired Delivery Date: __February 15, 19X6__

Equipment to be located at: __123 North Street__

Owner of premises: __123 North Realty Corp.__   __Same__

(Name)   (Address)

Will Equipment be attached to realty? If so, how? __No__

Shipping instructions: __Best Way__

CREDIT AND FINANCIAL

Trade References: _____ Address: _____

_____ Address: _____

_____ Address: _____

Bank References: __XYZ Bank__   Address: _____

_____ Address: _____

_____ Address: _____

STATEMENT ATTACHED FOR FISCAL YEAR ENDING __December 31,__, 19 __X5__ Interim statement attached for_____months period.

Other equipment presently leased   ☐ Yes   ☒ No   If so, total unpaid rent $_____ Term_____

DATE:

We hereby request you to acquire the above Equipment and lease the same to us on the terms hereof and of any lease submitted to you herewith. This Lease Request includes the terms and conditions appearing on the reverse side hereof.

XYZ Corporation

By_____

Title:

Fig. 11–1.   Lease Request

249

TERMS AND CONDITIONS

---

1. In consideration of your ordering or purchasing Equipment (of which no notice need be given to us) we agree that thereafter our offer to lease Equipment on the terms hereof and of any lease submitted to you herewith cannot be revoked. We agree to indemnify and save you harmless from any liability to seller and/or any other party arising from or in connection with this Lease Request and/or the purchase of Equipment and leasing thereof, and in case of dispute with seller or other party we will pay you on demand any amounts theretofore paid by you in respect of the purchase of Equipment (in which event we shall be subrogated to your claims, if any, against seller and/or any other party.)

2. All delivery, transportation, shipping, storage, installation and testing charges shall be paid by us.

3. We agree that all inquiries and communications directed to seller will be made through you.

4. We represent that execution, delivery and performance of this Lease Request and the lease have been duly authorized and will not violate any provision of law or our charter or by-laws or any indenture, loan or credit agreement or other instrument to which we are party or by which we or our property may be bound or affected; and that the financial statements submitted herewith have been prepared on the basis of generally accepted accounting principles, and are complete and correct and fairly present our financial condition as at the dates thereof.

Fig. 11–1. Lease Request—Continued

usually determined by the cost of the equipment, its usefulness to him, and its depreciable life, or any combination thereof.

Credit Analysis

The financer thereupon makes a thorough credit analysis of the prospect. This includes reviewing balance sheets, profit-and-loss figures and trade and bank references. The financer also analyzes the prospect's need for the equipment and the liquidation value of equipment itself. In short, the procedure parallels that for an application for purchase money security interest financing.

The Lease Agreement and Acquisition of Equipment

If satisfied, the financer prepares the lease agreement which is executed to ensure a commitment on the part of the lessee (see Fig.

DELIVERY-INSTALLATION AND ASSEMBLY CERTIFICATE

Dated February 21, 19X6

TO: XYZ LEASING CORPORATION

Gentlemen:

We hereby acknowledge complete and satisfactory delivery, assembly and installation of
the equipment supplied by XYZ Plastics Company
            and described in the Equipment
Lease Agreement, Number 12345   , between
us dated February 1   , 19X6   . We
approve payment for said equipment.

XYZ Corporation
Company

By (title)

Fig. 11–2.   Delivery Acceptance

11–3, page 253). Then the purchase order is accepted and the equipment ordered. In short, a commitment to lease is required from
the prospective lessee before a commitment to purchase can be given
by the prospective lessor. The prospect's purchase order is trans-
posed to the leasing company's form of purchase order (see Fig.
11–4, page 260) and submitted to the particular manufacturer with
instruction to bill the leasing company and ship to the lessee. Upon
completion, the manufacturer ships the equipment.

Acceptance of Delivery

Upon receipt and installation satisfactory to him, the lessee notifies the lessor thereof via a delivery acceptance form (see Fig. 11–2). The lessor-financer then pays the manufacturer, puts the lease on its books, and proceeds to bill the lessee on a monthly or other pre-determined basis.

Expiration of Lease

At the end of the lease period, the lessee may elect to buy the equipment from the financer for a pre-determined percentage of the agreed cost or re-rent for an additional period at some other percentage. These percentages will vary, but they will usually be tailored to the desires of the lessee. He will normally have paid during the term of the lease the cost of the equipment purchased on his behalf plus the desired return on the lessor's investment. Hence, the usual lessor does not consider the options part of the necessary return on its investment. This can be left open in the initial stages of the transaction.

In sum, therefore, equipment leasing has several facets. Financers and leasing companies make the techniques available. As is so frequently true in other matters, a decision based on full consideration of related facts and problems constitutes the soundest and most successful course.

XYZ LEASING CORPORATION

LEASE NO. 12345

EQUIPMENT LEASE

Lease, dated as of February 1 , 19 X6, by and between XYZ LEASING CORPORATION

("Lessor") and XYZ Corporation a New Jersey corporation ("Lessee").

1. Lessor hereby leases to Lessee, and Lessee hereby rents from Lessor, at a total rent for the term of this lease of One Hundred Ten Thousand Five Hundred and------------------00/100 Dollars ($ 110,500.00), which Lessee agrees to pay to Lessor as hereinafter set forth, the following personal property (hereinafter called "Equipment"):

One (1) XCO Model 123AB456 Plastics Molding Machine A/B 1234

2. This lease, upon the rents, promises, terms and conditions set forth herein, is for a term of Sixty months commencing on the date (the "Commencement Date") that Equipment or any part thereof is delivered to Lessee or shipped via common or other carrier for delivery to Lessee or------------------------, whichever date shall be earliest.

Fig. 11–3. Equipment Lease

3. Lessee hereby directs that Equipment (which Lessee has requested Lessor to purchase) be shipped via common or other carrier

to Lessee at ___123 North Street___,

___Newark___ (City) ___Essex___ (County) ___New Jersey___ (State).

(Street address)

4. Lessee agrees to pay to Lessor the total rent specified above in monthly payments as follows:

One (1) payment of $ ___1,822.00___ ; then ___59___ consecutive payments, each of $ ___1,842.00___ ; then

___ consecutive payments, each of $ ___ ; then

___ consecutive payments, each of $ ___ ; then

___ consecutive payments, each of $ ___ ; then

___ consecutive payments, each of $ ___ ; then

___ consecutive payments, each of $ ___ , constituting the payment in advance of the

Upon signing this lease, Lessee shall pay Lessor the sum of $ ·9,210.00

56th, 57th, 58th, 59th and 60th

monthly payments of rent stated above. On the first day of the month immediately following the Commencement Date, Lessee shall commence, and on the corresponding date of each month thereafter shall continue making the remaining monthly payments in the order and amounts stated above, until the total rent shall have been paid in full. All payments of rent shall be made at the office of Lessor, at the address set forth below Lessor's signature herein, or at such other place as Lessor may designate.

5. Time being the essence of this agreement, in the event that any payment required to be made hereunder is not received by Lessor within 10 days from its due date, Lessee agrees to pay, immediately, in addition to and with said payment, to the extent allowed by law, a delinquency charge equal to 5% of the amount of said payment in arrears, or such lesser amount as is the maximum permitted by law, such delinquency charge to be in addition to accrued interest, and attorney's fees and other fees incurred in connection with the collection of said payment and such delinquency charge.

6. Equipment shall be located at the address to which Equipment is to be shipped, as set forth in Section 3, and shall not be removed from such location without the prior written consent of Lessor. Lessee will not change or remove any insignia or lettering which is on Equipment at the time of delivery thereof or which is thereafter placed thereon indicating Lessor's ownership thereof, and at any time during the term of this lease, upon request of Lessor, Lessee will affix to Equipment, in a prominent place, labels, plates or other markings supplied by Lessor stating that Equipment is owned by Lessor.

7. In consideration of Lessor's ordering or purchasing the Equipment (of which no notice need be given to Lessee) Lessee agrees that thereafter its offer to lease Equipment on the terms hereof and any and all Lease Requests submitted to Lessor cannot be revoked. Lessee further agrees to indemnify and save Lessor harmless from any liability to any supplier of Equipment and/or any other party arising from or in connection with this Lease and/or the ordering and purchase of the Equipment and the leasing thereof, and in case of dispute with any supplier or other party Lessee will pay Lessor on demand any amounts theretofore paid by Lessor in respect of the purchase of the Equipment (in which event Lessee shall be subrogated to Lessor's claims, if any, against any supplier and/or any other party). Lessor shall not be liable for loss or damage occasioned by any cause, circumstance or event of whatsoever nature, including but not limited to failure of or delay in delivery, delivery to the wrong place, delivery of improper Equipment or property other than Equipment, damage to Equipment, governmental regulations, strike,

embargo or any other cause, circumstance or event, whether of like or unlike nature. Lessee shall inspect Equipment within 3 business days after its arrival at the address set forth in Section 3. Unless within said 3 business days Lessee gives written notice to Lessor, specifying any defect in or other proper objection to Equipment, Lessee agrees that it shall be conclusively presumed, as between Lessor and Lessee, that Lessee has fully inspected Equipment, that Equipment is in full compliance with the terms of this lease and in good condition and repair, and that Lessee is satisfied with and has accepted Equipment. In case Lessee gives such written notice with respect to any item of Equipment, Lessee shall on demand by Lessor, pay Lessor any amounts theretofore paid or owing by Lessor in respect of the purchase of such item of Equipment and upon such payment Lessee shall be subrogated to Lessor's claims if any against the manufacturer or other supplier thereof and Lessee shall become entitled to such item, as-is, where-is, without warranty, express or implied, by the Lessor with respect to any matter whatsoever, and Lessee shall indemnify and save Lessor harmless from any and all liability to the manufacturer or other supplier thereof. All delivery, transportation, shipping, storage, installation and tax charges shall be paid by Lessee to Lessor immediately upon notification thereof by Lessor.

8. Lessee shall use Equipment solely in the conduct of its business, and in a careful and proper manner, and shall not part with possession of or enter into any sub-lease with respect to Equipment or any part thereof or assign this lease or its interest hereunder without the prior written consent of Lessor. Lessee, at its own cost and expense, shall keep Equipment in good repair, condition and working order and shall furnish any and all parts and labor required for that purpose. Lessee shall not make any material alterations to Equipment without the prior written consent of Lessor. All equipment, accessories, parts and replacements for or which are added to or become attached to Equipment shall immediately become the property of Lessor and shall be deemed incorporated in Equipment and subject to the terms of this lease as if originally leased hereunder.

9. Lessee hereby assumes and shall bear the entire risk of loss of and damage to Equipment from any and every cause whatsoever, and effect. In the event of damage of any kind whatever to any item of Equipment (unless the same is damaged beyond repair), Lessee, at the option of Lessor, shall at Lessee's expense (a) place the same in good repair, condition and working order, or (b) replace the same with like Equipment of the same make and of the same or a later model, and in good repair, condition and working order. If Equipment, or any item thereof, is determined by Lessor to be lost, stolen, destroyed or damaged beyond repair, Lessee shall immediately pay Lessor therefor in cash an amount equal to the aggregate amount of unpaid total rent for the balance of the term of this lease or the amount of such unpaid total rent allocated by Lessor to the item or items involved, as the case may be. Upon such payment this lease shall terminate with respect to the Equipment or items thereof so paid for, and Lessee thereupon shall become entitled thereto as-is-where-is, without warranty, express or implied, with respect to any matter whatsoever.

No loss of or damage to Equipment or any part thereof shall impair any obligation of Lessee under this lease, which shall continue in full force

10. Lessee shall indemnify and save Lessor harmless from any and all liability arising out of the ownership, selection, possession, leasing, renting, operation, control, use, maintenance, delivery and/or return of Equipment, but shall be credited with any amounts received by Lessor with respect thereto from liability insurance procured by Lessee.

11. Lessee shall keep Equipment insured against all risks of loss or damage from every cause whatsoever for not less than the aggregate amount of unpaid total rent for the balance of the term of this lease, and shall carry public liability insurance, both personal injury and property damage, covering Equipment. All said insurance shall be in form and amount and with companies satisfactory to Lessor. All insurance for loss or damage shall provide that losses, if any, shall be payable to Lessor, and all such liability insurance shall be in the joint names of Lessor and Lessee. Lessee shall pay the premiums therefor and deliver to Lessor the policies of insurance or duplicates thereof, or other evidence satisfactory to Lessor of such insurance coverage. Each insurer shall agree, by endorsement upon the policy or policies issued by it or by independent instrument furnished to Lessor, that it will give Lessor 30 days' prior written notice of the effective date of any alteration or cancellation of such policy. The proceeds of such insurance payable as a result of loss of or damage to Equipment shall be applied, at the option of Lessor, (a) toward the replacement, restoration or repair of Equipment which may be lost, stolen, destroyed or damaged or (b) toward payment of the obligations of Lessee hereunder. Lessee hereby irrevocably appoints Lessor as Lessee's attorney-in-fact to make claim for, receive payment of, and execute and endorse all documents, checks or drafts received in payment for loss or damage under any said insurance policy. In case of the failure of Lessee to procure or maintain said insurance or to comply with any other provision of this lease, Lessor shall have the right, but shall not be obligated, to effect such insurance or compliance on behalf of Lessee. In that event, all moneys spent by and expenses of Lessor in effecting such insurance or compliance shall be deemed to be additional rent, and shall be paid by Lessee to Lessor with the next monthly payment of rent.

12. Lessee shall comply with all laws and regulations relating to, and shall promptly pay when due, all license fees, registration fees, assessments, charges and taxes, municipal, state and federal, excluding, however, any taxes payable in respect to Lessor's income, which may

Fig. 11-3. Equipment Lease—Continued

now or hereafter be imposed upon the ownership, possession, leasing, renting, operation, control, use, maintenance, delivery and/or return of Equipment, and shall save Lessor harmless against actual or asserted violations, and pay all costs and expenses of every character in connection therewith or arising therefrom. If compliance with any law, ordinance, rule or permit by any Government agency requires changes or additions to be made on or to Equipment, such changes or additions shall be made by Lessee at his own expense. Lessee covenants that it will make lawful use of Equipment.

13. Title to Equipment shall at all times remain in Lessor, and Lessee, at its own cost and expense, shall protect and defend the title of Lessor. Lessee shall at all times keep Equipment free and clear from all levies, attachments, liens, encumbrances and charges or other judicial process of every kind whatsoever, shall give Lessor immediate written notice thereof and shall indemnify and save Lessor harmless from any loss or damage caused thereby. Lessee will cooperate with Lessor, and take whatever action may be necessary, to enable Lessor to file, register or record, and refile, re-register or re-record, this lease in such offices as Lessor may determine and wherever required or permitted by law, for the proper protection of Lessor's title to Equipment, and will pay all costs, charges and expenses incident thereto. Equipment is and shall remain personal property irrespective of its use or manner of attachment to realty, and Lessee will not cause or permit Equipment to be attached to realty in such manner that it might become part of such realty without securing the prior written consent of Lessor and the prior written agreement of the owner (if other than Lessee) and of the mortgagee, if any, of such realty, that Equipment shall remain personal property and may be removed at the option of Lessee or Lessor. Lessor's books and records showing the account between Lessor and Lessee shall be admissable in evidence in any action or proceeding, shall be binding upon Lessee for the purpose of establishing the items therein set forth and shall constitute prima facie proof thereof. Lessor may at any time examine the books and records of Lessee and make copies thereof.

14. If Equipment is removed, with the consent of Lessor, from the address specified above, Lessee shall, whenever requested, advise Lessor of its exact location. Lessor may, for the purpose of inspection, at all reasonable times enter upon any job, building or place where Equipment is located and may remove Equipment forthwith, without notice to Lessee, if Equipment is, in the opinion of Lessor, being used beyond its capacity or in any manner improperly cared for, abused or misused.

15. If (a) Lessee shall default in the payment of any rent or in making any other payment hereunder when due, or (b) Lessee shall default in the performance or observation of any other covenant herein and such default shall continue for five days after written notice thereof is sent to Lessee by Lessor, or (c) Lessee shall default in the payment when due or any indebtedness of Lessee to Lessor arising independently of this Lease, or Lessee shall default in the payment of any other debt or obligation or the performance of any other covenant in connection with any other contract (hereinafter called "other indebtedness") between Lessee and Lessor or any parent, subsidiary or affiliate of Lessor (hereinafter collectively called "Affiliates"), which would permit Lessor or such Affiliate to exercise any rights or remedies under such contract, or (d) Lessee becomes involvent or makes an assignment for the benefit of creditors, or applies for or consents to the appointment of a receiver, trustee or liquidator of Lessee or of all or a substantial part of the assets of the Lessee, or if such receiver, trustee or liquidator is appointed without the application or consent of Lessee, or (e) a petition is filed by or against Lessee under the Bankruptcy Act or any amendment thereto (including, without limitation, a petition for reorganization, arrangement or extension) or under any other insolvency law or law providing for the relief of debtors, or (f) if the condition of the Lessee shall change, or if Lessee shall undergo any change, as to in Lessor's sole opinion materially increase Lessor's risk, then, if and to the extent permitted by applicable law, Lessor shall have the right to declare the entire amount of unpaid total rent for the balance of the term of this lease due and payable, whereupon the same shall become immediately due and payable, and, if and to the extent permitted by applicable law, Lessor, acting for itself or any Affiliate in its own name or in the name of such Affiliate, or otherwise, shall have the right (A) without demand or legal process, to enter into premises where Equipment may be found and take possession of and remove the same, whereupon all rights of Lessee in Equipment shall terminate absolutely, and (i) retain Equipment and all prior payments of rent made hereunder; or (ii) retain all prior payments of rent and sell Equipment at one or more public or private sales, with or without notice to Lessee and with or without having Equipment at any sale, at which sale Lessor may purchase all or any of Equipment, the proceeds of such sale, less expenses of retaking, storage, repairing and reselling, and reasonable attorneys' fees incurred by Lessor, to be applied to the payment of the unpaid total rent for the balance of the term of this lease and then to be applied to the payment of all unpaid rents or other moneys due under any other lease or on account of any other indebtedness due Lessor or Affiliates, Lessee remaining liable for the balance of said unpaid total rent and for any deficiency and for the balance of rent due under any other lease and for all other indebtedness due Lessor or Affiliates, and any overplus thereafter remaining to be paid to Lessee, its successors or assigns, or to whomsoever may be lawfully entitled to receive the same, or as a court of competent jurisdiction may direct; or

balance of the unpaid total rent for the balance of the term of this lease and for the balance of rent due under any other lease and for all other indebtedness due Lessor or Affiliates, together with all of the above-mentioned expenses, including reasonable attorneys' fees incurred by Lessor, it being agreed that the amounts to be retained by Lessor and the balance to be paid by Lessee under this sub-section shall not be as a penalty but as liquidated damages for the breach hereof and as reasonable return for the use of Equipment and for the depreciation thereof; (B) to pursue any other remedy available to Lessor at law or in equity. Upon default Lessor may without removing Equipment render it unusable. Lessor may dispose of Equipment on the Lessee's premises and shall not be liable for rent, damages or costs therefor. Lessee hereby irrevocably authorizes any attorney of any court of record to appear for and confess judgment against Lessee (except in Indiana and any other state where such action is not permitted by law) for all unpaid rents and other moneys due under this and any other lease or on account of any other indebtedness due Lessor or Affiliates, plus expenses and an amount for attorneys' fees not exceeding 15% of such, rents, moneys and other indebtedness, without stay of execution, and Lessee hereby waives and releases relief from any and all appraisement, stay or exemption laws of any and all obligations of Lessee under this lease or any indebtedness to Lessor or Affiliates, Lessor shall have the right to apply to or hold as security for the payment and performance reserves or money, paper, instruments, funds, securities or other property of any kind owned by Lessee or in which Lessee shall have any right or interest which is now or may hereafter come within the possession, custody or control of Lessor or Affiliates, including, without limitation, the right to retain any overplus arising from the sale of Equipment.

16. All remedies of Lessor hereunder are cumulative, and may, to the extent permitted by law, be exercised concurrently or separately, and the exercise of any one remedy shall not be deemed to be an election of such remedy or to preclude the exercise of any other remedy. No failure on the part of the Lessor to exercise, and no delay in exercising, any right or remedy hereunder shall operate as a waiver thereof; nor shall any single or partial exercise by Lessor of any right or remedy hereunder preclude any other or further exercise thereof or the exercise of any other right or remedy. Damages occasioned by Lessor taking possession of Equipment are hereby expressly waived by Lessee. Lessee hereby waives and releases all rights to stay of execution and Lessee waives all rights to trial by jury in any litigation with Lessor, Affiliates and their assigns.

17. Lessor covenants to and with Lessee that Lessor is the lawful owner of Equipment, free from all liens and encumbrances, and that, upon Lessee's paying the rents and performing the promises, terms and conditions hereof, Lessee shall peaceably and quietly hold, possess and use Equipment during the term of this lease without hindrance. Lessee agrees to procure for Lessor such estoppel certificates, Landlords' and Mortgagees' waivers or other similar documents as Lessor may request. Lessee agrees to furnish to Lessor its certified annual financial statement, certified without qualification by independent certified public accountants, and such interim statements as Lessor may require.

18. Should Lessee fail to pay any part of the rent herein reserved or any other sum required to be paid by Lessee to Lessor hereunder, Lessee shall pay Lessor interest on such delinquent payment at the highest lawful rate, not to exceed 1% per month, from the date when such payment was due until paid, along with expenses of collection, including reasonable attorneys' fees.

19. On termination of this lease, and on request of Lessor upon default, Lessee shall, at its own cost and expense, return Equipment to Lessor at an address specified by Lessor in the same condition as received, reasonable wear and tear and normal depreciation excepted, and shall assemble the equipment at an address specified by Lessor.

20. All notices relating hereto shall be in writing and delivered in person to an officer of the party to which such notice is being given or mailed by certified mail to such party at the address specified below its signature hereto, or at such other address as may be hereafter specified by like notice by either party to the other. Lessee agrees that Lessor has made no representation or warranty of any kind, nature or description, express or implied, with respect to Equipment. This lease contains the entire agreement between the parties, and may not be changed, modified, terminated or discharged except in writing. Lessee warrants and represents that the execution, delivery and performance of this lease and any Lease Requests submitted to Lessor have been duly authorized and will not violate any provision of any governmental or quasi-governmental law, rule, regulation or ordinance or Lessee's charter or by-laws or any indenture, loan or credit agreement or other instrument to which Lessee is a party or by which Lessee or its property may be bound or affected; and that any and all financial statements submitted and plete and correct and fairly present Lessee's financial condition as at the date thereof.

21. Lessee shall have the option, if Lessee is not in default hereunder, upon giving written notice to Lessor at least 30 days prior to the termination of the original or any renewal term of this lease, to renew this lease for such annual terms as may be specified in such written notice at an annual rent, payable in advance at the beginning of each such annual or renewal term, of $ 1,700.00

Fig. 11-3. Equipment Lease—Continued

22. Lessee shall have the option, if Lessee is not in default hereunder, to purchase Equipment as a whole but not in part, as-is, where-is, at the end of the original or any renewal term of this lease, upon giving at least 30 days' prior written notice to Lessor and upon payment simultaneously with the giving of such notice of $ 4,250.00 _____

23. This lease or any Equipment or any rent or other sums due or to become due hereunder may be transferred or assigned by Lessor without notice, and in such event Lessor's transferee or assignee shall have all the rights, powers, privileges and remedies of Lessor hereunder and Lessee's obligations hereunder shall not be subject to any defense, offset or counterclaim available to Lessee against Lessor.

24. If any provisions of this lease are in conflict with any statute or rule of law of any state or territory wherein it may be sought to be enforced, then such provisions shall be deemed null and void to the extent that they may conflict therewith, but without invalidating the remaining provisions hereof. For the sole purpose of resolving any problem of conflict of laws with respect to filing or recording hereof, it is agreed that this instrument shall be deemed to be executed, completed and effective when Equipment is received at the address at which it is to be located, and that questions of filing or recording shall be determined by the law of such place. In all other respects this lease shall be governed by the law of the State where accepted by Lessor as hereinbelow set forth. This lease shall be binding upon Lessor and Lessee and their respective legal representatives, successors and assigns.

IN WITNESS WHEREOF, and intending to be bound hereby, Lessee has caused this lease to be executed by a duly authorized person as of the day and year first above written and Lessor has accepted the same as set forth below.

ACCEPTED by Lessor at Newark, New Jersey

on February 3 _____, 19 X6

TALCOTT LEASING CORPORATION

By _____
    Its: _____ Vice President

Attest: _____
        Assistant Secretary

[Seal]

Lessor's Address:

XYZ Corporation   L.S.
           LESSEE

By _____
    Its: _____ President

Attest: _____
           Secretary

[Seal]

Lessee's Address: 123 North Street
                  Newark, New Jersey

ACKNOWLEDGMENT OF LESSEE

State of _____ } ss.:
County of _____

ACKNOWLEDGMENT OF LESSOR

State of ....

County of .... } ss.:

On ...., 19......., before me, notary public, personally appeared ....

to me personally known and known to me to be a .... of Talcott Leasing Corporation, a Delaware corporation, the corporation that executed the foregoing instrument as Lessor and to be the person who executed the same on behalf of said corporation and being by me duly sworn did acknowledge and say that said corporation voluntarily executed said instrument as the free act and deed of said corporation, that he knows the seal of said corporation, that the seal affixed to said instrument is the seal of said corporation, and that he freely and voluntarily signed, executed, sealed and delivered said instrument as such on behalf of said corporation for the uses, purposes and consideration therein expressed and with full authority to do so pursuant to resolution of its board of directors.

(Notarial Seal) ....

.... (Notary Public)

My Commission Expires: ....

(For Corporation) On..........., 19......., before me, notary public,

personally appeared ....

to me personally known and known to me to be the........... of the corporation that executed the .... (Title) (attorney-in-fact) foregoing instrument as Lessee and to be the person who executed the same on behalf of said corporation and being by me duly sworn did acknowledge and say that said corporation voluntarily executed said instrument as the free act and deed of said corporation, that he knows the seal of said corporation, that the seal affixed to said instrument is the seal of said corporation, and that he freely and voluntarily signed, executed, sealed and delivered said instrument as such on behalf of said corporation for the uses, purposes and consideration therein expressed and with full authority to do so pursuant to resolution of its board of directors.

(For Individuals) On..........., 19......., before me, notary public,

personally appeared ....

each to me known and known to me to be the person described in and who executed, and whose name is subscribed to, the foregoing instrument as Lessee and duly acknowledged to me that he/she duly signed, executed and delivered the same as his/her free and voluntary act and deed for the uses, purposes and consideration therein mentioned.

(Notarial Seal) ....

.... (Notary Public)

My Commission Expires: ....

Fig. 11–3. Equipment Lease—Continued

PURCHASE ORDER

DATE February 3, 19X6

ORDERED FROM

XYZ Plastics Company
First and Main Streets
Wheeling, West Virginia

SHIP TO:

CARE OF:

XYZ Corporation
123 North Street
Newark, New Jersey

(LESSEE)

SHIP VIA	F. O. B.	SHIPPING CHARGES ARE PAYABLE BY LESSEE STATED ABOVE	TERMS	DELIVERY DATE
Best Way				2/21/X6

QUANTITY	DESCRIPTION	UNIT PRICE	TOTAL
	XCO Model 123AB 456 Plastics Molding Machine A/B 1234	85,000.00	85,000.00

SPECIAL TERMS AND INSTRUCTIONS: USE NON-NEGOTIABLE BILLS OF LADING, AND INSTRUCT CARRIER (1) TO NOTIFY BOTH LESSEE AND TALCOTT LEASING CORPORATION, OF ARRIVAL OF EQUIPMENT AND (2) TO DELIVER EQUIPMENT EITHER ON OUR RECEIPT OR LESSEE'S RECEIPT.

PLEASE FURNISH PROMPTLY
TO TALCOTT LEASING CORPORATION

1. SERIAL NUMBERS
2. INVOICE IN TRIPLICATE
3. ORIGINAL BILL OF LADING ON DAY OF SHIPMENT
   (COPY TO LESSEE STATED ABOVE.)

THIS ORDER IS SUBJECT TO THE TERMS AND CONDITIONS APPEARING HEREON INCLUDING THE REVERSE SIDE.

BY

62-1043 PLEASE SIGN AND RETURN ACKNOWLEDGMENT COPY   ORIGINAL

Fig. 11–4. Financer's Purchase Order

TERMS AND CONDITIONS

TITLE: RISKS IN TRANSIT. Unless this order is by its terms f.o.b. Seller's shipping point, title to the equipment furnished hereunder (hereinafter called "Equipment") shall not pass to Buyer until arrival at address stated and Buyer shall not be responsible for any loss or damage in transit.

INSPECTION BY BUYER AND CONSIGNEE. Equipment shall be subject to inspection and approval by Buyer and Lessee, either of whom shall have the right to reject and return Equipment at Seller's expense if defective or not in compliance with Buyer's specifications. Defects shall not be deemed waived by Buyer's or Lessee's failure to notify Seller upon receipt of Equipment or by payment of invoice. In the event of rejection, this order shall be deemed to have been submitted by Lessee, and Seller shall indemnify Buyer against all claims arising from such rejection or from Seller's delivery of defective or non-complying Equipment and on demand shall forthwith pay Buyer from Lessee's account all payments theretofore made by Buyer to Seller for Equipment.

DELIVERY AND INSTALLATION. If this order by its terms requires Seller's assistance in assembling or installing Equipment, Buyer shall be under no obligation to Seller until Equipment is assembled and installed as directed and put in operating condition. Nor shall Buyer be under any obligation to Seller if delivery is delayed by Buyer's or Lessee's inability to take delivery for any reason beyond Buyer's or Lessee's control. Buyer reserves the right to cancel this order with respect to any undelivered Equipment and if this order is not filled as specified.

MISCELLANEOUS CHARGES. Seller will not charge Buyer or Lessee for any of the costs of packing, drayage, installing, readying or for any other costs in addition to the purchase price of the Equipment, and if Equipment is rejected Seller will pay all charges incurred in transporting Equipment to Lessee and back to Seller.

SELLER'S AGREEMENTS. Seller agrees that all inquiries and communications directed to Lessee will be made through Buyer. Seller will: prior to delivery, affix to Equipment at a conspicuous place a decalcomania or plate to be supplied by Buyer; on the date of shipment, mail original of the bill of lading covering Equipment to Buyer at Buyer's home office or as Buyer may direct and copies to any other place designated by Buyer; indemnify, defend, protect and save harmless Buyer, its customers and the users of Equipment against all suits and from damages, claims and demands arising from failure of Equipment, injuries to persons or property caused by defects therein, actual or alleged infringement of any patent, trade mark or copyright by reason of its sale or use, and/or any other cause whatsoever; refer to the order number hereof on all correspondence, packing slips, bills of lading, etc., pertaining to this order; and mail invoices in triplicate to Buyer, upon which Seller will certify that Equipment was produced in compliance with all applicable requirements of Sections 6, 7 and 12 of the Fair Labor Standards Act of 1938, as amended and of regulations and order duly issued under Section 14 thereof. Seller shall not assign this order, nor any interest therein, nor subcontract any part hereof, without Buyer's prior written consent.

SELLER'S WARRANTIES. Seller warrants to Buyer and Lessee that Equipment: is new unless otherwise stated by Buyer on the face thereof; will conform to specifications, drawings and other descriptions to be furnished by Buyer or Lessee; will be merchantable, of good material and workmanship and free from defect; and will have been produced, sold, transported and delivered under terms and conditions satisfying all requirements of all applicable laws and regulations. All warranties and service normally accompanying Equipment shall be extended by Seller directly to Lessee or, at Buyer's direction, to Buyer or any other user of Equipment.

OTHER MATTERS. No variation in any of the terms, conditions, deliveries, prices, quality, quantity or specifications of this order, irrespective of the wording of Seller's acceptance, shall be effective without Buyer's written consent, and no local, general or trade custom shall be deemed to effect any variation therein. Unless special terms of payments are noted on the front of this form, Buyer will pay the net amount of invoices dated from the first to the 15th inclusive on the 25th of the same month and Buyer will pay the net amount of invoices dated from the 16th to the last inclusive on the 10th of the following month, deducting any applicable discount for prompt payment. No specifications or drawings submitted in connection with this order shall be reproduced or copied in whole or in part and all shall be treated as confidential and returned upon completion of work. Special features of design or construction peculiar to such specifications, drawings, samples and other descriptions shall not be incorporated in orders or projects of others without Buyer's permission. All dies, molds, patterns, jigs, and fixtures furnished to Seller by Buyer, or specifically paid for by Buyer, shall be the property of Buyer, shall be retained, returned or disposed of upon completion of the order only in accordance with Buyer's directions, shall be used only in filling orders from Buyer. shall be held at Seller's risk and shall be kept insured by Seller while in its custody or control in an amount equal to the replacement cost thereof with loss payable to Buyer.

Fig. 11–4.   Financer's Purchase Order—Reverse

12

Interim Real Estate Financing

Joseph S. Lesser
Senior Vice President, Federated Mortgage Investors

DEVELOPMENT AND NATURE OF INTERIM REAL ESTATE FINANCING

Since a substantial portion of this country's wealth is invested in real estate, the study of short-term credit devices properly includes a discussion of the interim real estate financing field. By making available large amounts of needed operating cash, this type of financing has contributed greatly to the dynamic growth of the real estate industry.

Development

Historically, this field—often called second mortgage or secondary financing —was originated by individuals with limited funds who were familiar with real estate values and were attracted to the field by the higher prevailing yields. Today, however, as a result of the enormous growth in the real estate industry and the large funds required to commence and complete projects, publicly-held companies with substantial resources dominate the field. The experience gained over the years by the individual second-mortgage lenders has now been adapted and combined with the latest practices and innovations of the larger firms. This accumulated knowledge and experience has led to the present principles and credit devices of interim real estate financing.

Commercial finance companies and banks are making substantial amounts of loans secured by real estate. Generally, such accommodation is granted during periods of relatively easy money in order to diversify profitably the lenders' activities, expand their portfolios, and supplement their other financing services.

An example of this use of real estate financing as an adjunct of banking and commercial financing is the device, in accounts receivable financing or in factoring, of securing over-advances by taking a second mortgage on property owned by the borrower. Another procedure is to have an individual guarantor of a corporate borrower pledge or lien his individual real estate assets as additional security for loans made to the corporation. The purpose is to bolster a weak credit or enable the lender to advance additional funds not justified by the assets of the borrower-corporation. Furthermore, particularly in state-chartered institutions where the regulations regarding real estate lending are more flexible, banks are making direct second-mortgage loans completely apart from the real estate transactions tied to other types of accommodation. Because of the rising costs of attracting funds, coupled with higher operating costs, it can be anticipated that banks will continue to expand into this higher gross yield area of financing.

This chapter, however, is concerned primarily with those interim real estate financing firms that operate as separate and distinct specialized lending organizations, with their own principles of credit and administration which are peculiar to the real estate field.

Definition

Interim real estate financing can be defined as short-term loans or commitments to make loans secured by a lien on interests in real property. The proceeds of such loans are utilized primarily in the acquisition, development, modernization, completion of existing and commencement of new real estate projects. The interest in the property may be a fee position, a leasehold interest, or merely an assignment of an option to purchase land. The properties subject to the lien devices described below may range from single-family dwellings to 60-story, high-rise apartments, from giant shopping centers to the neighborhood market, form the local single-story law office to the Empire State Building. They may be garden apartments, warehouses, manufacturing plants, condominiums, industrial parks, or parking lots. Any property with a cash flow (see page 269) or potential cash flow via development and leasing may be the subject of interim real estate financing. Vacant land or land in the process of development, if properly located, is also acceptable.

The term "interim" generally is defined to cover a term not exceeding five years, although most financers prefer a three-year term. Some financers will, however, stretch their loans for a period of seven or eight years, particularly where the income from a property is very stable.

The purpose of this financing is to supplement other types, i.e., short- and long-term bank and "permanent" institutional funds which are also available to the real estate industry. Interim real estate financing only fulfills its function if it provides funds not available or insufficiently available from these conventional sources. Interim real estate financing provides, in essence, *senior equity funds* for projects that might otherwise have to be postponed indefinitely.

Mortgages

The most commonly used legal device is the mortgage, and in most instances—with some major exceptions—it is a second mortgage. Before examining this financing device, it is necessary to describe the legal effect and economic purpose of the first mortgage.

First Mortgage. The interim financing field generally presupposes the existence of a first mortgage on the property or a commitment by a bank, insurance company, or other institutional lender to make a long-term first mortgage some time in the future. The first mortgagee, or conventional "permanent" lender, is usually one of the insurance companies, savings banks, savings and loan associations, pension funds, or other investment institutions that make long-term commitments for investment of their continuous inflow of savings and retirement funds. By law or charter provisions, such lenders are prohibited from making conventional first-mortgage loans for more than a specified percentage—usually 66⅔% or 75%—of the appraised value of the property. This restriction, consequently, requires either one-third or one-fourth of the funds to be supplied by the owner-developer of the project. Today, real estate projects such as the building of a 1 million sq. ft. regional shopping center, the construction of a 60-story office building or a 35-story apartment house, the development of twenty thousand single family dwellings, or the demolition and development of an urban renewal project in the center of a large city may each require many millions, and the one-third or one-fourth requirement is beyond the means of all but a few.

Second Mortgage. With the aid of the second mortgage, however, the owner's requirement of initial capital funds to commence a project can be substantially reduced. The interim real estate financer meets this need for funds by "matching" the capital of the owner-developer on a senior equity basis, usually via the second mortgage route. It is, of course, possible in order to raise additional capital to take in partners, thus giving up a portion of the equity. Most entrepreneurs prefer, however, to pay the higher rates of the interim real estate lender, retain 100% of the equity, and also retain full control of their project.

Priority of Mortgages. A second or junior mortgage is in all respects subordinate to the claims of a first mortgage. Revenue or gross income from a real estate project is applicable first to the payment of first-mortgage charges. Foreclosure of a second mortgage in no way disturbs the position of the holder of the first mortgage, unless the first mortgage by its terms provides for acceleration in the event of a default in a subordinate lien. If the first mortgagee forecloses, he wipes out the claim of the junior mortgage holder. Accordingly, it is vital to the junior mortgage holder that the first mortgage be kept current. If the first is accelerated upon default in payment, then the junior mortgage holder must satisfy the first mortgage in order to protect his interest.

Conventional Permanent Mortgage. This is the normal long-term first mortgage (15 to 25 years) made by institutional lenders. It usually provides for monthly or quarterly amortization whereby the mortgage is reduced over the life of the loan.

Building or Construction Loan Mortgage. This is given as security for loans made during the course of construction of a building. These loans, which are utilized for the construction, are generally made by banks and more recently by insurance companies, savings banks, and savings and loan institutions. They usually mature upon completion of construction. *Stage advances* are periodic advances made under a construction loan based upon the progress of the construction.

"FHA" mortgage. This is a conventional permanent mortgage that qualifies for insurance under one of the provisions of the Federal Housing Administration, an agency of the United States government. This agency does not make loans. To encourage certain types of construction and the financing thereof, it will for a small fee (usually ½ of 1%) guarantee first mortgages made by permanent lenders. Like a few of the conventional lenders, the FHA insists that no subordinate liens may be placed on the property. However, this restriction has been circumvented by the secondary lender's taking a pledge of the stock of the corporation owning the building which secures the FHA guaranteed mortgage.

Purchase Money Mortgage. A purchase money mortgage is created where a property is sold and the seller takes back a first or second mortgage as part of the purchase price (hence the term *purchase money mortgage*). This is a common device used in the sale of real estate, and may be illustrated as follows: A purchases XYZ office building from B for $12 million. Making up the purchase price, he takes subject to an $8 million institutional first mortgage on the property, puts a new second *purchase money mortgage* on the property, which he gives to B for $2 million and pays $2 million in cash, thus making up the total purchase price. See the marketability and leverage factors discussed below.

Leasehold Mortgage. A *lease* is a contract between an owner of real estate, called the lessor, and a tenant, called the lessee, providing for the payment of rent for the use of the real estate. The lessee has a *leasehold estate* in the property. Another lien device utilized in financing is a *leasehold mortgage*. This is similar to a regular second mortgage, except that the lien is on the lease rather than on the property. Assume a first mortgage and a second mortgage on a piece of property. Subsequently, the property is leased by the owner to a tenant for 99 years. The tenant can place a leasehold mortgage on his leasehold interest. However, it is incumbent on both the tenant and the holder of the leasehold mortgage to insure that the first and second mortgages are kept current and in good standing. Foreclosure of either mortgage would terminate the lease and thereby extinguish the leasehold mortgage. The life of the latter obviously depends upon the existence of a good lease.

Debt Service

"Debt service" means the interest and amortization payable on the first mortgage and the second, if any. This is usually reflected in a "constant payment" to be made monthly, quarterly, or semi-annually. (For example, the normal 8% constant would include 6% interest and 2% amortization, the 2% being applied in reduction of the principal.) Generally, the constant payment is calculated on the original principal amount of the loan. Accordingly, during the early years, the major portion of the "constant" consists of interest which is deductible for income tax purposes. During the later years, the "constant" is comprised of primarily amortization, which is not deductible. Where accelerated methods of depreciation are being used, this treatment accounts for the economic desire of high bracket taxpayers to dispose of projects after several years. They thereby also seek to convert prior ordinary income deductions into capital gains. Of course, under present tax laws, these owners must have held the property for a minimum of ten years in order to fully justify this treatment.

Cash Flow

The most important term in interim real estate financing is "cash flow." For the purposes of this discussion, it is defined as the gross revenue of a property less all *cash* expenses of operating the property, less "debt service" on the first mortgage, and less real estate taxes. The resulting net figure after these deductions is the "cash flow." There is no deduction of Federal income taxes in arriving at net cash flow; nor is depreciation considered, since the latter does not represent a cash expense. Federal income taxes and depreciation are ignored in the calculation because, after deduction of the depreciation allowance, there generally are no Federal income taxes payable for the first six or seven years. This, of course, assumes that the owner is taking accelerated depreciation on his project. During this period, the interim lender's loan has been either paid off entirely or substantially reduced. Federal income taxes cannot be ignored, however, if the present owner and potential borrower has held the property for several years. In such event, not all the cash flow will be tax free; and taxes must first be deducted to arrive at the true cash flow.

DETERMINANTS OF PROPERTY VALUE

Status of First Mortgage

It is axiomatic in this field that the value and marketability of a property are greatly dependent upon the existence of a realistic first mortgage. To protect this value, it is therefore essential that the first mortgage be current and in good standing.

This axiom may be illustrated as follows: An office building with a $4 million first mortgage is in temporary financial difficulty. The interim lender has a short-term second mortgage on the property of $500,000. Assume he does not cure a default to the extent of $50,000 of unpaid interest and amortization on the first mortgage; thereupon the first mortgagee accelerates his first mortgage and forecloses. At the foreclosure sale, the second mortgagee, to protect his interest, must pay off the first mortgage of $4 million or induce a buyer to do so. This is an almost impossible task for all but the strongest lenders. However, it is not as difficult (assuming the property has the intrinsic value) to induce a buyer to pay the $50,000 to bring the first current, take subject to the $4 million first mortgage and the $500,000 second mortgage, and try to weather the temporary financial difficulty. (In this situation, the lender will accept interest only on his $500,000 loan for a two or three year period, in order to induce a new purchaser to take over the property.) Even in today's affluent society, there are many more purchasers with $50,000 than with $4.05 million.

Leverage. The above example also leads to a discussion of marketability and the effect that "leverage" has on that marketability. A property is always worth more to a potential buyer if he can keep his investment to a minimum.

Assume that the property in the preceding example has, after the financial difficulty has been alleviated, a gross rental income of $800,000. Expenses of operation and real estate taxes amount to $300,000, and the interest and amortization payable on the first mortgage for each year are $320,000. The second mortgage bears an interest rate of 10% per annum, or $50,000 per year. Deducting all these charges from the gross rental income leaves $130,000 of "net cash flow." Assume further that, in addition to the $50,000 arrears in interest and amortization, it costs the purchaser another $210,000 to put the property back into a normal operating position so that it will again earn gross rentals of $800,000. At this point, the buyer has $260,000 invested in the property and is receiving net cash flow of $130,000, or a return on his investment of 50%.

Contrast the above to a situation where he purchases the property for $4.05 million and takes subject to the second mortgage of $500,000. Here his return is increased to $450,000 since he no longer has to pay interest and amortization on a first mortgage. However, his investment is now $4.26 million ($4.05 million incurred on the payment of the first mortgage and $210,000 to put the property back in shape), for a net return of just over 10%.

By keeping the first mortgage current, the new owner has kept his investment at a minimum and "leveraged" his income from 10% to 50% per annum on that investment. Further, he does not face the difficulty of raising the $4.26 million from banks, partners, etc. This ease of purchase, due to the existence of a current first mortgage, is exactly what makes the property more marketable. It increases the number of potential buyers.

Adequate Cash Flow

The existence of cash flow will generally determine the return on the owner's equity and, except for vacant land, the value of the property. Potential investors will purchase the property on the basis of the return that the cash flow will yield on their investment. Some properties sell at five times cash flow or a 20% capitalization rate, others at ten times the cash flow or a 10% capitalization, and still others at 16 times the net cash flow, depending upon the nature and stability of the income comprising the cash flow.

Needless to say, an office building or warehouse with a net income of cash flow from a 30-year General Motors lease covering 100% of the rental space will sell at a higher value than property with cash flow generated from the rentals under a lease from a small dry cleaner. Conversely, a lease for even 30 years, if cancellable by its terms at any time, has little stability of cash flow. Thus, "cash flow" and its stability are the most important factors considered in interim real estate financing, since they determine to a great extent the value of the property involved.

Ability of Management

Some properties depend for their success on the ability of management to run the business operating within the bricks and mortar, rather than on their location or value as real estate. This is particularly true in properties such as bowling alleys, motels and hotels, restaurants, night clubs, nursing homes and hospitals. In such situations, regardless of the intrinsic value of the project as real estate, the dominant factor in generating income will be the managerial ability of the entrepreneur. In the eyes of the interim lender such "management" properties possess greater risk than properties that can be appraised by past results and by the income stability derived from leases to creditworthy lessees. Because the management talents of individuals and companies vary greatly, it is more difficult to judge this type of property. This increased risk does not disqualify the management properties. They do, however, require scrutiny and detailed analysis of considerable magnitude, which not all interim financers are willing to undertake.

OPERATIONAL PROCEDURES

To illustrate the operation of interim real estate financers and their method of analysis, it may be helpful to follow the financing of a project from its inception to its successful conclusion.

Vacant Land and Site-Acquisition Loans

Consider the financing of vacant land or site-acquisition loans. Prior to building anything, an owner-developer must first acquire land. Normally, vacant land has no cash flow and, therefore, no readily ascertainable market value. (Parking lots are an exception.) That is why institutional lenders are generally prevented by law, charter, or credit policy from making loans secured only by un-developed vacant land. (There are exceptions. Some insurance and other institutional lenders will make loans secured by vacant land in order to tie up the future financing of the projects to be built on the land.)

Amount and Repayment of Loan. As a result of this restrictive policy, unless the owner-developer can purchase the land at very favorable terms by giving the seller a long-term purchase money mortgage for most of the purchase price, he would require all cash to complete the purchase. This, of course, may require a substantial amount of capital which the particular purchaser may not possess. In this event, the interim real estate financers will lend, as a general rule, up to 50% of the value of the land as determined by the lender and will take back a first mortgage on the property to secure the loan. The lender will normally require the owner-developer to put up the other 50% of the purchase price. In a considerable number of cases, the owner-developer may not possess the cash to meet the 50% requirement. In lieu thereof, he may have an equity in other properties, with or without a cash flow, which can be utilized as collateral security for an additional loan by the interim lender. This procedure may obviate the necessity of the owner-developer putting up any cash for the purchase of the land.

Normally, site acquisition loans are repaid from the proceeds of construction loans (see below). Occasionally, however, if the interim lender feels that the completed project will be very successful, he may subordinate his acquisition loan to the construction loan.

Occasionally, the interim lender is asked to finance not only the site of the present project, but the acquisition of adjacent land as well; in that event, only the portion of the loan applicable to the actual site is reduced with the construction loan proceeds. By acquiring additional land now for future use, the owner-developer has the advantage of fixing his future site costs. This may enable him to enjoy hoped-for increased values of the contiguous land based upon its proximity to the potentially successful office building, apartment house, or shopping center he is now building.

Another variation of vacant land loans occurs when the interim financer makes available funds for large tracts of land to be improved and developed for single family dwellings. In addition to the acquisition, he may finance the installation of offsite and onsite improvements such as roads, curbs, utilities, grading, sewage treatment plants, etc.

Risk. Site acquisition and development loans are considered the most hazardous of interim loans because the "ascertainable value" has not yet been created. The owner—and, over his shoulder, the lender—must await the sale of the lots and homes, or the construction and leasing of the apartment house, office building, or shopping center. In short, the venture must be successfully completed before money can be earned and loans repaid. If problems arise in the sale of the lots or the houses, or in the construction, or in the leasing then the ability to repay the loans at maturity is seriously affected.

Financer's Appraisal. In applications for vacant land or site acquisition loans, the prime considerations are location and the immediate demand for the project being built on the land. Further questions are: Is the site being best utilized to generate optimum cash flow? Is it zoned properly? Is the general area where the property is located improving, its population increasing, its location and labor supply attracting new industry? Is the site in or convenient to the main stream of traffic and to neighboring commerce or industry or residential areas? If these questions can be answered affirmatively then, depending upon the intended use of the property, and the demand therefor, the owner probably has a good location, and the site may well qualify for financing.

Construction Loans

Most interim real estate financers, with some major exceptions, do not make construction loans. Historically, this has been the province of commercial banks and institutional lenders. They provide, at lower cost than interim lenders, construction funds generally against permanent "takeouts" of insurance companies, savings and loan institutions, savings banks, pension trusts, etc. The long-term permanent lenders "take out" these loans from the bank upon completion of construction in order to invest their funds for the long term, i.e., 15 to 25 years. Commercial banks with their stringent requirements of liquidity generally desire repayment upon completion of construction.

These construction lender banks maintain large staffs well versed in real estate, including appraisers, engineers, and consulting and supervising architects. They must approve the original plans and specifications of the project prior to making advances and then follow construction closely to insure that the project conforms to those plans and specifications. Such compliance is essential, since the retirement of the bank loan is dependent upon the first-mortgage institutional lender's purchasing the loan upon completion of the project. It was upon these original plans and specifications that the permanent lender based its decision. Hence the permanent lender will not purchase the loan unless the property is completed substantially in accordance with these original "plans and specs." Accordingly, the short-term construction lender follows (or should follow) the job through every stage of construction to insure compliance with these specifications.

Generally, the more sophisticated construction lenders enter into a "buy-sell agreement" with the permanent lender. Under this arrangement the permanent lender agrees to purchase the loan made by the bank and the bank agrees to sell the loan to the institutional lender. The reasons for this agreement are obvious. The bank wants to be sure that there will be as few obstacles as possible to the institutional lender's taking over the loan. Therefore, all title questions, all plans and specifications, and even the form of the note and mortgage are approved by the permanent lender in advance of construction or completion. The permanent lender also desires this arrangement, for it is thereby assured of a desirable loan.

In the past, the interim financers have not made construction loans due to their inability to compete with the banks on rate. An increasing number of the interim real estate lenders, however, are entering the field, particularly during tight-money periods, when banks are forced to restrict their accommodations in this area. Higher rates are then available and make such loans more attractive to interim financers.

Commitment Financing

In recent years real estate financers have engaged in commitment financing. Here the interim lender, instead of making immediate cash advances, agrees to make loans in the future. Such commitments are sometimes unconditional and sometimes predicated upon compliance with certain conditions, including completion of the project. In effect, the interim lender lends his credit in lieu of money.

Commitment financing is utilized when an owner-developer decides to proceed at once with construction without waiting the expensive months until the insurance company or pension fund issues its permanent commitment for a long-term loan. This commitment the owner normally must have in order to obtain a construction loan from a commercial bank. By proceeding immediately, the owner-developer avoids delaying the construction of the shopping center or office building during the time required to obtain sufficient signed leases to qualify for a maximum institutional loan.

Takeout Commitments to Construction Lender. Some of the major finance companies have made available their credit in the form of "takeout commitments" to the construction bank lender. These takeouts are conditioned upon completion of the office building, apartment house, or shopping center in accordance with the original "plans and specs" approved in advance by the interim lender. They are agreements by the financer to purchase the bank's loan when the project has been fully completed. Against the takeout, the bank—which normally only desires short-term construction loans—advances construction funds to the owner-developer, and the project moves forward immediately.

In the case of a shopping center or office building, the takeout device enables the owner to be more patient and selective, thereby attracting national and local tenants at considerably higher rents. He does not have to accept any tenant at any rental in order to reach the minimum rental provisions required by the normal long-term institutional loan. As a result, the completed project, because of the higher rent roll, can ultimately qualify for a long-term mortgage substantially higher than might otherwise have been available at the inception of the project.

To illustrate the effect of commitment financing, assume a project costing $6 million to build. A first mortgage could be obtained for $4 million, or two-thirds of the cost of the project. Hence an addi-

tional $2 million would be required of the owner-developer. The
construction bank lender will advance only $4 million because this
is the commitment from the first mortgage long-term lender.
Now, assume the interim real estate lender gives his commitment
to the construction lender to "take out" a $5 million *first mortgage*.
The construction bank lender, if satisfied with the credit and reliability
of the interim lender, will advance against the takeout the full $5
million of construction funds. Obviously this has the effect of reducing the initial capital necessary for the project by 50% or $1 million.
In a great number of cases, the financer will enter into a buy-sell
agreement with the construction lender similar to that previously
discussed.

The "takeout" enables the owner to build the project immediately.
Since most takeouts are given for two to three years, or at least for
the period of construction, it should enable him to lease the project
without pressure. Accordingly, if the project is successfully leased,
he should be able to obtain a $5 or even $6 million institutional
mortgage. The institutional lender can now justify a larger long-term
mortgage loan based upon the value created by established cash flow
rather than the mere bricks-and-mortar cost of the project.

Second-Mortgage Takeout Commitments. Another refinement of
commitment fee financing is the situation where the owner-developer
already possesses a permanent first mortgage commitment providing
for a two-disbursement loan. The last disbursement is contingent
on the project's being leased substantially.

For example, the institutional long-term permanent lender may
agree to lend $4 million upon completion without regard to rentals,
and an additional $1 million when the building is 80% leased. While
such a total permanent mortgage will be quite satisfactory when the
property is leased, $5 million is still required to construct. The bank
construction lender, however, will only lend against the firm non-con-
tingent portion of the permanent commitment, or $4 million. Fur-
thermore, the construction lender may not even be willing to advance
the $4 million since he may not be satisfied that the project will
be completed without an additional $1 million of construction costs.
As indicated above, without completion, the permanent lender will
not take out the bank loan. Therefore, the owner is still short $1
million, and the land lies idle. To solve this problem, the financer
may make available a second-mortgage takeout commitment for $1
million which, when coupled with the permanent lender's commitment,

will enable the borrower to safeguard the construction bank lender in advancing full construction funds, or $5 million.

Financer's Appraisal.   Before extending a commitment to a short-term construction lender, the financer will analyze the project thoroughly.   Obviously, the most important questions are the quality of construction and the demand for the proposed project.   In the case of an office building, shopping center, or apartment house, many of the questions about location raised in connection with site financing will again have to be answered in the affirmative.   In addition, assuming the property is leased, other questions arise.   Will it, after a realistic reserve for vacancies, develop sufficient cash flow from operations to pay all normal operating expenses, real estate taxes and interest and amortization on the projected institutional first mortgage? This mortgage will have to be in a principal amount sufficient to replace the financer's commitment.   Needless to say, a loan application for an apartment-house takeout commitment where the building cannot operate profitably even if fully occupied, or at least yield a fair return on the owner's investment, should never be considered.

Furthermore, the lender giving the commitment must determine the following: Are the principals experienced in this business?   Do they have the ability to procure and retain tenants?   Can they operate the property well and maintain the status quo?   All these must be answered in the affirmative.   This analysis should be made by the lender independently and not based on figures or opinions given by the proposed borrower.

Non-utilization of Commitment.   In the case of both first- and second-mortgage takeout commitments granted by the interim financer, the commitment is usually never utilized.   It is normally replaced by an institutional first-mortgage commitment in a like amount or by the actual purchase of the construction loan directly from the bank by the permanent lender.   In the case of a second-mortgage takeout commitment, a successful project will have been leased to an extent sufficient to trigger the escalated amount.   In the case of a first-mortgage takeout commitment, it now has proven income, or projected income based on signed leases, to attract a higher institutional first mortgage than was available when the property was merely a gleam in the builder's eyes.   Hence, the device of the commitment takeout has fulfilled its function.   It has enabled the construction bank lender to advance a greater share of the necessary operating funds to commence the project.

Fees. The fees for commitment financing generally range from 2% to 4% of the amount of the commitment. Accordingly, if a first-mortgage commitment is given in the amount of $5 million, the commitment fee may be $150,000. However, on a $6 million project, this commitment credit device has enabled the builder to obtain an additional $1 million of operating cash less, of course, the commitment fee, or a net of $850,000.

A typical commitment agreement appears in Fig. 12–1 (p. 281).

Completed-Project Financing or "Cash-Flow" Loans

Now that the project is complete or nearing completion, the critical question is whether the property is economically successful. Has it created a value over the actual cost thereof, thereby justifying the construction of the project. This creation of value is illustrated by the following: A project costs $6 million to build, including the cost of the land. The building is leased to tenants creating gross rentals of $1 million. After deducting a reserve for vacancies of 5% or $50,000, expenses of $350,000 including real estate taxes, and debt service of $400,000 (8% constant on a $5 million first mortgage, usually five times the gross rentals), the property possesses a cash flow of $200,000. Using a capitalization rate of 10% (10 × $200,000), the property has a value of $2 million over the first mortgage. This includes the $1 million put in by the owner and $1 million of *created value*—or a total value of $7 million, including the first mortgage of $5,000,000. The cash flow generated by the leasing of the property has created this value and therefore the project is successful.

Analyzing Stability of Income. Now the interim lender must examine and analyze the income derived from the leases to insure "stability of income" in order to determine the amount of loans, if any, to be made against this cash flow. To begin the analysis, it is necessary to consider the type of property involved.

SHOPPING CENTERS. In shopping centers, the fundamental question to be answered is what percentage of the aggregate rentals of the center are with strong-rated concerns? The lender is actually lending against the stability of the lessees rather than on the bricks and mortar comprising the shopping center.

Further inquiry will determine how much of the rentals payable under the leases are fixed mandatory rentals and whether the leases are non-cancellable. Do these leases provide for escalation in the event that real estate taxes or other operating expenses are increased?

In short, will the owner of the center (the borrower) be able to pass along increased real estate taxes to the tenants and thereby preserve the stability of his cash flow? The same question applies to any expense, an increase of which would have the effect of decreasing the cash flow.

The lender should also make a quick market analysis, including an examination of existing and potential competition, population, income, employment and retail sales in the area. He should check the design of the center and tenant selection by type of business. All of this may have an effect, good or bad, on the success of the center over the years and, therefore, a beneficial or adverse effect on the stability of the cash flow.

APARTMENT HOUSES. When analyzing cash flow of an apartment house, determine whether the leases are for the normal two- or three-year term or on a month-to-month basis. Have concessions been given and will it be necessary to give additional concessions to renew the leases? These concessions, if made, will, of course, decrease the future cash flow. Will the expenses of operating the apartment house go up? Has the property been well maintained, or is there deferred maintenance to be incurred in the future? Is the property now being operated in a proper manner so that the tenants will be retained on renewals?

OFFICE BUILDINGS. When viewing the stability of the income of an office building, it is again essential to analyze the individual leases comprising the total gross rentals. To a considerable extent, the analysis is similar to that of a shopping center except that in some sections of the country short-term leases on office space are normal rather than the exception. Some of the questions asked previously are raised again: Is the area where the office building is located improving; is population increasing; is the site convenient to the mainstream of traffic and to neighboring commerce or industry? Is there a surplus of office space? Can new space be readily absorbed in the market? Needless to say, competition breeds lowering of prices, and this affects renewals. What is the condition of repair? Is deferred maintenance required? Is management efficient? Is the property being maintained at proper standards with minimum operating costs? Would a business desiring to lease office space in this city consider this site favorably?

Size of Loan. Assuming a completed and successfully leased project, the owner should have created a value evidenced by the net cash flow. To repeat, this is gross revenue after deduction of all cash operating expenses, including real estate taxes, and after servicing the first mortgage (both interest and amortization). This cash flow determines the value, the marketability, and, more important from the point of view of the interim lender, the existence of an equity in the asset to serve as collateral security for a loan. For example, a property with a net cash flow (or, as it is sometimes called, cash throwoff) of $100,000, if all other factors are favorable, will generally justify a second-mortgage loan of $400,000 or $500,000, or five times the cash flow.

The principle is that property possessing either a full or partial tax shelter as a result of depreciation will, for the life of the loan, throw off the same cash flow each year, assuming the property remains rented and properly maintained. On the basis of a loan of five times the cash flow, the loan by the second-mortgage lender has the effect of accelerating the borrower's cash flow for a period of five years. Assuming the cash throwoff continues, the loan could be repaid (after allowing for interest) out of the cash flow within a six- or seven-year period.

Terms of Repayment. To illustrate the principle involved, as well as the usual terms of the lender, assume a loan of $450,000 against a cash flow of $100,000 at an interest rate of 10% per annum with a term of three years. Most second-mortgage lenders, having accelerated the cash flow by making the loan, will not return any portion of it to the borrower. They will require that the future flow be applied in full toward interest and amortization on their loan. Therefore, at the end of the first year the principal loan will be reduced by $55,000 (the remaining amount of cash flow, after paying interest of $45,000), at the end of the second year by an additional $60,500, and at the end of the third year by an additional $66,550, or a total for the three years of almost half the loan. Furthermore, as the loan has now been reduced by almost 50 per cent over the three year period (assuming the stability of the cash flow is unimpaired), the balance of the loan is easily refinanced by another lender, or more likely, the existing lender will refinance the reduced balance for another three years under the same terms and conditions. As a practical matter, however, if the income is extremely stable (based, for example, on a long-term, high-rated lease) the lender may require little or no amortization over the life of the loan.

Completing the Financing Cycle. The property's ability to generate a cash flow sets the value of that property. The cash flow determines the return an investor receives as a result of his ownership. It also determines the amount a potential purchaser is willing to pay. This is not the case, of course, in vacant land investments, where the owner does not wish to develop the property himself, but merely desires to hold it for investment. Here he offsets the expenses of holding—real estate taxes and carrying charges (interest, etc.) of his cash investment—against the anticipated increase in value of the vacant land. He hopes for gradual increments in value on the theory that "fools predict the end of the earth and wise men continue to invest in real estate."

With cash flow, the owner of property has an asset with an easily determinable fair market value. He may desire to sell the equity represented by the value of the cash flow and with the proceeds commence another project. Conversely, he may desire to retain his ownership and convert this non-liquid asset into cash again via the route of second-mortgage lending.

To illustrate, if property possesses a cash flow of $100,000, the owner could borrow $500,000 on a second mortgage. With the $500,000, he then proceeds to acquire another site to develop another shopping center, office building, apartment house, etc. Assume the owner-developer wishes to buy another tract of land for $1 million. Returning to vacant land loans, the interim financer, on the basis of the owner's cash investment of $500,000 (received from his second-mortgage, cash-flow loan described above), would match this investment with a $500,000 first-mortgage acquisition loan for the full purchase price. The financing cycle is now complete, from the financing of the initial site by the interim lender to the placing of the second mortgage on the completed cash-flow project thus freeing the equity of the owner for future projects.

COMPARISON WITH OTHER SHORT-TERM FINANCING

Analogies can be drawn between interim real estate financing and other types of short-term credit. Vacant land or site-acquisition loans are similar to raw and finished inventory financing, for vacant land is also "warehoused." Commitment financing in real estate is similar to letter of credit financing, and construction loans correspond to the financing of work in process. Cash-flow financing or the granting of second mortgages on completed projects is comparable to accounts receivable financing. In accounts receivable financing, the lender accelerates the cash flow, enabling borrowers to produce and sell in larger volume. Such increased volume within the same time span increases profits. By providing second mortgages on successful projects, the lender similarly accelerates cash flow. The borrower, therefore, can build more projects simultaneously and thus increase his profits.

Both the time-sales lender (making loans against income producing chattels) and the second-mortgage real estate lender are primarily looking to the fruits of the property for repayment. The producer in both instances has received immediately what it normally would have taken him five years to receive. For the immediate and profitable use of these funds he is willing to pay an interest rate of from 10% to 12% per annum. He utilizes the funds "freed" or accelerated by the interim lender to produce additional products or projects.

As seen above, it is difficult to distinguish—except in terminology and form of collateral—between interim real estate financing and other types of short-term credit. The tools and analytic procedures may differ, but the credit and legal principles and devices, while they may bear different names, are in substance the same.

Construction Loan
Stand-By Commitment

DEF·LENDING CORPORATION
40 Wall Street
New York 5, N. Y.

XYZ Realty Corp.   May 3, 19X6
500 Fifth Avenue
New York, New York   re: ABC Office Building
                                500 Park Avenue
                                New York, New York

Gentlemen:

We hereby confirm our agreement to lend (or to cause our subsidiary to lend) to you the amount of $5,000,000.00, to be secured by a First   mortgage on the premises described in Schedule A annexed hereto, subject to the terms and conditions set forth below:

1. *Principal Amount of Indebtedness*: ($5,000,000.00)

   Five Million .... Dollars

2. *Term*:   Two years

3. *Interest*:   10 % per annum, payable monthly

   If the prime rate of interest charged by Chase Manhattan Bank shall increase beyond the present rate of 5-1/2% per annum, interest shall be increased, effective as of the date of such increase in the prime rate, by the amount of such increase in the prime rate; and if said prime rate is subsequently decreased, interest shall be similarly decreased, effective as of the date of such decrease, but in no event shall interest on the loan be less than 10 % per annum.

4. *Amortization*: $50,000.00 per month payable monthly.

5. *Prepayment*: None. - except from the proceeds of an institutional long-term loan bearing an interest rate of not more than 6-1/2% per annum.

6. *Guarantees*: This loan shall be guaranteed jointly and severally by John Doe and Richard Roe.

Fig. 12–1. Commitment Agreement

7. *Other Security*:

    (1) A first chattel mortgage covering all items of furnishings, fixtures and equipment contained in the ABC Office Building or on the plot of ground known as 500 Park Avenue;

    (2) Conditional assignment of rents of all leases entered into covering space in the ABC Office Building.

7a. *Insurance*: You shall supply and maintain fire insurance and extended coverage and public liability covering the premises referred to above in a company or companies satisfactory to us and in an amount or amounts meeting with our approval. Such fire and extended coverage policy or policies, endorsed to show our interest as mortgagee (or certificates where such policies are held by prior mortgagees), and proof of issuance of such liability policies shall be delivered to us at the closing. All policies shall provide that they may not be altered or cancelled except on ten days written notice to us. We shall have the opportunity to pay any monies or to do any acts necessary to prevent such alteration or cancellation, the cost thereof to be added to your indebtedness.

8. *Title Insurance*: You shall supply title insurance covering the premises referred to above in the amount of this loan and in such form and with such company or companies as may be approved by us free of exceptions objectionable to us.

9. *Costs*: You shall pay, at the time of closing, all title examination and title insurance costs, legal fees of our attorneys, plus disbursements, appraisal fees, survey costs, recording and filing fees and taxes, revenue stamps and all other expenses incurred by us in connection with this transaction. In the event of your failure to close this loan, due to your inability to submit good title, or your failure to comply with the terms hereof, you shall pay for all expenses incurred.

10. *Closing*: The closing of this loan shall be held at our office or the office of our attorneys, Davis, Davis, Stone and Davis   , not later than eighteen months   from the above date of this commitment, and unless extended in writing by us, this commitment shall at our option, expire on such date.

11. *Use of Proceeds*: Proceeds of this loan shall be used to satisfy an indebtedness to a bank or other lender satisfactory to us in an amount not less than the amount of this loan, which indebtedness shall have been incurred for the purpose of financing the cost of the improvements described in paragraph 12 G hereof.

12. This loan is subject to the following conditions:

  A. You shall have good and marketable title to the premises referred to above, as well as any and all other collateral to be assigned, pledged or mortgaged hereunder, subject only to the matters expressly set forth in Schedule A.

  B. The stockholders, officers and directors of your corporation, and all other corporations guaranteeing this loan, shall agree that no dividend shall be payable on any of the stock of said corporations so long as there shall remain any unpaid balance of principal and interest on this loan, and shall further agree to subordinate to this loan any indebtedness owing or to be owing from said corporations to any of them. No payment of any kind shall be made on any such indebtedness to any such stockholder, officer or director until the entire principal balance and interest of this loan shall have been paid.

Fig. 12–1. Commitment Agreement—Continued

C. All obligations on our part are expressly subject to the approval of our attorneys, Davis, Davis, Stone and Davis , with respect to all matters pertaining to title, the form and substance of all proceedings and documents necessary to consummate the loan in compliance with the terms and conditions stated herein, and other legal matters, including the validity and effectiveness of any security or guarantee given hereunder. We shall have received copies of all documents and other evidence we may reasonably request, to establish compliance with all the terms and conditions hereof, the sufficiency of all corporate proceedings, the consummation of the transactions contemplated hereby and the legal validity and effectiveness of all such proceedings and transactions, all in the form and substance satisfactory to our attorneys.

D. You agree that all representations, warranties and covenants made to us in this agreement or in any other instrument delivered pursuant to the provisions hereof shall be deemed to have been relied upon by us and shall survive the closing hereunder, regardless of any investigation made by us or on our behalf.

E. You agree to pay all brokerage commissions, if any, payable in connection with the issuance of this commitment, whether or not the transactions hereby contemplated are consummated and you do hereby indemnify us and save us harmless from any and all claims which may be asserted against us or any liabilities which may be imposed on us by reason of any claim for brokerage commissions in connection with this transaction. This obligation shall survive the closing and the payment of the principal and interest of the loan.

F. You and all guarantors shall furnish us with financial statements quarterly and audited statements annually until full repayment of the loan.

G. The improvements described in Schedule A shall have been completed in accordance with plans and specifications initialed by us. No material changes may be made in said plans and specifications without our prior written consent. All work provided for in said plans and specifications shall have been done in a good, workmanlike manner, free of any mechanics or materialmen's liens, in accordance with the requirements of all Federal, state and municipal authorities having jurisdiction thereof. Said improvements shall be free of all violations of law, municipal ordinances, orders or requirements noted in or issued by any Federal, state or municipal authority having jurisdiction thereof. An architect's certificate of completion and the final certificate of occupancy shall have been issued with respect to such improvements and all licenses, permits and other approvals (Federal, state or municipal) required for the occupancy and operation of said improvements shall have been obtained and the originals thereof exhibited to us.

13. This commitment is intended by us as a "stand-by" in order to enable you to obtain an interim construction loan from a bank or other lender satisfactory to us. By "stand-by" we mean that, while our agreement to make the loan to you on the terms and conditions herein set forth is firm, you have no obligation to conclude this transaction.

   In the event you desire to conclude this transaction, you shall give us thirty (30) days prior written notice of your intention so to do, which notice shall be accompanied by a deposit of $500.00 , to be applied toward the costs and expenses referred to in paragraph 9 of this commitment, and by a notice from the construction lender that it desires to call its loan. Unless we receive such notices and deposit not less than thirty (30) days prior to the date set forth herein for the closing of this transaction, this commitment shall terminate and become null and void.

14. As consideration for the making of this commitment on the conditions above specified, you hereby agree to pay to us $ 150,000.00 upon the signing of this agreement, as a non-refundable fee therefor.

Fig. 12–1. Commitment Agreement—Continued

15. This agreement may not be changed or terminated orally.

Please indicate your acceptance by signing and returning to us two enclosed copies of this letter, together with payment of the commitment fee hereinabove referred to.

SCHEDULE A

A twelve-story office building to be built including all furnishings, fixtures and equipment on a plot of ground owned in fee comprising approx. 28,000 sq. ft. known as 500 Park Avenue, said office building to contain approx. 400,000 sq. ft. of gross rentable area. The building shall be fully completed pursuant to plans and specifications previously approved by DEF Lending Corporation, said plans and specifications are attached to this commitment marked Exhibit A.

Very truly yours,

DEF LENDING CORPORATION

By ....
                Vice President

ACCEPTED AND AGREED TO:
XYZ Realty Corporation

By ....

Fig. 12–1. Commitment Agreement—Continued

13

Financing Acquisitions and Mergers

Harry L. Goldstein
Executive Vice President, The Mastan Company, Incorporated

DEVELOPMENT AND NATURE OF ACQUISITION FINANCING

Credit grantors have long recognized the diversity of commercial finance company operations. The variety of activities discussed in this book concretely evidences them. The flexibility of finance company techniques is best demonstrated by acquisition financing which began in the early 1940's with the entry of the United States into World War II. Interestingly, this commercial finance company device is one of the few that commercial banks have not emulated to any great extent. Perhaps the difficulties described below may indicate why.

Development

In the 1940's the soaring volume and burgeoning profits of many small companies encouraged many entrepreneurs, for reasons discussed below, to dispose of their businesses. Finance companies thus were confronted with a challenge to their imagination, ingenuity, and versatility. It is fair to say that, after a relatively slow start, this new challenge was met effectively. Since the early 1940's literally hundreds of such acquisitions have been handled by finance companies, with advantages accruing to sellers, purchasers, and finance companies alike. Of greater importance is the resultant continuation

285

of businesses that might have been otherwise liquidated, with loss of jobs to many. Even more significant is the contribution made to many communities and to the entrepreneurial structure itself.

During the war an excess profits tax was enacted. By the end of the war, this tax became one important reason why owners of businesses considered disposing of their companies. In some cases, the heavy tax impact could be mitigated by sale to a company having higher earnings for the base years on which the excess profits were computed. Thus the war-born prosperity resulted in many sales of businesses, especially those owned by men of advancing years, who felt that the continuity of the business in the family was not assured. Indeed, more businesses have been sold because of the age of management-ownership and because of taxes than for any other single reason.

Role and Considerations of the Financer

The willingness of entrepreneurs to sell their businesses must be matched by the willingness and the capacity of the buyers to acquire them. Generally, such buyers have been relatively young men with some business background and anxious to expand their own business or to take advantage of an attractive purchase. Obviously, the companies involved, especially those whose acquisitions were facilitated by commercial finance company money, have been moderate sized. Normally, the purchaser makes a modest contribution of capital and relies on the finance company to provide the bulk of the funds. In most cases the business is acquired at a price less than its book value. Frequently, it is acquired at a price equal to its working capital; substantial asset value in machinery and equipment and plant is acquired for no consideration. These bargains are not as common today, however, as they were in the 1940's.

The considerations that are paramount to a purchaser, however, are not necessarily conclusive to a financer. The financer is primarily interested in the management capability of the purchaser, particularly his grasp of the financing problems. Also important are the purchaser's capacity and strength in all other phases of the business. Obviously, the financer must feel that it has a viable customer on its books in spite of the borrower's undercapitalized position, for the very process of financing an acquisition implies the substantial substitution of debt for equity. In the jargon of the trade this is called "bootstrapping," "stripping," or, more colorfully, "buying the cow with its own milk." Notwithstanding the reduction in capital of the com-

bined surviving company, the resultant entity must be strong enough
to meet its obligations and retain sufficient working capital to operate
properly. Many acquired companies, however, are overcapitalized
so that reduction in capital, per se, is not necessarily injurious.

Two types of financing are here involved. First, financing the
acquisition and, second, the continuing financing of the business acquired. The first kind of financing is called acquisition financing
and involves a turn-around or facilitating loan; the second, continuing
financing, involves conventional financing secured by accounts receivable and other assets. It should be emphasized that financers are
primarily interested in conventional financing and are only inciden-
tally interested in acquisition financing. To put it in another way,
financers are interested in acquisition financing only as a stepping
stone to the conventional financing that thus becomes available. As
above indicated, the reduction of equity in the acquired company
necessitates debt financing in the form of secured borrowing.

Form of Transaction

Depending on its form, an acquisition may or may not include
a merger. The merger process is only required where the acquisition
is effected by the purchase of the capital stock of the acquired company rather than a purchase of assets subject to liabilities. Only
in the purchase of capital stock is a so-called "turn-around" loan
or a "facilitating" loan required. Here such a loan is necessary to
effect the purchase of the capital stock. In the purchase of assets
subject to the assumption of liabilities, there is no merger and hence
no need for a turn-around loan. This kind of acquisition begins with
conventional financing secured by assets acquired from the selling
company. The legal procedures in such a transaction are less complex, and the financer is not burdened with as many operational,
credit, and analytical problems. The essential differences in the
handling of these two kinds of acquisition (which are subject to
other qualifying characteristics) will be discussed below.

In either type of acquisition, the acquiring entity may be either
an active operating company or a new corporation especially organized for the purpose of the acquisition. The purchaser, however,
must be a corporation because of state usury laws (see Chapter 3,
page 39). The merger step can follow the creation of a new corporate entity (if required) within several hours or, possibly, as many
as thirty days. Acquisition of the stock of a company and the neces-

sary merger can be effected "around the table." The time element depends to a large degree on the merger laws of the state involved and to a lesser degree on operational considerations. The legal requirements involved are discussed at greater length below (see page 297).

(see page 297).

PRELIMINARY ANALYSIS OF ACQUISITION

Agreement of Sale

The form of the transaction is determined by the agreement of sale between the seller and the purchaser. In many cases this agreement is not in final form when the financer is first approached. Usually negotiations are in progress and some material points still may be unsettled. It is essential that the financer review the final agreement to purchase before it makes any commitments.

The agreement to purchase provides for (a) 100% cash, or (b) a combination of cash and deferred payment, or (c) a combination of cash and a profit-sharing participation over a period of years based on specified formulae. If any part of the purchase price is deferred, or if there is a profit-sharing arrangement for the sellers who continue to manage, the agreement may contain prohibitions against assigning or pledging receivables or inventory or mortgaging fixed assets. In some cases there will be no such express prohibitions, but there may be negative covenants tantamount to prohibitions. These prohibitions or covenants can preclude the possibility of secured financing.

If capital stock is being purchased, then the acquisition of 100% of the capital stock is desirable. The agreement should then contain representations in that regard. If there are minority shareholders who are not parties to the sale, care should be exercised regarding their proper handling. Even in a purchase-of-assets transaction there may be dissenting shareholders. They may demand a right of appraisal or some other remedy.

Financial Statements

The financer must also have balance sheets and profit and loss statements of both the company to be acquired and the acquiring company for periods of at least three years prior to the date of closing. The importance of a detailed analysis of the balance sheets of both the acquiring and the acquired companies cannot be overemphasized.

Many situations involve an acquiring company already established in business. Where this is so, that company's financial weakness can be a deterrent to the acquisition financing. The reasons are obvious. Not only is there a poor balance sheet, but it can be reasonably assumed that the management of the acquiring company leaves something to be desired. In such situations, the purchase price conceivably may be very attractive. Nevertheless, financing such an acquisition would be imprudent. Conversely, if an established acquiring company shows a reasonably good financial statement with a good record of earnings, the financer's disposition to consider financing the acquisition is obviously stronger.

Consider a purchase-of-capital-stock (and therefore merger) type of acquisition. In the interest of clarity and simplicity, it has been assumed that the acquiring company has been specifically organized to make this acquisition. Mr. A organizes a Pennsylvania corporation called the A (acquiring) Corporation. The company to be acquired will be called the S (sold) Corporation, a New York Corporation.

Obviously, the purchasing A Corporation and the financer view the acquisition of S Corporation from substantially different perspectives. The purchaser is interested in a good purchase in terms of the *real* value of the S Corporation, distinguishing between book value and so-called fair value. This involves a critical evaluation of each of the assets on the balance sheet as well as a determination that all liabilities, including contingent liabilities, are fully disclosed. Of even greater significance than the going value of the business, as reflected in its balance sheet, is its profitability. An apparent bargain price, based on balance-sheet figures, may prove to be a mirage if the acquired company has been sustaining operating losses regularly.

The financer's analysis of the balance sheets, and the ultimate consolidated balance sheet, is directed to the viability of the pro forma company after reflecting the payment of the purchase price to the sellers and the financing required to consummate the transaction. The financer is also interested in making a tough-minded evaluation of all assets on the S Corporation's balance sheet and being assured that all liabilities are fully disclosed. Since the form of this transaction is an acquisition of S Corporation by purchase of 100% of its capital stock, any undisclosed liabilities or overstated assets are a distinct risk. Usually, in the agreement, the selling shareholders make certain representations and give warranties concerning both assets and liabilities. This is discussed in greater detail below (see page 297).

Balance Sheets. The balance sheets of the two corporations are presented in Fig. 13–1. A Corporation is capitalized at $100,000, represented by a cash investment in 100% of the capital stock of A Corporation by Mr. A. The S Corporation has capital stock and earned

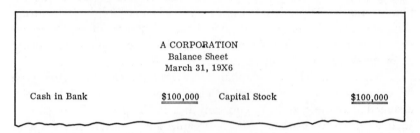

A CORPORATION
Balance Sheet
March 31, 19X6

| Cash in Bank | $100,000 | Capital Stock | $100,000 |

S CORPORATION
Balance Sheet
Dec. 31, 19X5

Cash		$ 50,000	Notes Payable-Bank		$100,000
Accounts Receivable		250,000	Accounts Payable		200,000
Inventory:			Current Portion— '		
Raw Materials	100,000		Mortgage Payable		5,000
Work in Process	175,000		Accruals		35,000
Finished Goods	75,000	350,000	Income Taxes Payable		25,000
Prepaid Items		25,000			
		675,000			365,000
Machinery & Equipment			Mortgage payable—		
(net of depreciation)		150,000	Real Estate		45,000
Real Estate (net of depre-			Capital Stock	100,000	
ciation)		100,000	Retained Earnings	415,000	515,000
		$925,000			$925,000

Fig. 13–1. Balance Sheets of Merging Corporations

surplus totaling $515,000, as evidenced by its balance sheet dated December 31, 19x5.

The balance sheet of A Corporation is very simple and needs no analysis. There should be, however, confirmation of the cash investment and the issuance of capital stock. The cash in bank also should be confirmed. The balance sheet of S Corporation requires more detailed examination:

CASH IN BANK. This item requires confirmation with bank deposi-
taries which can be buttressed by internal reconciliations.

ACCOUNTS RECEIVABLE. Inasmuch as this asset represents the
largest and most liquid item of security to be taken by the finance
company, it should be given detailed study. A proper analysis should
disclose concentrations in individual debtor accounts exceeding 5%
of the total accounts receivable. A detailed aging of the receivables
should be obtained (preferably on a comparative monthly basis for

```
                    MEMORANDUM OF FINANCER


        Funds Required for Purchase of Stock
            Purchase Price—100% of Stock of S Corporation    $400,000
            Less—Deposited by A Corporation with Financer      100,000
               To be Advanced by Financer                    $300,000

        Availability—Conventional Financing (After Merger)

            To Repay $300,000—"Turn-around Loan"             $300,000
            Pay Off Bank Loan                                  100,000
               Total                                         $400,000

        From:

            Cash Account                                     $ 25,000
            80% Advance on Eligible Accounts Receivable        200,000
            Loan on Inventory                                   75,000
            Mortgage on Machinery and Equipment                100,000
               Total                                         $400,000
```

Fig. 13–2.   Financing Required for Merger

the last twelve months) which will indicate the collection turnover
of the receivables and generally reflect the quality of the debtors. In
addition, credit agency ratings of the accounts should be indicated
for all of the larger balances and for a sampling of the smaller
balances.

An analysis of ineligible accounts is important. This would include contra accounts, consignment receivables, and certain debtors
that exceed their credit limits. The total of this ineligibility should
be deducted from the total amount of receivables to determine the
collateral base on which the advances will be made.

The conventional financing required in this transaction, as indicated in Fig. 13–2, shows an advance of $200,000 on an 80% advance basis. This loan is self-liquidating and requires no maturity schedules. Indeed the analysis here corresponds to that for the financing of accounts, discussed in Chapter 3.

INVENTORY. The S Corporation is a manufacturing company. The inventory therefore should be broken down into raw materials, work in process, and finished goods. The inventory turnover as represented by the average inventory in relation to annual sales is an important consideration.

In many acquisitions, there are hidden inventory reserves which should be ferreted out and substantiated. Another typical element is excessive inventory that can be quickly converted into cash. This can be helpful in considering the real cash flow.

Of overriding importance is the currency and marketability of the inventory. A physical inspection of the inventory and inventory records is necessary to establish both the quantitative and qualitative aspects of the inventory.

The financing against inventory in Fig. 13–2 amounts to $75,000. This is a conservative advance against a total inventory of $350,000, all of which will be pledged. The raw material element in the inventory exceeds the amount of the inventory loan. Amortization of this loan should be provided on a monthly basis with a complete payout within two years.

MACHINERY AND EQUIPMENT. Inasmuch as the ultimate financing requires a loan against chattels and equipment, a professional appraisal establishing a so-called knockdown, forced-sale, or auction value is usually required. This physical inspection will also verify the presence of the machinery and equipment on the premises, and indicate its condition and the general quality of housekeeping.

A loan of 75% can be made on appraisal value. This will provide a reserve for depreciation during the term of the loan and for possible liquidation expenses. Inasmuch as a loan of $100,000 is required, as indicated in Fig. 13–2, the appraisal value should be not less than $133,000. The term of this loan should be between three and five years and should be amortized monthly together with interest on declining balances.

REAL ESTATE. We have assumed that the real estate mortgage will remain and become an obligation of the surviving consolidated company. This presupposes that there are no prohibitions against merger in the mortgage. Regarding the value of the real estate, both a physical inspection and a professional appraisal are desirable. The value of completely owner-occupied real estate is patently less than buildings which are multiple tenanted.

NOTES PAYABLE TO BANK. As indicated in Fig. 13–2, notes payable to the bank will have to be paid off. With the secured financing involved and the reduced equity implications of the acquisition and merger, a bank normally would insist on such repayment.

ACCOUNTS PAYABLE. A detailed list of accounts payable should be obtained, preferably aged. For comparative purposes such lists of accounts payable should be obtained for previous periods. Such listings reflect credit sources and the paying habits of S Corporation. Concentrations in a few suppliers might be a basis for concern. Both the purchaser and the finance company should ascertain whether the credit formerly extended to S Corporation will continue to be available to the surviving consolidated corporation. If old management remains, under contract or otherwise, the continuity of the credit relationships is better assured than if the purchaser takes over and old management retires from the scene.

INCOME TAXES PAYABLE. Aside from consideration of the adequacy of the income tax liability as stated on the balance sheet, there are, as noted below (page 299), additional tax implications in such an acquisition.

For a number of reasons it is desirable to obtain income tax returns for a period of at least three years. The returns should confirm the balance sheets submitted as well as the income statements for the periods involved. Disparities or discrepancies should be checked. In addition, the liability indicated on each of these returns should be checked against the company's accounting records. There also may be loss carrybacks or losses that can be carried forward. All of these require careful attention.

RETAINED EARNINGS. The consolidation of the two companies will result in a reduction of earned surplus. Hence as a matter of law it is vital that the earned surplus be sufficient to absorb such reduction. In the present case, it is fairly close. Great care must be taken therefore to be certain of its adequacy. Further ramifications of this point are discussed below (page 297).

Profit-and-Loss Statement. The profit-and-loss statement of S Corporation (Fig. 13–3) is obviously a matter of basic interest both to

A Corporation, the purchaser, and to the financer. Notwithstanding the attractiveness of the purchase at a price below book or real value, the viability of the surviving/consolidated company (whose net worth has been substantially reduced) requires a reasonably good record of profits. The S Corporation's profit-and-loss statement for the last year showed sales of $2 million, a gross profit of $500,000, a net profit before tax of $146,000, and a net profit after tax of $76,000. Volume and profits for the two prior years were somewhat smaller, reflecting a gradual improvement in each of the last two years over the prior year. This favorable trend is important to both the purchaser and the financer.

The initial financing will amount to $375,000 and will fluctuate seasonally. On average, by virtue of profit realized, it should be somewhat less than $375,000 for the first year. The additional cost represented by this financing, as compared with bank interest formerly paid, would represent a net reduction of profit before tax of about $40,000 and after tax of about $20,000. Notwithstanding the heavier financing charges, the profit will be about $60,000 after tax for the year, a very attractive return on the investment of $100,000 made by the purchaser.

THE FINANCING TRANSACTIONS AND RESULTS OF MERGER

Financing Purchase of Stock

Figure 13-2 reflects what are in effect two separate financing transactions. The first is the financing of the purchase of the capital stock of S Corporation by A Corporation. The financing required is commonly referred to as a "turn around" loan or a "facilitating" loan. In this instance, in addition to the $100,000 contribution of A Corporation, the financer would provide its $300,000, making a total of $400,000 representing the total purchase price.

Security. The security for the loan of $300,000 is an assignment to the financer of 100% of the capital stock of A Corporation and 100% of the capital stock of S Corporation. As evidence of this indebtedness, A Corporation will deliver its collateral note in the amount of $300,000, plus fees and interest, to the financer. This note will recite the securities deposited as collateral, as well as the due date, fee (if any), and interest on the note.

```
                         S CORPORATION
                     Profit and Loss Statement
                   For Year Ended Dec. 31, 19X5


     Net Sales                                        $2,000,000
     Cost of Goods Sold                                1,500,000
       Gross Profit on Sales                             500,000
     Operating, Selling and
        Administrative Expenses        $325,000
     Depreciation                        20,000
     Interest—Bank                        6,000
     Interest—Mortgage                    3,000            354,000
        Profit before Taxes                              146,000
     Provision for Federal Income Taxes                   70,000
        Net Profit after Taxes                          $ 76,000
```

Fig. 13–3. Acquired Company's Profit-and-Loss Statement

Provision for Taking Control on Default. In addition to the capital stock of the two companies, the financer should also obtain resignations in blank of all of the directors and officers of both companies. This will enable the financer to take over the operations of the companies in the event of a default by the borrower.

Fees. Formerly, financers generally charged a flat fee for a turn-around loan, covering a specified maximum period in which the turn-around loan could be outstanding. This period would normally range from one to thirty days. In the event that at the maturity date of the note such loan had not been liquidated, additional interest at a specified rate was charged for the period following such maturity date. More recently, and particularly where both turn-around and conventional financing are handled by the same financer, the turn-around fee has been abandoned. A simple per diem rate, usually similar to the rate on the conventional financing, is charged.

Conventional Financing

The second or conventional financing follows the merger. Simply stated, S Corporation has been merged or liquidated into A Corporation, its parent. The stock of S Corporation has been surrendered and canceled in exchange for its assets, subject to the liabilities of

S Corporation. Effectively, A Corporation has acquired the assets of S Corporation and has assumed its obligations. This becomes clearer in analyzing the pro forma balance sheet of the merged consolidated company. The A Corporation now liquidates its turnaround loan of $300,000 and repays the bank loan of $100,000 by resorting to the conventional financing detailed in Fig. 13–2. Notice that $25,000 of the company's cash is also thus used.

Pro Forma Consolidated Balance Sheet (Merged Company)

Figure 13–4 reflects the result of the merger by S Corporation into A Corporation. The combined capital and surplus of the two

A CORPORATION (AFTER MERGER)

Pro Forma

Cash	$ 25,000	Due Financer Current	$300,000
Accounts Receivable	250,000	Accounts Payable	200,000
Inventory	350,000	Current Portion—	
Prepaid Items	25,000	Mortgage Payable	5,000
		Accruals	35,000
		Income Taxes Payable	25,000
	650,000		565,000
Machinery & Equipment	150,000	Due Financer Machinery &	
Real Estate	100,000	Equipment	75,000
		Mortgage—Real Estate	45,000
		Capital Stock 100,000	
		Retained Earn-	
		ings 115,000	215,000
	$900,000		$900,000

Fig. 13–4. *Pro Forma* Balance Sheet After Merger

corporations prior to the merger was $615,000. The *pro forma* balance sheet now reflects a total capital and surplus of $215,000. The purchase price of $400,000 has been extracted from surplus and the same amount of financing has been substituted therefor.

There has been a substantial reduction in the working capital of the combined companies, which is implicit in such situations. However, the continued generation of new sales, against which the financer will supply funds, will insure the liquidation of accounts payable and other obligations. The profit from operations, described in Fig. 13–2, will provide funds for amortization of fixed obligations. It should be noted that the company real estate, on which there is an outstanding mortgage of $50,000, remains unchanged and un-affected by the financing.

Cash-Flow Projection

In all acquisitions it is important that a cash-flow projection, sup-plementing the *pro forma* balance sheet, be prepared. No exhibit reflecting the cash flow projection has been included here, inasmuch as the assumptions and projections are usually hypothetical. Further, they are not necessary to an understanding of the principles involved. Suffice it to emphasize the importance of adequate working capital to liquidate trade payables, meet payroll and other operating costs.

LEGAL CONSIDERATIONS

As stated above, the purchase transaction can take either of two forms: (a) a purchase of assets subject to liabilities or (b) a purchase of stock.

Purchase of Stock

Among the items of the purchase and sale agreement requiring attention are the following:

1. Representations concerning important balance sheet items
2. Warranties by sellers in connection with balance sheet and re-lated items
3. Specification of indemnities in the event that there are breaches of warranty, including amounts and dates of payment
4. Certified schedules supporting balance sheet items
5. Certified schedules of all contracts outstanding, including union agreements, leases, purchase agreements, etc.

As previously noted, an examination should be made of the surplus accounts of both the acquiring and selling corporations.

Distributions Exceeding Surplus. Generally, the rule is that any divi-dend or other distribution to shareholders of any amount exceeding the surplus constitutes a violation of creditors' rights. It is considered a depletion of the capital upon which the creditors have relied in extending credit to the corporation. Hence the financer must ascertain whether the payments to the selling shareholders exceed the corporate surplus. This legal provision is found in most of the large commercial states. A review of applicable state law is required.

State Merger Laws. The merger must also comply with applicable state law. In many cases the acquiring and selling corporations are incorporated in different states. Normally the law of the state of the acquiring corporation applies. This, however, should be checked carefully.

Financer's Liability to Creditors and Minority Shareholders. The question of the liability of financers of acquisitions, should a merged company encounter financial difficulties, has been the subject of much discussion. If a bankruptcy or insolvency ensues, there may be problems for the financer, especially if the acquired corporation's liabilities at the time of the merger remain unpaid. This risk may be minimized by the prompt issuance of a new financial statement of the merged companies. Strict observance of the legal provisions regarding reduction of surplus is also vital. Notwithstanding such care, some experts state that an acquisition and merger that entails the pay-out of substantial funds to selling shareholders thereby reducing the surplus of the selling corporation would be vulnerable to attacks by unpaid creditors. It is asserted that both the acquiring company and the financer would be liable to such creditors.

It is of the utmost importance therefore, that a financer of an acquisition be certain that the liabilities of both the acquired and the acquiring company will be fully repaid in the normal course of business. For the same reason, some attorneys have questioned the wisdom of one financer's doing both the turn-around loan and the ensuing conventional financing. They have insisted that the turn-around loan be made by one lender and the conventional financing done by another. Superficially, such an arrangement would appear to obviate the risk mentioned above. The rationale is that the later conventional financer is not involved in the pay-out to selling shareholders of the acquired corporation. The question, however, still persists: Is the conventional financer not on notice that creditors of the acquired corporation remain unpaid, notwithstanding the fact that it did not handle the turn-around financing? These matters should be reviewed by counsel in the light of the total situation, legal and practical.

A related matter concerns the liability of a financer that becomes unduly involved in the management of a company whose acquisition it has financed. Usually such involvement is the result of bad technique and worse judgment. A number of cases have arisen charging the financer with liability to creditors on the basis of its putative role as owner-manager of the company financed. Obviously a strong caveat is in order regarding the assumption by the financer of any ownership or management functions.

Sometimes the acquisition involves less than 100% of the capital stock of the company acquired. This usually results from the refusal of minority shareholders to accept the price offered to the majority shareholder(s). Wherever possible, the financer should insist that 100% of the stock be acquired. If that is not possible, then a reserve should be provided for the possible liability to dissenting shareholders who assert their right to an appraisal of their stock.

Purchase of Assets Subject to Liabilities

This form of acquisition transaction is much simpler than the purchase-of-stock transaction. Essentially the financing is conventional. No turn-around loan is involved. Here, too, the purchase agreement should contain representations concerning the assets acquired and the liabilities assumed. In addition, there should be warranties and provision for indemnity as in a purchase-of-stock transaction.

Bills of sale referring to the assets acquired, together with proofs of title, and so on, should be obtained; certified schedules supporting these items should also be submitted.

Under this form of purchase, compliance with the Bulk Sales Law is generally required. It is one of the articles of the Uniform Commercial Code, which has been adopted by almost all states.

Frequently, the acquiring company assumes the name of the selling corporation. It is desirable that creditors of the selling corporation, whose liabilities have been assumed, have public notice of the sale. Normally, this is accomplished by bulk sale notice, but sometimes such notice is not given. In any event, a new statement of the acquiring corporation should be issued at the earliest possible date.

Tax Considerations

Among the important reasons for acquisitions is the consideration of their tax implications. This is especially true where the selling corporation has a substantial loss carry-forward. Purchases of assets would make unavailable any possible tax saving. In a purchase-of-stock acquisition such tax savings are available, subject to quite complicated provisions of the Internal Revenue Code.

Need for Counsel

A final word, essentially cautionary: The unusual complexity of acquisition financing now should be apparent. The material herein obviously has been reduced to its simplest terms in order to convey the fundamental concepts. However, each financing of an acquisition is truly unique; no two are alike. It therefore behooves anyone engaging in acquisition financing to enlist the best available legal, accounting, and analytical know-how. There are serious risks and pitfalls in such financing, and the prudent financer should proceed with exceptional care.

Index